CO 1 35 59706 22

MW00337809

THE PRACTICAL ENCYCLOPEDIA OF

THE MARINE AQUARIUM

Yellow Tang (Zebrasoma flavescens).

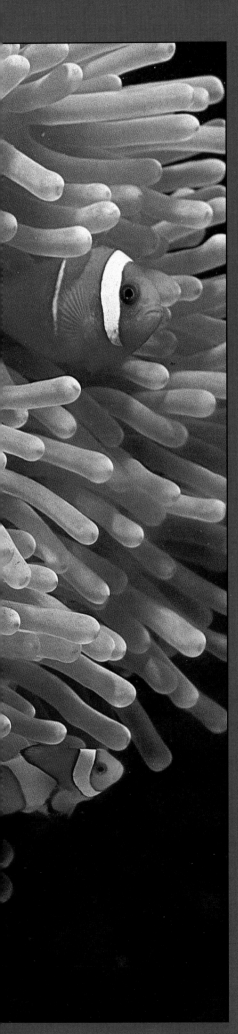

THE PRACTICAL ENCYCLOPEDIA OF
THE MARINE AQUARIUM

Dick Mills

Consultants
Dave Keeley
Terry Evans

DURHAM COUNTY LIBRARY
ACC. No. 3559706
CLASS No. 639.34

Left: *Tomato Clowns* (Amphiprion frenatus) *at home in their sea anemone.*

a Salamander book
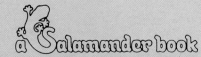
Published by Salamander Books Limited
LONDON • NEW YORK

A Salamander Book

© 1987 Salamander Books Ltd.,
52 Bedford Row,
London WC1R 4LR,
United Kingdom.

ISBN 0 86101 306 9

Distributed in the UK by
Hodder and Stoughton Services,
P.O.Box 6, Mill Road,
Dunton Green,
Sevenoaks, Kent TN13 2XX.

All rights reserved. No part of this
book may be reproduced, stored in a
retrieval system or transmitted in
any form or by any means, electronic,
mechanical, photocopying, recording
or otherwise, without the prior
permission of Salamander Books Ltd.

All correspondence concerning the
content of this volume should be
addressed to Salamander Books Ltd.

Credits

Editor: Geoff Rogers
Design: Stonecastle Graphics
Colour reproductions: Scantrans Pte Ltd.
Filmset: SX Composing Ltd.
Printed in Singapore.

THE AUTHOR

Dick Mills has been keeping fish seriously for more than 25 years, during which time he has written many articles for aquatic hobby magazines, as well as twelve books. A member of the local aquarist society, for the past 16 years he has been a Council Member of the Federation of British Aquatic Societies, for which he regularly lectures and produces a quarterly News Bulletin. He has also found time to appear on television pet-orientated programmes, a medium with which he is equally at home as his profession is composing electronic music and sound sequences for both radio and television. A noisy job to contrast with fishkeeping, the quietest of hobbies.

THE CONSULTANTS

Dave Keeley has been a practising aquarist for over 20 years, professionally since 1971. Having run a successful shop in the Midlands for 15 years, he now imports specialist aquatic equipment, in particular for marine aquariums. Marines are his true interest; he has kept them since 1973 and is fascinated by the ever changing and developing aspect of the hobby. Dave regularly contributes to British and American journals and lectures on marine fishes at clubs and shows throughout the U.K.

Terry Evans has been involved with both freshwater and marine fishes for 25 years, both as an importer and, for the past ten years, as a highly successful and respected retailer. He can claim particular success with keeping marine invertebrates and is an authority on all aspects of marine fishkeeping.

SPECIALIST ADVISERS

Dr C. Agius, BSc., MSc., Ph.D., Reader in Fisheries Biology, Kingston Polytechnic.
Peter W. Scott MSc., BVSc., MRCVS, MIBiol.

A Long-nosed Filefish (Oxymonocanthus longirostris) *amid* Goniopora *coral.*

CONTENTS

PART ONE PRACTICAL SECTION

A complete guide to setting up a marine aquarium, from selecting and furnishing a tank to choosing and introducing compatible fishes, their feeding, routine maintenance, breeding and health care.

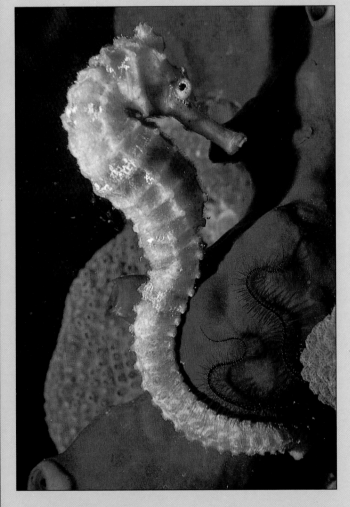

Left: *A magnificent display of ornate fins, a cryptic colour pattern and a graceful slow-swimming action, belie the true nature of Pterois volitans, the Lionfish. This species is a venomous-spined predator from the Indo-Pacific.*

Above: *To maintain the Seahorse, Hippocampus sp. successfully in the marine aquarium, provide it with a quiet environment, either in a tank of its own, or with non-boisterous fishes, and a plentiful supply of small live foods.*

PART TWO SPECIES GUIDE

This part of the book is divided into three main sections: tropical marine fishes, tropical invertebrates, and coldwater fishes and invertebrates.

Tropical Marine Fishes 64-185
A detailed survey of 200 marine fishes from the tropical waters of the world. The fishes are presented in A-Z order of scientific family name, and in A-Z order of species name.

Tropical Invertebrates 186-193
A practical introduction to these fascinating creatures – from crabs to sea anemones – with basic advice on how to keep them in the aquarium.

Coldwater Fishes and Invertebrates 194-199
A brief survey of temperate species suitable for display in a marine aquarium.

PART ONE
PRACTICAL SECTION

Marine fishes, particularly the tropical species, have to be seen to be believed. With the realization that these vivid and striking fishes exist in a multitude of shapes and sizes in the wild comes the urge to encapsulate part of this marine world in the aquarium. Newcomers to fishkeeping might think this an impossible dream, but developments over the past twenty years would prove them wrong.

Tropical marine fishes have one big drawback: they are not bred in huge commercial numbers like their freshwater counterparts and, therefore, must be caught from the wild. This labour intensive activity obviously increases the cost of each fish and cutting costs only results in the importation of poor-quality stock. However, thanks to years of experience, caring exporters now appreciate the problems posed by long and stressful journeys and generally handle marine fishes with greater understanding, thus improving their chances of arriving at their destination in good health. Another immense technological leap forward – the development of fast, modern aircraft – has cut down potentially stressful journeys from days to hours.

Once these beautiful creatures are safely installed in the aquarium, the fishkeeper assumes a vital role. This entails learning about the conditions the fish require and how to provide these ideal conditions on a long-term basis. Over the years, research has resulted in the development of reliable systems and equipment for keeping marine fishes. These advances, together with a greater understanding of the fishes' requirements, mean that we can embark on the splendid hobby of marine fishkeeping with much more confidence than did the early pioneers.

Brittle coral decorations need careful handling.

WHY KEEP MARINES?

Electric-blue Damselfish, justifiably popular.

If you are already a fishkeeper, then you will find no difficulty in answering this question. However, not all marine fishkeepers come into the hobby with previous experience of freshwater aquarium keeping. One real advantage of this is that they bring no prejudices with them and will not need to unlearn or amend their thinking. Whatever your fishkeeping background, expert or beginner, you are embarking on a truly grand adventure with delightful rewards for your earnest efforts. But back to answering the question: the most common reason put forward is probably the best: 'They're so colourful, who could resist them?' After reading this encyclopedia, you will find it hard to disagree.

Why keep marine fishes? There are at least two answers: the fishes are very colourful and they present a challenge. No one could deny the beauty of the brilliant colours and intricate patterns of the fishes, but this is only part of the attraction of marines. Many have quite distinctive lifestyles, often in association with other marine animals; the sea anemones share a close relationship with the Clownfishes; the Wrasses clean parasites from other, larger, species. As well as the fishes, there are a number of equally colourful and active invertebrates that can be kept in the aquarium, either alongside the fishes (to create a genuine underwater scene) or in an aquarium by themselves.

Marine fishkeeping raises other questions: why are juvenile fishes often a totally different colour to their adult parents? Why does the male seahorse incubate the eggs? Why are the fishes' colours so intense? We already have the answers to some of these questions, others await perhaps your answer.

Meeting the challenge

Do not underestimate the challenge of keeping marines. It is probably an advantage to have some previous experience of fishkeeping before taking on marines. Many freshwater fishkeepers assume that one 'graduates' to marines in time. However, it is not obligatory for the simple reason that marine fishkeeping is a more exact science; you can 'get away' with a degree of laxity in freshwater aquarium keeping, but marine fishes demand almost total dedication if they are to survive for an appreciable length of time. Furthermore, some aspects of marine fishkeeping have no direct equivalent in the freshwater world, and these skills need to be learnt from scratch.

Marine fish come from a very stable environment with a natural stability that cannot be exactly duplicated in the confines of the modest home aquarium, despite modern 'salt-mixes' being almost indistinguishable from the real thing. As their natural environment changes so little, marine fishes have not evolved a tolerance to cope with any such change, hence the need for marine fishkeepers to keep a constant check on the water quality conditions in the aquarium.

The availability of marine species is becoming less of a problem. (Except fishes on the list of endangered species; check your local regulations on import and sales.) More retail outlets are including marine fishes in their stock, and fishkeeping magazines will help you to find your nearest marine dealer, who should not be more than a car journey away.

Is marine fishkeeping expensive?

At first, it may look as if marine fishkeeping is relatively expensive, but closer examination shows that there is only a small premium to be paid for the privilege of going marine. Marine fishes may be more expensive than freshwater ones simply because they are caught in the wild and often transported halfway round the world. On the other hand, you won't be keeping marine species in the same numbers as freshwater species, for reasons that will be explained later. The cost of an all-glass aquarium plus the essential *basic* heating, lighting and filtration equipment will be approximately the same as for a freshwater aquarium of the same size. However, there are many options available and you should discuss them with your local dealer before making a firm decision. You may decide to opt for a larger financial outlay at the outset, for example, to avoid the nuisance and inconvenience of 'upgrading' your system within a short space of time.

You cannot expect a marine aquarium to succeed if it is set up on exactly the same lines as the freshwater aquarium. Although the basic principles are the same, some modifications will be necessary. After all, there is far more to marine fishkeeping than simply adding salt to a freshwater aquarium. Your expenses may include additional lighting to encourage the growth of algae; electric powerheads instead of air-operated systems for biological filtration; and coral sand to cover the aquarium base costs more than freshwater aquarium gravel (although some 'total' systems need very little substrate on the aquarium floor). Coral decorations can be expensive, but on the other hand you will not be buying aquatic plants, although nowadays it is possible to get marine algae to flourish in the aquarium. These need bright lighting to thrive – see pages 18-19 for further details.

Above: Even coldwater invertebrates, with their more subtle colours, have their own appeal for the fishkeeper. Specimens from the local seashore make interesting aquarium subjects.

Left: Anemonefishes are aptly named; many of the genus *Amphiprion*, such as these *Amphiprion frenatus*, never venture far from their home within the tentacles of a sea anemone.

Running costs will include the salt water mix, which enables you to make up replacement sea water for regular partial water changes. Food for marine fishes ranges (as it does for freshwater fishes) from flakes and pellets to live foods. It is much safer to use gamma-irradiated frozen and other specially formulated foods than to prepare your own. Cutting corners to cut expenses hardly ever succeeds, especially in the delicately balanced world of the tropical marine aquarium. As in all fishkeeping, neglecting regular maintenance may lead to eventual disaster.

Why not try temperate marines?

There is another way of keeping marine life that need not be too expensive at all; if you are sufficiently near to the seashore, you can quite easily set up a coldwater (or ambient temperature) marine aquarium and stock it with wildlife that you can capture yourself. The equipment required to keep them need not be too sophisticated. We discuss this aspect of marine keeping more fully on pages 194-199.

Above: The fully established tropical marine aquarium soon becomes the ambition of any newcomer to the hobby. Brilliantly coloured fishes share the tank with delicately shaded hard and soft corals and green marine algae. Such an aquarium will need both sound basic theory and regular maintenance to succeed.

Reaping the rewards

Whatever form of marine fishkeeping you decide to follow, the rewards are really quite self explanatory. You will enjoy no little sense of achievement, you will be the envy of fellow fishkeepers who were less confident in their own capabilities to emulate your path to success, and you will have a truly magnificent living underwater display within reach of your armchair. One side effect might even be the urge to visit your fishes' native habitat, particularly those from tropical areas! On a deeper level, it is quite likely that by studying marine fishes in the aquarium, further knowledge about their lifestyles will be forthcoming, leading to the widening distribution of information that will benefit both science and conservationists alike.

EXPLORING THE OPTIONS

Lysmata amboinensis, a fine Cleaner Shrimp.

Taking up marine fishkeeping involves more than just parting with a seemingly large amount of money, returning home with the hardware and fishes, and hoping it will all turn out right; if it didn't, then the hobby would be neither so challenging in its demands nor so rewarding – and maybe there wouldn't be a need for this encyclopedia! You should first explore what it's all about, to find out not only what you need to buy, but also what lies beyond your probably incomplete assumptions. You will soon discover a wide diversity of fishes and other animals that far exceeds your original aims and ambitions, and you will want to learn how to keep these animals looking their best in a splendid marine aquarium.

Compared with other systems of aquarium culture, marine fishkeeping is still in its infancy. However, it is not as narrowly defined as, say, coldwater freshwater fishkeeping. Within certain temperature limits you can choose to keep not only a range of fishes, but also other forms of animal life that will thrive in the marine aquarium.

Coral reef fishes

For most aquarists, 'going marine' means only one thing: keeping fishes from tropical coral reefs. This is admittedly the major area of interest for hobbyists and accordingly takes up a substantial part of this book. We have already seen that the principal attractions are the vivid colours and forms of the fishes, usually viewed against a background of strangely shaped but decorative 'skeletons' of once living corals. However, this is only part of the picture and there are other areas to be explored.

Tropical invertebrates

Apart from the fishes, a wide range of invertebrate life can be kept in captivity. These include shrimps, sea anemones, starfish and tubeworms that make their home on and around the rocks and corals. A piece of 'living rock' will have minute polyps attached to it that represent extra lifeforms introduced into the aquarium, although these are liable to be eaten by the fish or other animals larger than themselves. If species for the marine aquarium are carefully chosen, many of them can be kept in association with fishes; indeed, some fishes enjoy a particularly close relationship with invertebrates, as we shall see in later sections. Alternatively, you can keep invertebrates in an aquarium by themselves; protecting them from the unwelcome attentions of predatory fishes allows you to study their lifestyles more easily. Most tropical invertebrates are every bit as beautiful as the fishes and reward the patient viewer with intriguing behaviour patterns.

Coldwater fishes and invertebrates

It would not be fair to assume that the above selection of tropical animal life presents the whole picture. Fishes and inver-

Above: This is the typical home of our tropical marine fishes; a coral reef in the Maldive Islands set in the Indian Ocean about 350km(220miles) south east of Sri Lanka. Happily, your home aquarium will be more brightly lit.

Below: This strange-looking creature is a nudibranch, or sea slug. These shell-less, brilliantly coloured molluscs spend their time moving slowly over coral and rock surfaces in search of the algae on which they feed.

tebrates found in cooler waters can also be kept in captivity, sometimes with less difficulty! One advantage of tackling this aspect of marine fishkeeping is that, very often, collecting specimens is not only free, but also a most enjoyable activity – depending on how near you live to the coast. Another bonus is that you can keep native marines in a spare aquarium at reasonably low cost. Such a tank will require no heating equipment and can develop along DIY lines.

The only drawbacks are that the animals you catch may lack the bright colours of their tropical relatives and that, during the summer, the water temperature in the aquarium may rise too high for their well-being. (In fact, you may need to install some form of cooling system for a cold-water tank during very warm weather.) As we have seen, exploring the local seashore can be a useful lesson in conservation; should your specimens start to outgrow their aquarium, you can simply release them into their natural home and at the same time capture some smaller replacements to replenish your display.

The systems

In a 'domestic-scale' freshwater aquarium, it is possible to produce natural conditions using only 'organic' elements, i.e. keeping

Marine life in temperate waters

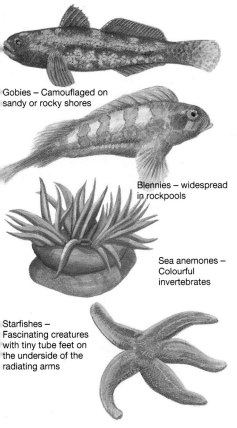

Gobies – Camouflaged on sandy or rocky shores

Blennies – widespread in rockpools

Sea anemones – Colourful invertebrates

Starfishes – Fascinating creatures with tiny tube feet on the underside of the radiating arms

Above: Local seashore rockpools in the temperate regions are teeming with life, waiting to be discovered. Small fishes, sea anemones and starfishes make for interesting collecting trips and fine aquarium displays.

Above: The simple clean lines of this aquarium enhance the magnificent display of the marine life it contains. There are no visible electrical cables and the filtration equipment needed to maintain the system is well hidden, housed in a cabinet below the aquarium.

the correct number of aquatic plants and fish to create a 'balanced' aquarium. This is impossible in the marine aquarium.

In the sea, the 'waste disposal' problem is solved by the sheer vastness of the water, wave action and the activity of filter-feeding animals, such as living corals, sponges, tubeworms, etc. At the same time, there is massive bacterial activity on the equally large surface area of rocks, corals and seabed that serves to 'purify' the water. An aquarium designed to function in the same way would be so large, and the number of animals in it so small, that it would be beyond the scope of, and be of little interest to, the average fishkeeper. Furthermore, such an aquarium would be very susceptible to 'explosive pollution' if the fishes were overfed or a decaying body were to go undetected.

Conversely, logic might suppose that a constantly monitored, automatically controlled smaller marine aquarium is possible in this 'hi-tech' day and age (albeit at a proportionately large financial cost). This may be true to some extent but, while theoretically everything may be under control, there are always seemingly unpredictable factors to be considered when keeping live animals in captivity that tend to upset even the best laid plans, with the occasional 'wipe-out' occurring. Speculation suggests that the animals within such a system could become 'over-protected' by the technological aids and lose their natural resistance to disease should any be inadvertently introduced into the aquarium or the fish removed to other, less 'sanitary' quarters. A further drawback with this type of aquarium is that it may not be possible to keep filter-feeding animals, their food being

removed most effectively from the water by the constant action of very powerful filter systems. Efficient removal of vital minerals from the water may also preclude the growth of marine algae.

Marine fishkeeping has developed a middle path between these two extremes. An understanding of the natural cleansing processes that occur within the ocean (and, indeed, in freshwater systems as well) has led to the development of relatively low-cost solutions to the equivalent problems in the aquarium. Modern filtration systems – particularly those based on bacterial activity – use natural methods of processing wastes and this is the key to the increasing popularity and success rate of marine fishkeeping around the world.

Complete aquarium set-ups based around efficient, but essentially 'natural', filter systems are discussed in a later chapter. However, armed with a basic understanding of water management, there is no reason why you should not be able to build up an aquarium system from separate components. In fact, this usually proves more satisfying, and probably suits the needs and finances of the average hobbyist more closely. At the very least, doing things 'bit by bit' offers a good chance to absorb some knowledge along the way. If you buy everything in one package, you may not understand or even care why it works; if it develops a fault and the system fails, you may not know enough to put it right.

SELECTING A TANK

Choose a tank size to suit you and the fishes.

Now you've decided to keep marine fishes, you must decide on the type and size of tank in which to keep them. You may choose a 'complete system', a tank built into a cabinet, or a more simple, less expensive aquarium for that spare alcove. In any case, the aquarium will soon become a focal point of the room, so be sure to make it a tidy arrangement free from trailing wires (which could be a safety hazard) and with the equipment hidden. Always bear in mind that the aquarium is a living space for fishes: the size and design of the aquarium will be important considerations. Choose sensibly, put the fishes' requirements first and you will have the beginnings of a successful system.

Choosing a suitable marine tank demands more thought and care than selecting a freshwater aquarium. Not only must you consider the size, shape and design of the tank, but also the type of materials used in its construction.

Tank construction

The most important thing to remember is that, apart from being watertight, a marine tank must be made from materials that are neither affected by corrosion caused by sea water nor, conversely, introduce toxic materials into the sea water. This immediately rules out a tank that includes metal in its construction. The normal all-glass tank is ideal, although you can use tanks made from reinforced fibreglass, plastics or even suitably treated wood or concrete. Some of these may be made in larger sizes than the average home aquarium.

The obligatory ban on metals extends to the hood, light fittings and any other equipment likely to be in direct contact with the aquarium; even objects that are not in the tank but just nearby are sometimes subjected to saltwater spray and can be damaged by corrosion. You can protect metal hoods with several coats of varnish if necessary, but it is far better to omit metals right from the start. With modern materials, this should be straightforward.

Tank design

The aesthetic appeal of different tank designs is a subjective topic, but we will touch briefly on 'designer aquariums' or complete systems. Your choice of tank and equipment will depend largely on how impatient you are and on your financial capabilities, but probably the soundest advice is to get the best equipment you can afford at any one time. Superbly equipped total systems are available for the fishkeeper who wants a complete set-up straight away without any unsightly external 'add-ons'. The less ambitious hobbyist can choose a basic tank and then fit a complete filter system, together with the necessary heating and lighting equipment.

If you are just starting to set up a marine aquarium, variations on the latter theme are usually a more realistic and practical option. There is the added advantage that a certain degree of 'do-it-yourself' brings a more complete understanding of the theoretical and practical operations involved. In the long term this is far more reliable than having blind faith in a complex total system, which may in itself be a total mystery! Furthermore, you can design the aquarium to suit your space requirements exactly, which is not always possible with commercially available standard-sized tanks. Bear in mind that whatever the design, most

aquariums benefit by having a proportional sense of depth and avoiding a long shallow 'letter-box' appearance.

Glass tanks

At first sight, the all-glass tank seems to be much more fragile and subject to stresses than the unsuitable (but stronger) angle-iron framed tanks of yesteryear. However, this is not the case if the glass tank is correctly constructed and installed.

The glass must be thick enough to withstand the considerable water pressure on it and thicker than that used in a 'framed' tank of the same dimensions. Top-braces across the tank reduce the chance of the front or rear glass panels bowing outwards unduly under the pressure of the water. Ledges positioned around the inside of the tank just below the top not only add strength but also form a shelf on which to stand the cover glass and hood. Avoid cheap tanks which may be made from thin glass, and thus be less robust.

Below: All-glass tanks are now standard for marine fishes. The panels of glass are bonded together using aquarium silicone sealant and there are no toxic materials exposed which might otherwise leach into the salt water or be corroded by it. The narrow shelves, likewise fixed in place with aquarium silicone sealant, will support both the cover glass and lighting hood.

All-glass tank construction

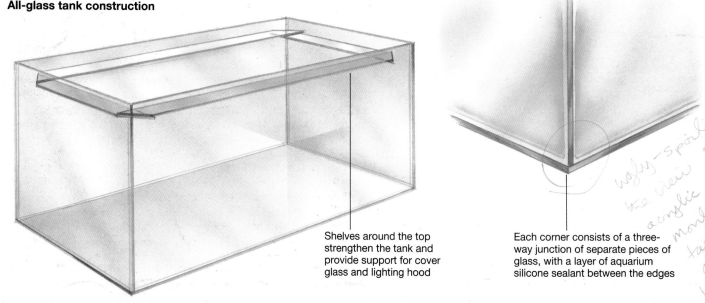

Shelves around the top strengthen the tank and provide support for cover glass and lighting hood

Each corner consists of a three-way junction of separate pieces of glass, with a layer of aquarium silicone sealant between the edges

Selecting the correct size

When considering the size of the aquarium, remember the principle that 'large is good but big is better'. The larger the volume of water, the more inherently stable it is in terms of quality. The same rule applies to the filtration area if it is to be included within the tank.

If you intend to upgrade your aquarium at a later date, make sure it is capable of accommodating any new improved equipment. For instance, a protein skimmer often requires extra 'headroom' in a tank, a fact often overlooked when choosing the original tank. Similarly, extra room will be required if sophisticated 'above tank' filtration systems are to be used.

Stocking levels

The size of the tank obviously influences the number of fishes that can be accommodated in it and, in making this calculation, the principles that apply to the marine aquarium are slightly different to those that apply to the freshwater aquarium.

Experienced freshwater fishkeepers will already be familiar with the theory that the number of fishes that can be comfortably held in a tank of any given volume depends on three things: the amount of dissolved oxygen in the water and its replenishment rate capability, the temperature of the water, and what sort of fishes you are keeping. Warm water holds less dissolved oxygen than cool water, but coldwater fish require more oxygen than tropical species. The whole complex problem can be calculated in a convenient manner by allowing a certain total of fish body lengths (measured, excluding the tail, in centimetres or inches) per given area (measured in corresponding square centimetres or square inches) of water surface.

This theory is not entirely transferable to the marine aquarium, for many of the fishes we intend to keep are used to coral-reef water, which may be over-saturated with oxygen.

You can use one of two methods, or a combination of both to make the calculation. The area of the filter bed in a tank with internal biological filtration is usually the same as the water surface area. Allow 120cm² of water surface for every 1cm of fish body length (48in² of water surface for every 1in of fish). This formula gives you a theoretical maximum figure, but you should also consider the shape and body weight of the fish and consult your dealer if in doubt. Always build up the stocking level gradually to avoid overloading the filtration system. Alternatively, in a new aquarium with a built-in filtration system (whose area may be difficult to calculate) you should proceed along the lines of 1cm of fish per 7 litres of water (1in of fish per 4 Imp gallons/5 US gallons). After six to twelve

Calculating fish-holding capacity

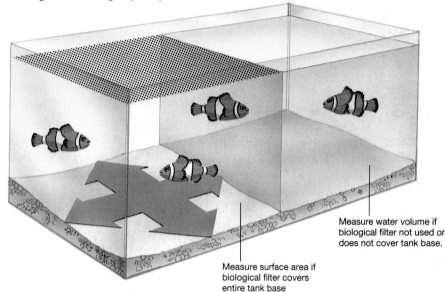

Measure water volume if biological filter not used or does not cover tank base.

Measure surface area if biological filter covers entire tank base

Above: You can calculate the aquarium's fish-holding capacity by allowing a certain number of 'fish lengths' either per square centimetre of water surface area or per litre of water volume. In either case, although the total figure arrived at may well represent the tank's holding capability, you should not introduce the full quota of fishes into the aquarium right at the start, but build up to this maximum figure over many months.

months you can double the number of fish in the tank. Do this progressively to allow the filtration system to adjust to the increasing load placed upon it.

Bearing in mind the above guidelines, the minimum size of a marine aquarium should be about 900mm long, 380mm high and 300mm front to back (36×15×12in). A tank this size will hold approximately 104 litres (23 Imperial gallons/27.5 US gallons) of water and will provide enough space in which individual species can stake out their chosen territories and 'co-exist' with neighbours without too much squabbling occurring. As long as each fish has an area it can retreat to, it will not feel threatened and will settle down more happily.

Siting the tank

When a tank of this size is fully furnished with corals, rocks, sand and is filled with water, it will weigh over 120kg (265lb) – an immovable object. You must therefore consider the tank's final planned position before you set it up.

Because it is so heavy, the tank must obviously be sited on a firm base and the base itself must be evenly supported on a strong floor. The tank stand should have a solid and flat top on which to place the tank – angle-iron stands that support only the edges of an all-glass tank may not be as safe. Cushion the tank against any unevenness in the supporting base with some absorbent material – expanded polystyrene is very suitable for this purpose. (Remember, however, that a layer of polystyrene will only compensate for minor irregularities; any major twist or warp in the supporting surface will stress the tank once it is full.) Try to arrange an even distribution of the weight, across floor joists if possible. It is not difficult to build the tank into the structure of the house and in fact you will have to do this if the aquarium is

very large. An aquarium used as a room-divider looks very impressive, but is not easy to decorate to suit all-round viewing.

The aquarium will need lighting, heating (if tropical) and electrically operated filtration equipment, so be sure to place it near an electrical power outlet.

Although tropical coral reefs are brilliantly lit, it is not a good idea to site the marine aquarium near a window. The tank will overheat in summer and cool down in winter. Overheating could be a critical problem if you keep temperate species and you may have to cool the tank in summer.

Excessive light falling on the tank will encourage growths of algae – a problem that freshwater aquarists avoid like the plague. However, in marine aquariums you can encourage algae growth and in this respect a little direct sunshine will not be harmful. In general, however, it is better to install sufficient lighting equipment rather than to rely on unpredictable natural sources of light (see Lighting, page 18).

Some fish are susceptible to external disturbances, so avoid a site opposite a constantly opening (and slamming) door. Always leave sufficient space above the aquarium to allow access to lighting and heating systems. Filtration systems can be integrated within, above or below the aquarium – another factor to consider when siting the aquarium. You must certainly leave enough room around and above the tank to facilitate feeding and regular maintenance duties. (See 'Setting Up', page 37.)

HEATING AND LIGHTING

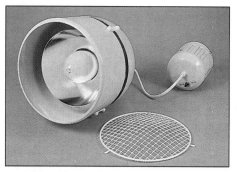

A mercury vapour spotlight for aquarium use.

The waters around the coral reefs of the world are warm, the lighting brilliant. Heating the water presents no problems: the equipment is reliable and inexpensive to operate – any freshwater fishkeeper will vouch for that. Of course, heating will not be required for coldwater fishes (see pages 194-199) and cooling may even be necessary during the summer months. Lighting may be a matter of personal taste but, as far as the fishes are concerned, it is a necessity, particularly to encourage the growth of algae for herbivorous fishes. Making use of various lighting combinations and suitable tank decorations will give the impression of a real underwater scene, the more realistic the better – for you and your fishes.

The water in a marine aquarium must be maintained at a reasonably constant temperature if fishes from tropical coral reefs are to survive. Animals collected from a local shore should thrive at normal ambient temperatures without the need for heating equipment. In summer, cooling measures may even be needed.

Types of heating equipment
Various forms of heating have evolved over the years. The most popular method of heating aquarium water, however, is by means of small, individual electric immersion heaters controlled by a thermostat. In a large fish house it may be more economical to heat the entire room rather than individual tanks. Paraffin (kerosene) heaters, electric thermostatically controlled fan heaters or gas-fired central heating radiators are all effective space heating methods. (When using paraffin heaters or other fuel-burning processes, be sure to provide adequate ventilation, both to keep up the supply of oxygen to the heaters and to the air around the tanks and to vent the fumes.)

Controlling and conserving heat
In an aquarium heater, the thermostat controls the supply of electricity to the heating coil by sensing the temperature of the surrounding water. This sensing may be achieved by means of a bimetallic strip that bends and straightens as the temperature changes or, in the latest designs, by microchip circuitry. Thermostats and heating elements combined in the same glass tube – so-called heater-thermostats – are available in fully submersible and semi-submersible designs. Microchip thermostats are usually isolated units that control separate heaters by way of a sensing probe hanging in the water. Both types of thermostat can be adjusted to a few degrees above and below a factory-set level. For most marines, set the thermostat to a temperature of 24°C (75°F). The combined heater-thermostats have a waterproof cover on the control knob and, depending on the design, you may need to remove this to make an adjustment. Allow some time to elapse before re-checking the temperature and making any further adjustments.

FOR YOUR OWN SAFETY, ALWAYS SWITCH OFF THE POWER SUPPLY BEFORE MAKING ANY SUCH ADJUSTMENTS.

To avoid stressing the fishes, always adjust the water temperature very slowly and gradually. Once the water has reached the required temperature, a relatively small amount of electricity is needed to maintain it at that level. The larger the aquarium, the slower the rate of heat loss from it.

Heating equipment may also be incorporated within the water treatment compartment of a built-in 'total system'. (A recent development in freshwater aquariums has been the inclusion of a thermostatically controlled heater within the body of an external power filter. These 'thermofilters' are not suitable for marine aquariums however, because there is a slight risk that the metallic heater-thermostat connections will be corroded by salt water.)

The heater must be able to maintain the water temperature without working continuously; for example, in a 900mm (36in) aquarium in a normally heated room you should allow 2 watts of heating per litre (10 watts per Imp gallon/8 watts per US gallon). Heaters are manufactured in standard ratings, usually in steps of 50 or 100 watts. To ensure an even spread of heat, it is advisable to split the total heat requirement between two heaters (or combined units),

Using heater-thermostats in the aquarium

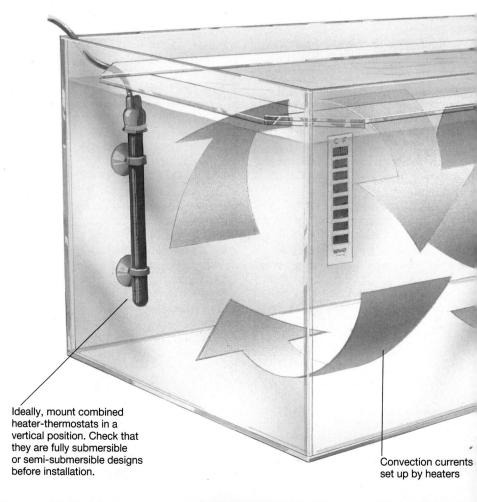

Ideally, mount combined heater-thermostats in a vertical position. Check that they are fully submersible or semi-submersible designs before installation.

Convection currents set up by heaters

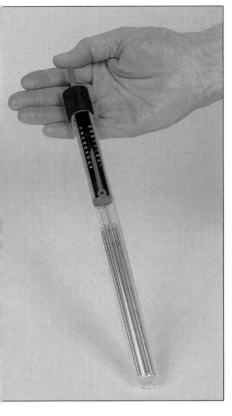

Above: This modern combined heater-thermostat unit has a clearly visible temperature scale which indicates the temperature setting in both Centigrade and Fahrenheit as the thermostat adjustment control is altered.

Micro-chip external thermostat

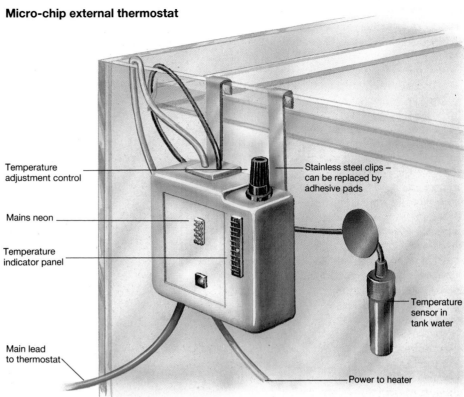

Temperature adjustment control

Mains neon

Temperature indicator panel

Main lead to thermostat

Stainless steel clips – can be replaced by adhesive pads

Temperature sensor in tank water

Power to heater

Above: This separate external thermostat, with a microchip circuit, does not necessarily need to be attached to the aquarium, as its remote sensor has sufficient cable to allow it to hang in the aquarium from a reasonable distance.

Use two heaters in a large tank for even heat transfer

Above: The aquarium water is heated by submerged heating coils, usually mounted in glass tubes. Some incorporate a thermostat in the same tube as the heater. They may be mounted vertically at each end of the tank or, if too long, mounted diagonally along the back.

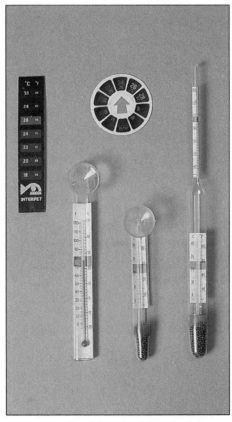

Above: Thermometers may be of various types. Clockwise from top left: two liquid crystal external designs, a floating combined thermometer-hydrometer, a free-floating or captive type, a simple spirit captive type. The green bands on the scales indicate safe ranges.

one positioned at each end of the aquarium. If you use multiple heaters controlled by one thermostat, ensure that the thermostat has a current-carrying capacity in excess of the total current demanded by the heaters. If you use two combined heater-thermostat units then one will provide an automatic backup system if the other one fails.

Some external thermostats are mounted on the aquarium with metal clips. Remember the dire warnings about the dangers of metal and salt water (and the subsequent toxic effect on the fishes), and ensure that fastening clips are waterproof. Cover simple spring-wire clips with plastic airline. Microchip controllers can be held in place with double-sided adhesive tape, thus avoiding the need to use the clips provided, even if the manufacturer claims they are made of stainless steel. These modern thermostats have a remote sensing probe hung in the aquarium; consequently they can be mounted anywhere convenient within easy reach of the tank. They do not have to be stuck or clipped onto the tank itself. Never use metal clips to anchor submerged heaters or combined units; always use plastic non-toxic fittings.

To conserve heat and reduce costs in particularly cool areas, you can lag an entire room or individual tanks with expanded polystyrene sheeting. Condensation drip trays and cover glasses fitted to the tanks will also minimize heat losses.

The thermometers used in freshwater aquariums are quite suitable for marine aquariums. Electronic systems of measuring temperature are also available.

Lighting

It is important to make an accurate assessment of the lighting you will need to install in your aquarium.

If you are setting up a 'clinical' system, then you only need sufficient light to see the exhibits. In such a system the growth of desirable green algae will be practically non-existent, although non-beneficial red, brown or blue-green algae will certainly occur. In other systems, you should encourage the growth of green algae, both for the benefit of browsing fishes and to help purify the water, since the algae will extract some of the nitrates and phosphates as 'plant food'. As any freshwater fishkeeper will tell you, algal growth is a sure sign of bright lighting and the marine aquarium requires a good supply of it to approximate to the lighting levels found on the coral reef. The intensity of the lighting in a marine aquarium may need to be three or four times that found in a conventional freshwater aquarium.

Types of lighting

You must decide at the outset whether to choose lamps that are cheap to install, but expensive to run and relatively short lived, or lamps that are more expensive to install but longer lasting and cheaper to run. The two basic options are tungsten or fluorescent, plus various types of spotlights.

Above: The lighting hood of this aquarium is mounted clear of the tank itself. Alternatively, you can dispense with the hood (but you should retain the cover glass) and use suspended spotlights, taking care to keep them at least 30cm(12in) above the surface of the water.

Tungsten lighting

Ordinary household incandescent (tungsten filament) lamps may appear to provide a cheap source of light, but they are entirely unsuitable as a form of illumination for any type of modern aquarium (freshwater as well as for marines). They do not give the optimum light spectrum for good plant growth; it may be difficult to accommodate the necessary number of lamps of the correct sizes in the aquarium hood; and they are inefficient, converting most of their energy consumption into heat, rather than into useful light output.

Fluorescent lighting

Fluorescent tubes are the most suitable form of aquarium lighting. They give an even spread of light, are relatively cheap to run and cool in operation. They are also available in different light spectrum outputs so that you can select the most suitable for your aquarium. Algae, like most plants, require light in the blue and red/orange regions of the light spectrum. Unfortunately, our eyes are not quite so sensitive in these areas and such lamps appear dimmer than other fluorescent tubes. By using three or four tubes, each with a different spectrum of light, it is possible to satisfy the requirements of the algae and the fishkeeper. 'Grolux' tubes, for example, are specially developed for growing plants, having the red and blue parts of the colour spectrum accentuated. They also give the fishes more intensified colours, although their overall light output is fairly low. Using Grolux tubes with brighter 'daylight-balanced' tubes, such as Truelight, is an

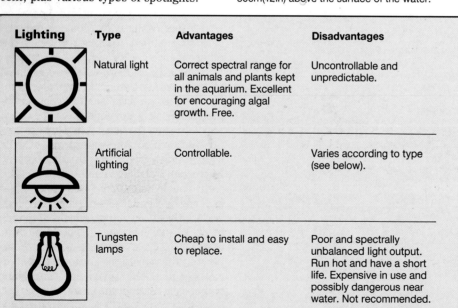

Lighting	Type	Advantages	Disadvantages
	Natural light	Correct spectral range for all animals and plants kept in the aquarium. Excellent for encouraging algal growth. Free.	Uncontrollable and unpredictable.
	Artificial lighting	Controllable.	Varies according to type (see below).
	Tungsten lamps	Cheap to install and easy to replace.	Poor and spectrally unbalanced light output. Run hot and have a short life. Expensive in use and possibly dangerous near water. Not recommended.
	Fluorescent tubes	Cool running, inexpensive in use and long lasting. Even light output. Available in a range of 'colours', many close to natural spectrum.	Relatively expensive to buy and install. Heavy starting gear. Performance may decline unnoticed. The ideal light source, however. Recommended.
	Spotlamps, such as metal-halide and mercury vapour	High light output, making them ideal for producing dramatic effects and for use with deep tanks. Good for encouraging algal growth.	Expensive. Depending on type, light may not be totally ideal in spectral balance. Must be used at least 30cm (12in) above an open-topped aquarium.

ideal combination. So-called 'actinic' tubes are also available to provide ultraviolet light, which is especially important for invertebrates in the aquarium. Used in association with conventional tubes, these provide an attractive 'glow' to the display.

Spotlights

As an alternative to the uniform spread of light from fluorescent tubes, the reflector hood can be removed from the tank and illumination provided by overhead individual lamps or spotlights. These lamps are ideal for creating dramatic effects and for emphasizing any surface water movement. They are particularly useful if you are keeping invertebrates, or using an overhead algal filter (see pages 29 and 30), and for punching light down into relatively deep tanks. Focusing a spotlight on a particular rock will benefit sea anemones, for example, which will migrate to that spot to bask in the brighter light.

It is important to choose the correct type of spotlights and to ensure that they are adequately protected against water splashes. It is best to opt for those with a higher light output than domestic tungsten spotlights and to choose models made specifically for aquarium use. Although these are more expensive than fluorescent lamps, suitable spotlamps can be chosen from a variety of types, including mercury vapour, metal-halide, high-pressure sodium discharge, etc. Here, we briefly review the possible alternatives.

Mercury vapour lamps

Lamps in this group use mercury vapour to produce light – whereas fluorescent tubes use a mercury vapour discharge in starting but depend on fluorescing phosphors that form a coating on the inside of the tubes for actual light output. Mercury vapour lamps have an electrical consumption of around 80-125 watts, well above that of fluorescent tubes used in domestic aquariums. The 'point-source' light produced is bluish white which, while giving a 'seabed' effect, will not show the fishes off in their best colours in the aquarium. These powerful lamps are more suited for large public aquariums, where their light output can be colour corrected with supplementary lighting of a different spectral balance.

Metal-halide lamps

Although this type of lamp does have a tungsten filament, it produces a more intense light than ordinary tungsten lamps. Any tungsten evaporated from the filament at the extremely high operating temperature combines with the 'halogen' vapour within the quartz envelope of the lamp and is re-deposited back on the filament, extending its effective life. Mounted 30cm (12in) above the tank, in a suitably designed reflector, a 150-watt lamp will illuminate an area of approximately 1800cm^2 (2ft^2). Metal-halide lamps are also referred to as tungsten-halogen or quartz-halogen types. Do not touch the quartz envelope when fitting these lamps and do not view directly.

Aquarium light housings

This illustration contrasts two different ways of providing aquarium lighting. The traditional hood over an aquarium is ideal for supporting fluorescent tubes. The hanging spotlight shown at left is an alternative approach, which is ideal for open-topped deep aquariums. It contains a mercury vapour lamp in a stylish housing.

High-pressure sodium

Familiar as street lamps, these emit an orange light. Other types of lamps can be used with them, supplying more light at the blue end of the spectrum and providing more conventional, colour-balanced illumination in the aquarium.

Duration and intensity of lighting

The lighting should be kept on for at least 12-15 hours each day, but the lighting level can be reduced from its full intensity to a lower level for evening viewing. The exact light requirement is best found by trial and error; in a semi-natural aquarium the aim is to have a reasonable algal growth that does not take over the whole aquarium. As a rough guide, you should allow 5 watts of light per 100cm^2 (16in^2) of water surface area. In a 900×300mm (36×12in) tank this works out to approximately 135 watts. Four 30-watt tubes should suffice, but you may need five shorter length, lower wattage tubes if the hood will not accommodate the longer tubes. It is quite permissible to mix different types of lamp if you prefer, for example a fluorescent mixed with suitable spotlights.

Care and use of lights

Whatever lamps you use you must protect them against water damage, either from direct spray and splashes, or from condensation. Waterproofed lamp fittings safeguard the electrics, and a cover glass fixed on the top of the aquarium between the lamps and the water surface will prevent damage and also cut down excessive evaporation losses. Be sure to keep the cover glass spotlessly clean so that none of the beneficial light is prevented from encouraging algae growth. For the same reason, you must maintain an efficient filtration system that will ensure the clarity of the water (see pages 26-31).

Even when you are satisfied that you have found the correct combination of lamps and have decided on the best lighting period, the lighting story is still not quite finished. Although you may have satisfied the requirements for algal growth, you should not forget the needs of the fishes and other tank occupants. One of the major contributory factors to aquatic ill-health is stress and marine fishes are equally susceptible to it. Turning the aquarium lights on or off suddenly can cause fishes to become stressed. Some authorities suggest leaving a low wattage lamp burning overnight to reduce stress. It is a good idea to switch off the aquarium lights several minutes before the main room lights, so that the fish can become acclimatized to darker conditions. On dark winter mornings, switch on the room lights a few minutes before the tank lights. This will slowly acclimatize them to brighter light.

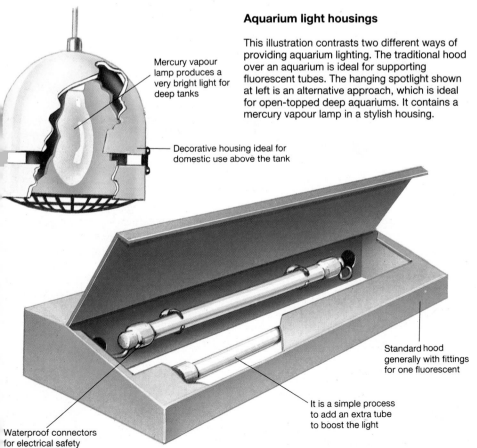

Mercury vapour lamp produces a very bright light for deep tanks

Decorative housing ideal for domestic use above the tank

Standard hood generally with fittings for one fluorescent

It is a simple process to add an extra tube to boost the light

Waterproof connectors for electrical safety

WATER–SIMULATING THE REAL THING

Clean-looking rockpool water may be polluted.

The majority of marine fishkeepers are not blessed with warm water oceans at their doorstep, and natural sea water presents far too many problems to be a viable proposition, being neither easy to collect nor completely safe when used in the aquarium. Fortunately, synthetic sea water is a perfect substitute for the real thing; you can buy all the necessary dry ingredients in a 'just add water' package. However, it will eventually become contaminated by the animal life in the tank, and new 'clean' water must be made up and used to replace it at periodic intervals. Various test kits are available for you to monitor the quality of the water – a vital consideration for marine fishes and invertebrates.

A shroud of mystery has surrounded marine fishkeeping during its relatively brief existence. Many people are fearful of attempting what to them seems well nigh impossible, and the main problem seems to be maintaining the water quality. To quote Stephen Spotte, one of the leading exponents of water management systems, success depends on 'How well you control the inevitable changes taking place in the sea water . . . The water, you see, is everything. It's as simple as that.'

Natural sea water
As 71% of the earth's surface is covered by sea water, you might expect it to be one of the most convenient commodities to obtain. Unfortunately, it is not suitable for the aquarium, for several reasons.

For most aquarists it is totally impractical to make regular trips to the coast to transport large quantities of natural sea water, even if the sea is within easy reach. Secondly, most marine fishkeepers do not live in a tropical climate, so that local sea water is too cool for tropical species. If local sea water is heated up for tropical fishes, there is a danger that the plankton in it will either die and cause pollution or propagate extremely rapidly and reduce the water's oxygen content. However, if locally collected livestock is kept in suitable sea water the results could be quite satisfactory as long as the necessary precautions are taken (see page 196).

Another point to consider is the difficulty of finding a source of unpolluted natural water. The volume of seagoing commercial traffic and effluent from industrial activity usually mean that coastal waters are not

entirely pure, to say the least!

It is clear from this that unless you are planning a native marine aquarium and are within easy reach of the coast, using natural sea water is not worth the trouble.

Synthetic sea water
The best way of providing sea water in the aquarium is to use a salt mix carefully balanced so that the final composition approximates as closely as possible to natural sea water. It is important to follow the manufacturer's instructions exactly when using such mixes. Although it was once essential to use up the complete package each time to maintain the desired salt balance, modern top-quality salt mixes are so well prepared and integrated in their composition that this is no longer the case. Be sure to reseal any unused salt mix in the packet and store it in a cool dry place to prevent

the absorption of moisture, which may upset your calculations when you use it again – for carrying out routine partial water changes, for example.

Preparing synthetic sea water
Always prepare the synthetic sea water before you set up the aquarium so that the water is ready for you to use. The following guidelines will help you to achieve the best results.

1 It is becoming more common for local water authorities to treat tapwater with chloramines instead of the more traditional chlorine. Using a dechlorinator – or even

Below: The majority of marine fishkeepers do not have a good supply of clean, fresh sea water like this within easy reach. It is safer to use modern synthetic mixes, which are almost indistinguishable from real sea water.

Composition of sea water
In addition to sodium chloride, sea water contains many other dissolved minerals – chiefly chlorides and sulphates of magnesium, chlorides of calcium and potassium, and sodium bicarbonate. Others, so-called 'trace elements', occur in very small amounts.

55% Chlorine 30.5% Sodium 7.5% Sulphate 3.5% Magnesium 1% Calcium 1% Potassium 0.5% Bicarbonate 1% Trace elements

Salinities around the world

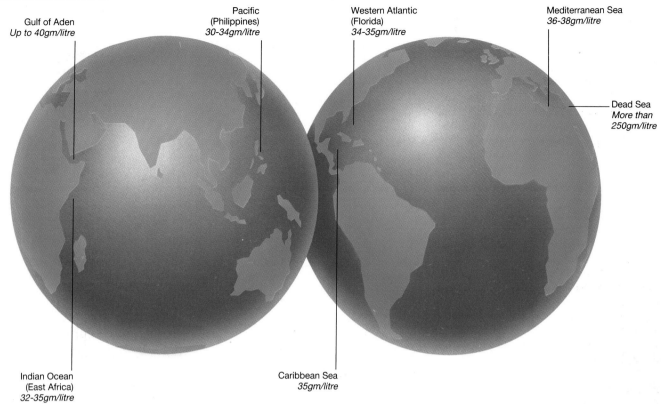

Gulf of Aden
Up to 40gm/litre

Pacific
(Philippines)
30-34gm/litre

Western Atlantic
(Florida)
34-35gm/litre

Mediterranean Sea
36-38gm/litre

Dead Sea
More than
250gm/litre

Indian Ocean
(East Africa)
32-35gm/litre

Caribbean Sea
35gm/litre

Above: These globes show how the salinity of sea water varies in different locations around the world. The main collecting areas for tropical marine fishes are the Philippines, Malaysia, Sri Lanka, the Red Sea and the Caribbean.

vigorous aeration – will remove the chlorine from tapwater before mixing in the sea salts. Once the salt mix has been added, however, it is not easy to remove the remaining ammonia, as chloramine removers may not be effective in sea water. You can test for the presence of choramines with an ammonia test kit and treat the water with a modern 'one-step' chloramine remover, which will remove both chloramine and (partially) ammonia, before mixing in the salt. You may wish to continue this practice of removing chlorine and chloramine when using tapwater to make up evaporation losses once the aquarium is fully functional. (See pages 52-53.)

2 Although you can use the aquarium for the initial mix, be sure to make subsequent mixes (for water changes, etc) in glass, plastic or other non-metallic containers. (As far as plastic is concerned, it is better to use polythene or polypropylene containers made specifically for home brewing or food use, rather than plastic dustbins made of recycled materials that might release toxins into the water over a period of time.) Mark the outside of the container with a line to indicate the amount of water needed to make up, say, 50 litres (11 Imp gallons/13 US gallons); this will save time in future.

3 Ideally, make up the sea water 24-48 hours in advance and follow the manufacturer's advice on aeration; some mixtures need vigorous aeration for several hours before use.

4 Turn on the aquarium pumps, airstones and filters to ensure thorough mixing and bring the water temperature up to the correct final reading before checking the specific gravity (S.G./see below). Add more salt if it is too low, or more *fresh water* if it is too high.

5 It is very difficult to assess the exact volume of water in a furnished aquarium, so measure the amount of water used during the setting up procedure and make a note of it for future reference. This information may one day help you to assess the required dosage of medication to treat your fishes, for example.

Specific gravity

Specific gravity is simply the ratio of the density of any liquid compared to the density of distilled water (which has a specific gravity of 1). Sea water is denser and contains far more dissolved minerals, so that the S.G. is greater than 1. (The concentration of total solids dissolved in a specified amount of water can also be expressed in terms of salinity i.e. grams/litre. The table shows the relationship between specific gravity and salinity.)

The salinity of sea water varies from one

Specific gravity/salinity at 15°C(59°F)	
Specific gravity	**Salinity (gm/litre:ppm)**
1.015	20.6
1.016	22.0
1.017	23.3
1.018	24.6
1.019	25.9
1.020	27.2
1.021	28.5
1.022	29.8
1.023	31.1
1.024	32.4
1.025	33.7
1.026	35.0
1.027	36.3
1.028	37.6
1.029	38.9
1.030	40.2

location to another. For instance, neither the Red Sea nor the Mediterranean is tidal and both have a high evaporation rate, therefore they are more saline than the open ocean. The Western Atlantic Ocean around the Caribbean also has a high salinity. The Dead Sea, of course, has the highest salinity of any sea in the world and no fishes can live there at all.

The salinity/specific gravity of water has an effect on the fishes living in it, and here we come to one of the fundamental differences between saltwater and freshwater fishes in terms of basic biology.

A freshwater fish is surrounded by water which is less dense than its body fluids.

Due to a phenomenon known as osmosis, water is absorbed into the body and a fish must excrete water constantly so that it does not burst. The marine fish faces the opposite problem: it is constantly losing water to its surroundings so that it must drink copious amounts of water and excrete only salts. A reasonably low S.G. of 1.020-1.021, which is slightly below that of their natural environment, will lessen the 'water-loss' stress on marine fishes in captivity. (Once an aquarium is fully stocked, some experienced marine aquarists allow the specific gravity to rise slowly to 1.022-1.023.)

Variations in S.G. will occur as a result of evaporation. Only pure water is lost during this process and so evaporation losses should be made good with fresh water and *not* a prepared salt-mix. Losses caused by evaporation are automatically replaced in 'total systems' which incorporate self-acting topping-up devices. A condensation tray or close-fitting cover glass will cut down evaporation losses as well as conserve heat in the aquarium.

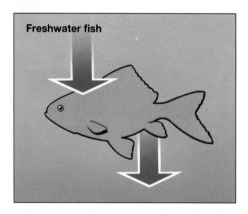

Above: An important difference between marine and freshwater fishes is the way in which they are affected by the water that surrounds them. Freshwater fishes absorb water through osmosis, and must pass copious amounts of urine to prevent themselves from bursting.

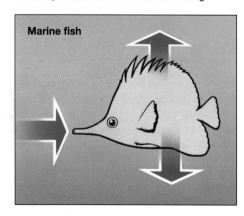

Above: The marine fish has to cope with the reverse situation; it is constantly losing water through its skin to the stronger concentration of sea water outside. Therefore, it has to drink large amounts of water to keep its body fluids at the correct concentration, and so passes only very small amounts of urine.

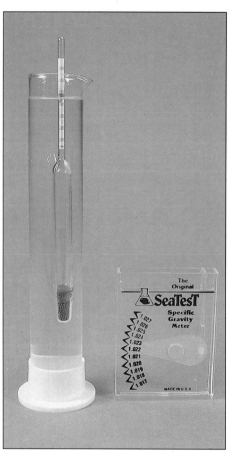

Above: Two methods of measuring specific gravity. Left: A floating hydrometer where the S.G. is read off at the water line. Right: A 'swing-needle' type of hydrometer indicates the S.G. of the water filling its container. Air bubbles on the needle will affect the reading and should therefore be removed by gentle tapping.

The pH of water

The pH of water is a measure of its acidity or alkalinity. It is measured on a logarithmic scale: values below 7 are acidic and values above 7 are alkaline. Sea water has a higher pH than fresh water or domestic tapwater and should be maintained at between 7.9 and 8.3. A falling pH often indicates that the water is aging and that its buffering capabilities (its ability to resist pH changes) is declining. In this case, a proportion – say 20% – of the aquarium water should be changed. Such partial changes are usually part of a regular, monthly routine and, in addition to stabilizing the pH, will also help to keep the nitrate level low in the absence of more sophisticated filtration equipment. (Since tapwater may contain appreciable levels of nitrate, be sure to check your local supply and allow for this when making water changes. Resin-filled treatment units are available for reducing nitrate levels in tapwater.) Although once believed to help stabilize the correct pH value of the water, a calcareous substrate – one rich in calcium – is probably of more use as an inert, 'bacteria-friendly' colonizing material vital in the biological filtration process (see Filtration, pages 26-31).

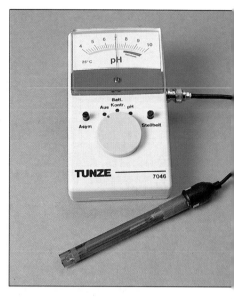

Above: A sophisticated method of measuring pH is to use an extremely accurate electronic pH meter. The probe is first calibrated, using a special solution, and then immersed in the aquarium water to give an immediate reading.

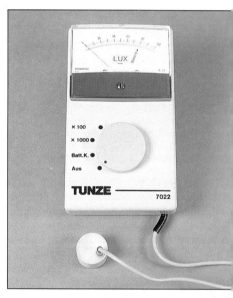

Above: The lighting level in the marine aquarium is critical if beneficial growths of algae are to be encouraged. This lightmeter has a remote probe that can be used to monitor light intensity. Clean water will help to keep light levels high.

Maintaining water quality

It is important for the marine fishkeeper to understand these details about the properties of water and the importance of maintaining water quality. Marine fishes are highly intolerant of poor conditions and of sudden changes in conditions brought about by the good, albeit drastic, and often last-minute intentions of the hobbyist. Any deliberate alteration to the quality and condition of the water must be made as gradually as possible to avoid stressing the fish. A case in point here is that newly bought fish introduced into an established aquarium may succumb to the levels of toxins (although relatively low) that the 'resident' fishes have become used to.

Testing the pH value of water

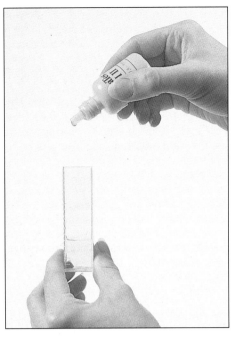

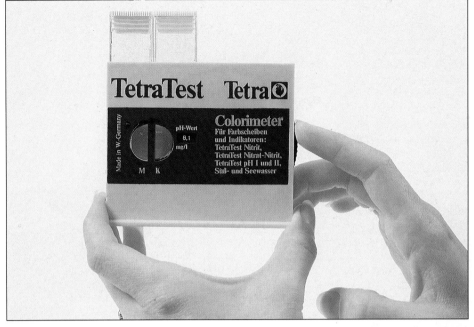

Above: For this pH test, add the required number of drops of reagent to a sample of aquarium water and gently shake the calibrated container to ensure complete mixing. Above right: Insert the container of mixed sample and reagent into a 'colour wheel' comparator. The second vessel (to the right) contains just aquarium water; this pre-colours the viewing window and so a true colour comparison is obtained that automatically takes into consideration the colour of the aquarium water. Rotate the colour wheel until you achieve a close colour match and read off the pH value. Right: Alternatively, you can compare the sample with a printed colour chart.

Below, below right: All pH test kits are based on the same principle, as shown in these further examples: a colour comparison between a mixture of water and reagent and a calibrated colour scale. It is a good idea to keep the colour chart out of strong light when not in use as faded colours make for inaccurate results. In order to obtain a true evaluation of water conditions, ensure that all factors, especially temperature and time of day, remain consistent.

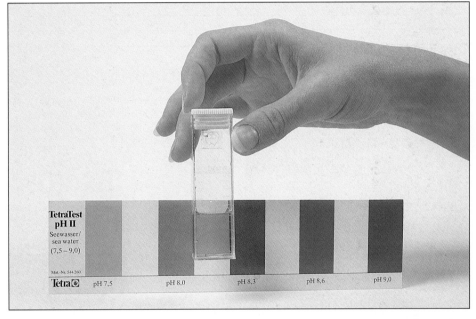

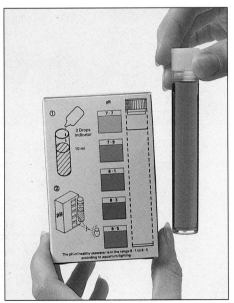

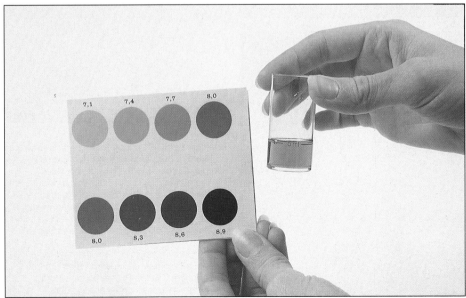

Testing for ammonia

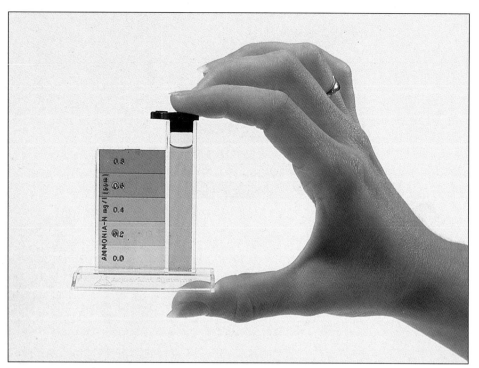

The marine aquarium is no more a slice of the ocean indoors, than the freshwater aquarium is a section of river or stream. The forces of nature in the aquarium may always seem to be against you, but a clear understanding of the problems, coupled with proficient management techniques should make for success.

In addition to periodically measuring pH and specific gravity, there are other tests that can, and should be performed to ensure that water quality remains at its optimum. Once water has been 'lived in' (for want of a better phrase), the resultant effect of the waste products of fish respiration, digestion and natural decay on the water quality can be measured. The main component of waste products is ammonia, together with two other important nitrogenous compounds, nitrite and nitrate. All three compounds are toxic to fishes and invertebrates to varying degrees (see Fil-

Left: The reagents used in this ammonia test kit are pre-packed in sachets. Simply add to a water sample as directed and interpret the colour change as ammonia level in mg/l(ppm).

Testing for nitrite

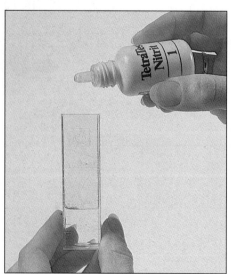

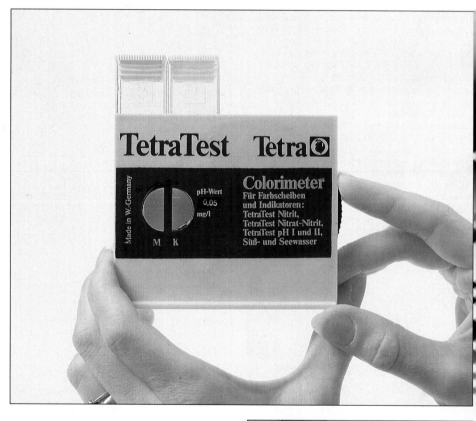

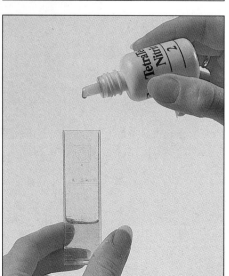

Above left and left: When testing for nitrite, you will need to add two reagents to the water sample in turn. Above: The colour wheel comparator is used again, but this time with the nitrite wheel. As before, a 'control' container of aquarium water is used in the viewing window. Rotate the wheel, find the closest colour match and then read off the nitrite level in mg/l(ppm).

Right: It is still possible to read the nitrite level without a colour wheel system; here a printed colour chart is used. Precautions taken for making pH readings apply equally here.

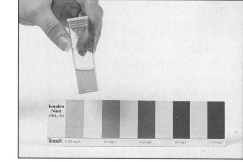

tration, page 26). By using the relevant test kit you can keep a check on the build-up of these unwanted byproducts, and also evaluate how efficient your filtration system and regular partial water changes are at keeping them down to a minimum. (Checking the carbonate hardness of the water periodically, for example, will provide an indication of its buffering capabilities.)

All these tests will indicate the state of your aquarium water, but be sure to interpret the readings correctly, otherwise you may implement the wrong remedial measures, with dire results.

Other test kits, such as those used to determine levels of copper in the water, can be of great value when treating the aquarium for disease. The usual disease treatments for marine fishes are copper based and, since copper is lethal at 'overdose' levels, it is important to administer a very accurate dose. By using a copper test kit to monitor the amount of copper given, you will avoid the 'kill or cure' method of old, in which dosing was based on correctly estimating the water content of your aquarium. This is not easy to do, especially allowing for coral and other decorations, and heater displacement. Since modern aquarium technology has provided the means of monitoring the water quality, you would be foolish to ignore these facilities, but do use them wisely. (See pages 57-58 for advice on using disease remedies.)

Testing for copper

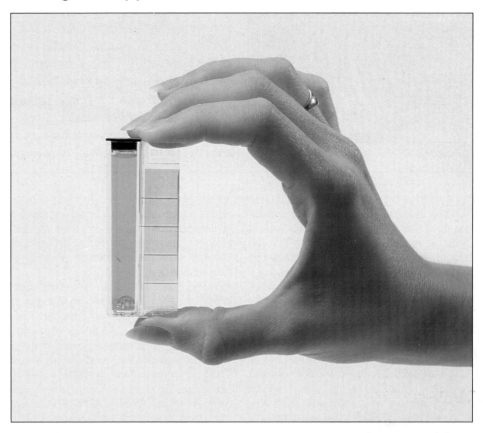

Above: Accurate measurements of the copper level will assist you to dose the water when treating for diseases. This test involves adding one sachet and then another to a water sample; the colour change shows mg/l copper.

Below: Invertebrates are less tolerant of low concentrations of copper than are fishes. Using a copper test kit is strongly advised, although it would be better to remove sick fishes from a fully stocked tank for 'copper-cure' treatment.

FILTRATION SYSTEMS

Regal Angelfish, thriving in clean water.

Clear water allows beneficial light to reach the algae, and enables you to see your fishes more clearly. 'High-tech' filtration systems look after everything but are expensive to install, and a more simple system is usually quite adequate. Visible or invisible waste materials can be removed either biologically (using the aquarium's base covering as a bacterial colony), chemically or mechanically, using miniature water pumps to drive the aquarium water through suitable filtration media. Filtration also aerates the water, circulates it throughout the aquarium, assists gaseous exchanges at the water surface and prevents 'cold spots' occurring. It can even bring food to sedentary invertebrates.

As we stated right at the outset, the key to success in marine fishkeeping is maintaining good water quality. Here, we look in detail at aquarium filtration systems and how they help to provide healthy conditions for a wide range of marine creatures.

Filtration systems
The purpose of the aquarium filtration system is to remove as much unwanted 'dirt' from the water as possible, thus delaying the need to replace water for as long as possible. As well as visible dirt and sediment stirred up by the actions of the fishes and other tank occupants, the water also contains invisible dissolved organic compounds (waste products and the result of their decomposition) and these too must be removed.

Many types of filters are used in the aquarium hobby, ranging from simple air-operated box filters to highly sophisticated water purification systems. Filters vary

External power filter

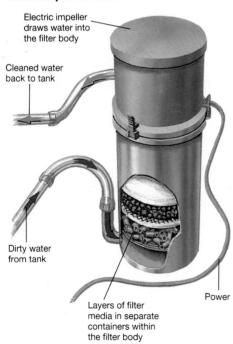

Electric impeller draws water into the filter body

Cleaned water back to tank

Dirty water from tank

Power

Layers of filter media in separate containers within the filter body

Above: External power filters, containing a variety of filter media, help to maintain excellent water conditions in the aquarium. Pieces of ceramic pipe, activated carbon and floss are among the media most commonly used.

not only in design but in their mode of operation, some providing simple mechanical straining while others exert a chemical or biological influence on the water flowing through them. Many filters perform all three functions.

In addition to these 'standard' filter types, many of which find a ready application in both freshwater and marine aquariums, there are a number of water treatment systems that are used more or less exclusively for marine creatures. These systems include algal filters, protein skimmers, ozonizers and ultraviolet sterilizers. We shall discuss the operation and merits of these filtration methods later in this section. First, we look at the options open to the marine aquarist among the more convential type of filters.

Mechanical and chemical filters
The simplest type of mechanical filter suitable for a marine aquarium is the external sealed canister power filter. Its basic advantage over air-operated designs widely used in freshwater fishkeeping is that it delivers a satisfactorily high throughput of water. An electric motor mounted in the top of the canister powers a pump that draws water through the filter media placed inside the body of the unit. By varying the media, it is possible to 'fine tune' the effect of the filter.

The most commonly used 'mechanical' filter medium is some form of floss made from spun nylon, dacron or some other man-made fibre. In order to prevent rapid clogging of the fibres it is normal practice to have some 'prefilter' medium ahead of the floss in the water flow. This can be small pieces of ceramic pipe, but many fishkeepers use squashed together plastic pot-scourers. Preformed foam pads that fit snuggly into the filter body not only perform a simple straining function but also act as biological filters once bacteria have colonized the foam (see below).

The most common chemical medium used in canister filters is activated carbon. This is basically wood charcoal that is 'activated' by being baked at a high temperature to open up tiny pores in the particles and to make the surface of the carbon more

'attractive' to certain substances. As aquarium water passes through the carbon pieces, dissolved waste products are adsorbed (i.e. taken up on the surface) over the very large surface area available (This also makes activated carbon an ideal site for bacteria to flourish and so provide a degree of biological filtration as well.) The carbon is usually sandwiched between two layers of floss in the filter body to prevent it from being drawn into the aquarium. Alternatively, the charcoal can be contained in a nylon bag, which serves the same purpose.

Other filter media include materials that help to remove nitrates from the water. One such type is readily colonized by nitrifying bacteria which, by increasing their numbers, provides an efficient biological action. Such a medium can be used within a canister-type power filter in addition to the other media used for mechanical and chemical filtration purposes.

As well as providing some biological filtration effect of its own, an external power filter is often used as a mechanical pre-filter to a reverse-flow biological filter, as described below.

Whatever type of mechanical or chemical filter you use, always clean or replace the filter medium regularly; a permanently dirty filter medium will redissolve much of the extracted dirt back into the aquarium.

Biological filtration
In the wild, the cleansing action of the sea disperses the waste substances produced by the fish. In the closed confines of an aquarium, the fish depend on the fishkeeper to provide an efficient system to purify the water. Biological filtration is a natural means of removing toxic ammonia-based wastes from the aquarium.

It is quite simple to summarise the reasons for the presence of ammonia in the water and the necessity of removing it. Fishes and invertebrates excrete ammonia from their gills. This is added to the ammonia produced by bacteria working on other waste materials in the aquarium, such as dead plants and uneaten food, and faeces. Ammonia is toxic to fishes and invertebrates; if it is not removed, or converted into other less harmful substances, then

Down-flow biological filtration system

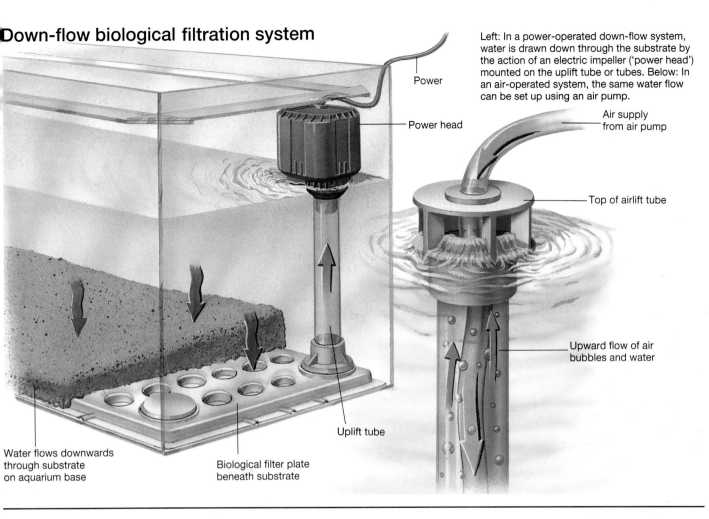

Power

Power head

Left: In a power-operated down-flow system, water is drawn down through the substrate by the action of an electric impeller ('power head') mounted on the uplift tube or tubes. Below: In an air-operated system, the same water flow can be set up using an air pump.

Air supply from air pump

Top of airlift tube

Upward flow of air bubbles and water

Uplift tube

Water flows downwards through substrate on aquarium base

Biological filter plate beneath substrate

Reverse-flow biological filtration system

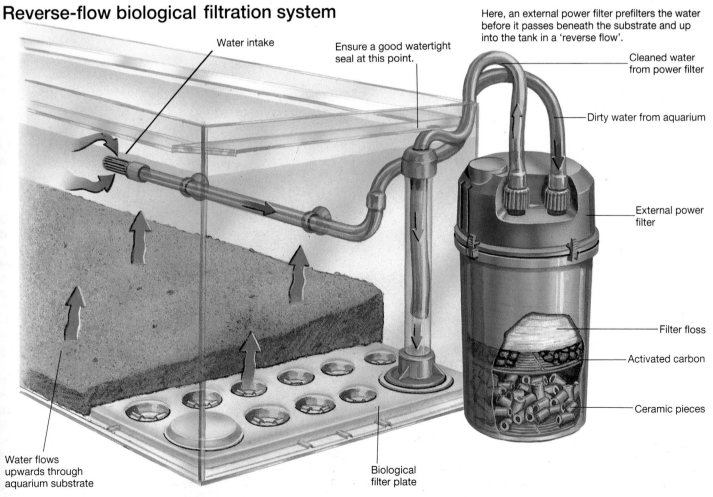

Water intake

Ensure a good watertight seal at this point.

Here, an external power filter prefilters the water before it passes beneath the substrate and up into the tank in a 'reverse flow'.

Cleaned water from power filter

Dirty water from aquarium

External power filter

Filter floss

Activated carbon

Ceramic pieces

Water flows upwards through aquarium substrate

Biological filter plate

aquatic life would soon perish. Fortunately, in Nature's Grand Plan, a substance that is poison to one living organism is food for another and thus there is a natural way of dealing with ammonia disposal.

Aerobic (oxygen-loving) bacteria, such as *Nitrosomonas* sp., convert ammonia to nitrite, a slightly less toxic substance but one that is still dangerous to fishes and invertebrates. A second group of bacteria, such as *Nitrobacter* sp., transform the nitrite to nitrate, a much safer substance but one that can still cause problems if it builds up in the aquarium. Different marine creatures vary in their sensitivity to these nitrogenous compounds. Nitrate levels, for example, should be maintained below 20ppm (parts per million/equivalent to mg per litre) for fishes and below 5ppm for invertebrates (and even lower for some).

If further anaerobic, or oxygen-hating, bacteria are allowed to get to work then the nitrate can be converted back to atmospheric nitrogen (by so-called denitrification) and vented from the aquarium. Herein lies a paradox, however, since if we are to provide ideal situations for the complete disposal of ammonia then it appears that we must provide two sets of conditions for opposite types of bacteria.

In the basic marine set-up it is usual to provide the conditions required by the first group of bacteria, i.e. those that thrive on oxygen. The inevitable subsequent build up of nitrate is kept under control by carrying out regular partial water changes – always assuming that the 'new' water has a lower level of nitrates than the tank water. Here, treating tapwater with a nitrate-reducing resin can be particularly useful. (In some modern 'total system' aquariums, the filtration system provides both aerobic and anaerobic conditions at different stages in the filtration process.)

Providing the necessary oxygen-rich environment for the *Nitrosomonas* and *Nitrobacter* bacteria is almost too simple: the aquarium water is pumped through a layer of coral sand (ideally about 5-7.5cm/2-3in) on the aquarium base. It does not matter to the bacteria whether the water is pumped downwards or upwards. Living on the surface of each grain of sand, and thus covering an immense total surface area, the bacterial colonies carry out their nitrifying task as long as oxygen-carrying water continues to flow. Once it stops, the colonies of beneficial bacteria begin to die, resulting in pollution of the tank.

In a marine aquarium containing fish, you must maintain a high rate of water flow through the gravel – around 50 litres per square metre per minute (approximately equivalent to 1 gallon per square foot per minute). In a system containing only invertebrates, filtration should be equally as efficient and, where possible, the turbu-

lence of the water should be increased.

In traditional 'down-flow' systems, water is drawn down through the sand and returned to the main body of the tank via vertical tubes. Powerheads fitted to the top of the return tubes leading from the undergravel filter plate are effective for this purpose. In a 'reverse-flow' system, an external canister-type power filter is used as the motive force to pump water into the space beneath the filter plate so that it then flows upwards through the sand. One advantage of this system is that the water is cleaned before it passes through the filter bed and so the sand does not clog up quite so quickly. Water currents rising from the substrate will help to keep food in suspension, to the benefit of bottom-dwelling invertebrates, and will help to maintain a clean tank floor by preventing detritus from settling. There is also the possibility that food will be filtered out of the water on its way to the sub-sand filter, but this should not be a problem if the water flow through the sand is not excessively fast.

In aquariums of more advanced design, the beneficial activity of nitrifying bacteria may take place elsewhere. Sometimes, instead of using the substrate as a filter bed, the water passes through a filter medium with a correspondingly large sur-

Below: The use of filtration and aeration in the aquarium need not necessarily result in a cluttered tank; notice how cleverly the air diffuser has been hidden in this sunken jug.

face area to support bacterial colonization. This could be a large sponge filter, for instance, located within the confines of the tank or outside it. Such filters can be easier to handle, maintain and control than undergravel types. Alternatively, a small portion of the water flow can be trickle fed through a chamber containing inert granules that support beneficial bacterial colonies. Such chambers allow the bacterial activity to occur before the water rejoins the main circulation system.

In a newly set up aquarium, the biological filter's bacterial colony will take time to become established and, until the colony has matured, it will have little control over the rise of ammonia and nitrite levels. *Nitrosomonas* and *Nitrobacter* colonies may take one and two months respectively to become established and the conversion of nitrite into relatively harmless nitrate does not begin until the ammonia-nitrite conversion process is well under way.

Fishkeepers may become impatient with this delay, but there are ways of reducing the biological filter's maturation period. Adding some sand or even water from an existing well-established aquarium will 'seed' the filter bed and get it off to a good start. Alternatively, introducing one or two inexpensive hardy fish – to provide waste products – will give the bacteria some raw material to work on.

Be sure to monitor the nitrite level regularly in the first few days and weeks and only start to add more fish and other

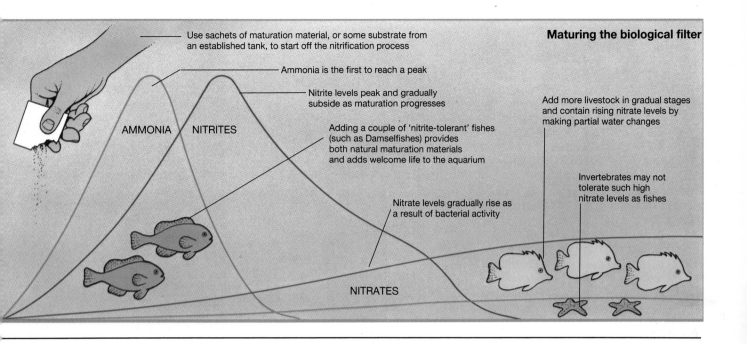

Maturing the biological filter

Use sachets of maturation material, or some substrate from an established tank, to start off the nitrification process

Ammonia is the first to reach a peak

Nitrite levels peak and gradually subside as maturation progresses

AMMONIA   NITRITES

Adding a couple of 'nitrite-tolerant' fishes (such as Damselfishes) provides both natural maturation materials and adds welcome life to the aquarium

Add more livestock in gradual stages and contain rising nitrate levels by making partial water changes

Nitrate levels gradually rise as a result of bacterial activity

Invertebrates may not tolerate such high nitrate levels as fishes

NITRATES

The nitrogen cycle

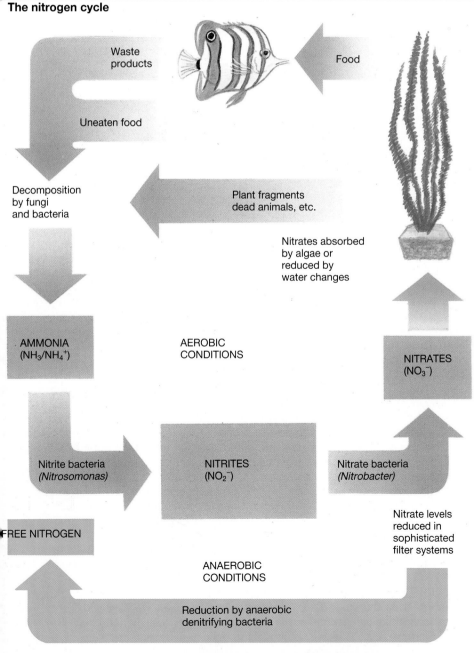

Waste products

Food

Uneaten food

Decomposition by fungi and bacteria

Plant fragments dead animals, etc.

Nitrates absorbed by algae or reduced by water changes

AMMONIA
(NH_3/NH_4^+)

AEROBIC CONDITIONS

NITRATES
(NO_3^-)

Nitrite bacteria
(*Nitrosomonas*)

NITRITES
(NO_2^-)

Nitrate bacteria
(*Nitrobacter*)

Nitrate levels reduced in sophisticated filter systems

FREE NITROGEN

ANAEROBIC CONDITIONS

Reduction by anaerobic denitrifying bacteria

Above: Accelerate the maturation of the biological filter by adding 'seeding' substances or one or two hardy fishes. Ammonia and nitrite levels rise to a peak then fall to a stable minimum. Nitrate levels rise slowly, but are kept in check by regular partial water changes.

Left: The establishment of a well-balanced nitrogen cycle is vital to the marine aquarium. Ideally, ammonia-based waste products are broken down by aerobic bacteria into nitrites and then nitrates, which are absorbed by algae and/or removed during partial water changes.

animals to the aquarium when the level falls to a minimum reading. Be sure to build up the full population capacity of the tank over a reasonably long period of time, ideally several months, so that the filter bed can keep in step with the increasing levels of waste materials it has to deal with.

Other types of filters

In a marine aquarium devoid of plant life, an algal filter is especially useful. A considerable amount of algae is required in marine tanks, so the filter will need to be a correspondingly large affair, which may not be practical in a domestic setting. If you are interested to pursue this aspect of filtration, the following description outlines the basic principles involved.

Aquatic plants utilize carbon dioxide in their photosynthesis processes and do much to keep this unwanted gas down to a minimum. The marine aquarium relies much upon water movement to expel carbon dioxide from the aquarium, particularly at the water surface. Unfortunately, the marine aquarium is not blessed with a profusion of conventional water plants, as is the freshwater aquarium, but it is possible to reduce the carbon dioxide levels by the use of the most primitive of plants – green algae. Although in theory this is quite reasonable, the practical applications are not without problems.

An algal filter can take two forms: an outside sand filter can be encouraged to produce an algal top layer by shining a bright light down on its surface; or the water from another type of filter can be returned across a shallow well-lit tray on which algae are again encouraged to grow. Algal filters are not commonly found in aquariums of home proportions, but may be incorporated in much larger aquariums, where there is sufficient space to accommodate the trays above the aquarium.

A more practical alternative to setting up bulky, difficult to install and disguise algal filters, is to encourage heavy growths of leaf algae, such as the various species of *Caulerpa*, in the main body of the aquarium (see pages 34-35 for a selection of algae).

Other forms of water purification

There are other water purification systems that are especially useful in the marine aquarium. However, they may not be absolutely necessary in tanks with a low stocking level, provided an efficient biological filtration system is present. Activated carbon also helps to remove organic matter, as does protein skimming, a singularly marine aquarium process often associated with the use of ozone. Ultraviolet light sterilization can also be used to keep the water free of parasites and other unwanted micro-organisms. Here, we look briefly at each of these purification processes.

Protein skimming

Protein skimmers literally 'skim off' organic matter from the aquarium water by making use of the natural tendency for the so-called 'surface-active' dissolved organic molecules to 'stick' to the air/water interface. If we can provide a good opportunity for air/water interfaces to occur within the aquarium water, then we should be able to remove the organic matter. Such a situation is provided by the protein skimmer, which introduces a column of air bubbles into a vertical 'contact' tube within the aquarium. The organic matter is adsorbed (in a similar manner to which organic material is adsorbed by activated carbon) onto the air/water interface of the bubbles and is carried up into a collecting cup at the top of the skimmer. Here, the foam collapses into a yellowish liquid, which is then discarded. The alternative name of 'foam fractionation' is perhaps a more apt description for the processes involved.

In practice, there are two basic designs of air-operated protein skimmers. In so-called 'direct-current' devices, the water and air bubbles flow in the same direction (i.e. upwards) in the contact tube. An airstone near the bottom of the tube provides both the stream of air bubbles and the

Counter-current protein skimmer

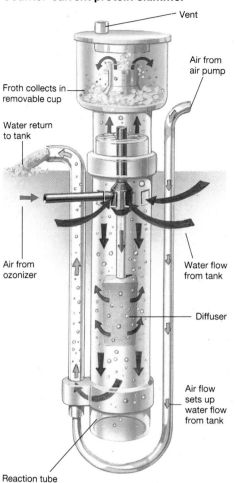

Vent

Froth collects in removable cup

Air from air pump

Water return to tank

Air from ozonizer

Water flow from tank

Diffuser

Air flow sets up water flow from tank

Reaction tube

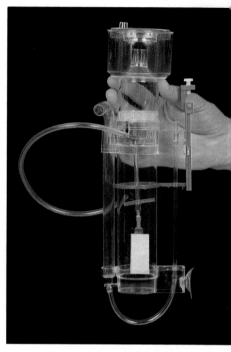

Above: An air-operated counter-current model of protein skimmer, considered by most marine aquarists to be a vital piece of equipment. Note the clip for attachment to the tank (top right) and the removable sediment cup (top).

Left: Water enters the protein skimmer through the small square holes, travels down against the upward flow of ozonized air bubbles, and returns to the aquarium via the airlift tube (left). Froth collects in the cup and settles into an organic-rich liquid that is discarded.

impetus to set up the water flow. In these designs, the water and air bubbles are in contact for a relatively short time. In 'counter-current' protein skimmers, two air-stones are used in different tubes of the device so that incoming water flows downwards through the rising mass of bubbles in the contact tube. In this way, water and bubbles stay in contact for a longer time.

A third design makes use of an electric pump to produce a high-pressure mixture of air and water in a venturi chamber. This produces froth, which is again collected in a chamber and the settled liquid discarded. This type of protein skimmer will not remove planktonic foods from the water (needed by filter feeders) since the protein wastes diffuse into the collecting chamber.

It has been suggested that the continuous use of a protein skimmer can cause a reduction of trace elements in the water. There is no real evidence for this, but it is as well to use proprietary trace element additives, particularly if filter feeders and seaweeds are included in the aquarium.

Using an ozonizer

Ozone (O_3) is an unstable form of oxygen gas (O_2). The extra atom of oxygen readily separates from the molecule and oxidizes toxins and other compounds in the aquarium water. This oxidizing action also makes ozone an effective disinfectant; it will kill bacteria and other free-swimming micro-organisms that come into close contact with the gas.

Ozone is formed by passing air (ideally dried and cooled) through an electrical discharge in a device known as an ozonizer. The ozonized air is then passed into the contact tube of a counter-current protein skimmer. In this way, the ozone has an immediate disinfecting action on the water passing through the skimmer, but does not harm fish and other living organisms in the main part of the tank. A carbon filter can be used to remove any surplus ozone before the water returns to the aquarium.

As you might imagine, it is very dangerous to use ozone directly in the aquarium water, by passing it through an airstone, for example. It could prove particularly harmful in a reverse-flow biological filtration system, since any build up of surplus ozone within the aquarium hood will adversely affect the bacteria in any overhead trickle filters.

Always use plastic airline when dealing with ozone; it will damage rubber tubing and pump diaphragms, and excessive levels will even make plastic brittle. Be careful when working with ozone; exposure over long periods may cause headaches, dizziness or even nausea. As a ough guide to the correct level, increase he amount of ozone until it is just detec- able by its rotting seaweed/bleachy smell and then reduce the supply slightly.

Ultraviolet light sterilization

Ultraviolet light will sterilize water exposed to it and is used as a mild disin- fectant. Like ozone, it is not without its dangers and must be used correctly. *Never look at the UV lamp without eye protection.*

A UV sterilizer consists of a UV lamp, which has a special quartz envelope, mounted within a water jacket. Aquarium water fed into the outer jacket is sterilized as it flows from one end to the other. The efficiency of sterilization depends, among other factors, on the contact time of expo- sure. The effectiveness of the lamp can be optimized by filtering the water well before passing it through the sterilizer. This pre- vents organic material and suspended mat- er from obscuring the quartz envelope and thus lessening the effect of the UV rays. Even so, the lamp has a definite lifespan; used continuously it will last between six months and a year. After this period, the lamp may appear to function properly, but in fact the UV light cannot penetrate the quartz tube and a replacement is needed.

Using filters with medications

The treatment of disease in the marine aquarium can be complicated by the pre- sence of sophisticated filtration systems. Activated carbon will adsorb many medica- tions, for example, and there has been some speculation in the past that the use of ozone and UV sterilization in conjunction with copper-based remedies could possibly prove dangerous. Recent professional ex- periences have not shown any problems, but some amount of caution might be pru- dent if you are in any doubt.

Using filters with filter-feeders

Invertebrates need a high water flow rate and clean water. A protein skimmer will take care of providing clean water. (Protein skimmers that do not damage plankton – an essential part of the invertebrates' diet – are particularly suitable. Check with your local aquarium dealer.) Reverse-flow bio- logical filtration has obvious benefits for the aquarium, but it is a good idea to turn off the water flow for a short time when feeding invertebrates. It is also beneficial to try and set up different directions of water flow from time to time to simulate natural tidal action. Many 'total systems' incorporate programmes such as 'food interrupt' or 'tidal pulse' and even reduced night-time power settings.

Right: This cutaway diagram shows how the aquarium water is sterilized by UV rays as it passes through the water jacket surrounding a UV fluorescent lamp. Replace lamp regularly.

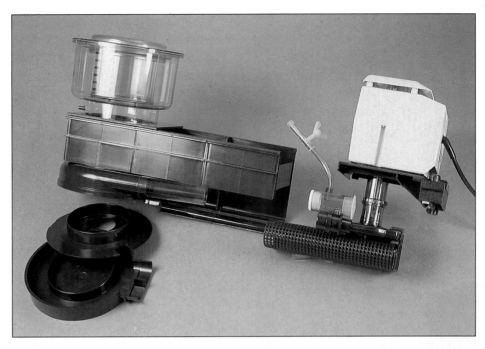

Above: This power-operated protein skimmer (seen partially dismantled) pumps water via a venturi, where it is mixed with air (right), into a circular chamber. The resulting froth collects in the large container at top left.

Below: The action of this particular skimmer causes protein, but not planktonic food, to diffuse into the collecting area. This type of skimmer is especially beneficial in aquariums housing filter-feeding animals.

UV sterilizer

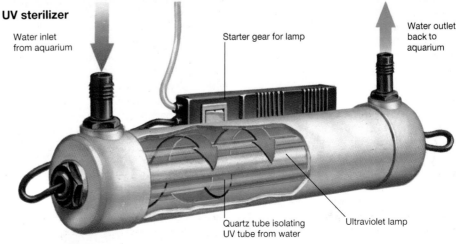

Water inlet from aquarium

Starter gear for lamp

Water outlet back to aquarium

Quartz tube isolating UV tube from water

Ultraviolet lamp

TANK DECORATIONS

Fishes and corals making a perfect display.

A bare tank may look the ultimate in cleanliness but how uninteresting for the observer! Fish, too, appreciate tank decorations, where they can find safety and rest. Pieces of coral create a pleasant scene for you and give the fishes peace of mind. Do not overdo the tank decorations, however; you will reduce the available swimming space, you'll never catch the fish and you may overlook a fish that dies hidden from view. It may also make it difficult to estimate the water capacity of the tank – vital for treatments. Use suitable materials to decorate the tank and stick to natural-looking pieces; plastic models of freshwater plants may add welcome foliage but are hardly realistic in a marine setting. Consider growing marine leaf algae.

A newcomer to marine fishkeeping might be forgiven for thinking that the sole function of tank decorations is to beautify the tank and disguise its artificiality. However, most of the materials used to decorate the aquarium play an integral part in maintaining good water quality. Therefore, this aspect of setting up the tank deserves to be treated as a priority and not as a last-minute consideration. Another reason for planning the decor in advance is that corals must be thoroughly cleaned and treated long before they are added to the tank.

When you come to decorate the tank, always work from the bottom upwards. An obvious statement perhaps, but if you are intending to use undergravel biological filtration it is vital to remember to install the filter plate at the base of the tank before adding any substrate on top.

Choosing the substrate

The covering of the aquarium base performs two important functions. Primarily, where it is used as part of a biological filtration system, it forms a huge surface area upon which nitrifying bacteria can thrive and carry out their purifying activity. Secondly, it is used by those fishes that bury themselves in the substrate at night, burrow into it by day, or sift through it in search of food.

Coral sand and coarser crushed coral are ideal materials for this purpose. Use the coarser material to form the lower layers of the substrate and separate this from the finer textured top layer with plastic or nylon netting. The netting will prevent burrowing fishes from exposing the subgravel filter plate and is useful in the event of a total strip down of the tank when you may want to wash the two materials separately. One problem of introducing substrate netting is that it will prevent adequate substrate cleaning using the modern siphonic 'gravel cleaners'. If you do not keep digging fishes, then use the cleaner at partial water-change times, partially removing water and cleaning the substrate at the same time. Alternatively, the lower portions of the substrate may be kept clean by periodically siphoning out water and dirt via the biological filter uplift tube.

The substrate should be sufficiently deep to allow efficient biological filtration to occur. A depth of at least 5-7.5cm (2-3in) is recommended, and the substrate can be sloped from the front up to the rear of the aquarium to an even greater depth. This not only makes it look interesting, but also causes dirt and detritus to collect at the front of the aquarium, where it can be seen and removed. In practice, however, dirt often gets trapped behind rocks and lumps of coral, so don't forget to siphon out this accumulated detritus too!

Left: The plastic 'gravel tidy' separates the lower layer of crushed coral from the coral sand. Allow a deep enough layer of substrate on top for the benefit of burrowing fishes and for filtration.

Choosing suitable rocks

Apart from deciding how to set out the tank, you must choose the correct materials to put in it. Once again, remember the importance of water quality control and use one of the wide range of calcareous substances available. Fortunately, there is no difficulty in obtaining such materials; hard sandstones, basalt, granite, lava rocks, limestone (dolomite), slate and tufa rock are all quite safe, but avoid any rocks that have metallic-ore veins showing. If you have any doubt about the suitability of a particular rock, seek advice from your local aquarium dealer.

Build up the rocks to form backdrops and multicreviced terraces for the cave-dwelling fishes. Flat-topped rocks placed on the aquarium floor become natural anchoring sites for sea anemones, and tubeworms will readily make use of rocks with suitable holes in them. (See pages 186-199 for a wide selection of suitable invertebrates.)

Corals as decorations

Although it is very tempting to try to create a finished aquarium that looks like a section of the Great Barrier Reef, resist the temptation to overdo the decoration. Corals

Above: Tufa rock is high in calcium content, will not adversely affect the water's chemical condition and may even help to stabilize the pH at the required level of around 7.9-8.3.

Above: You can glue large empty barnacle shells together to form interesting outcrops and these will also provide the necessary retreats for both smaller fishes and shy invertebrates.

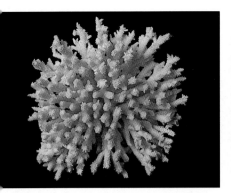

Above: This Staghorn Coral may be extremely decorative but it has one or two drawbacks: it is very brittle, requires very careful handling and can be awkward to clean thoroughly.

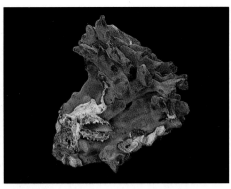

Above: Blue Coral, *Heliopora,* provides a welcome alternative to the normally white skeletal remains of most other corals. The coloration is caused by mineral deposits.

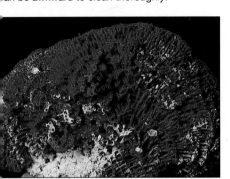

Above: Another coloured coral, *Tubipora musica,* or Organ Pipe Coral, is a favourite with marine fishkeepers. Like the Blue Coral, its brilliant colour does not fade as the polyps die.

Above: Another brittle, finely branched coral. You should wash such specimens thoroughly before placing them in the aquarium. Use your nose to discern if all is really clean!

look superb in their natural surroundings – as we know from the many television documentaries on the subject – but some of the more spectacular formations are quite impracticable in the aquarium. Apart from the fact that they are far too big, some pieces of coral are extremely brittle, or so convoluted that they are impossible to clean and become traps for uneaten food, which could pollute the water.

The corals you buy from aquatic stores are the skeletal remains of the original living polyps. Most corals are white; it is their physical shapes that provide the visual attraction. However, *Tubipora,* the Organ-pipe Coral, retains its red coloration. Sometimes you will see *Heliopora,* a fleshy-lobed blue coral for sale.

In time, the objection to the 'too-white' colour of coral becomes meaningless as you realise that it will soon become naturally discoloured with, hopefully, a covering of beneficial green algae after a reasonable period in the aquarium.

Imported corals may have been superficially cleaned, but very often organic remains still cling to them. Always clean corals yourself before using them in the

Below: The variety of different structures and colours of corals will provide you with plenty of raw material from which you can construct an attractive coral reef in your own aquarium.

aquarium (see page 36).

You can avoid the risks of cleaning and perhaps breaking corals, by placing them dry in a box behind the tank and leaving the back panel of the tank unobscured. When you illuminate this feature with a spotlight you create not only an effective diorama (three-dimensional backdrop) but also appear to increase the front-to-back dimensions of the aquarium.

Yet another approach is to decorate the aquarium with synthetic copies of corals. These are made using rubber moulds and coloured resins that will not break down in salt water.

If you wonder why real coral is expensive, try to imagine how you would bring home that visually stunning piece from the local store without damaging it, let alone transport it all the way from its original habitat! Less spectacular coral forms can make equally interesting layouts and offer excellent refuges and clearly defined areas for territorial fishes.

To anchor the coral, glue it to a base rock with aquarium silicone sealant. You can join several separate pieces together, but do not build up too large a display. Once constructed and glued, you may well have difficulty in moving it around the tank, or removing it if necessary. Furthermore, when it comes to catching the fish, those wonderful coral structures soon make short work of the net – as well as providing the fish with too many frustrating safe retreats from your attentions.

To make a coral display, apply aquarium silicone sealant to each piece as here

Build up the display on a firm base. Keep the arrangements simple and compact

Above: You can use aquarium sealant to glue separate pieces of coral together to form interesting outcrops, or you can glue them directly on to rocks to give them a more stable foundation in the aquarium.

Creating a coral diorama

Below: A dry, well-lit diorama of corals and rocks behind the aquarium will provide a natural-looking background to the underwater scene. Leave the tank's rear glass clear.

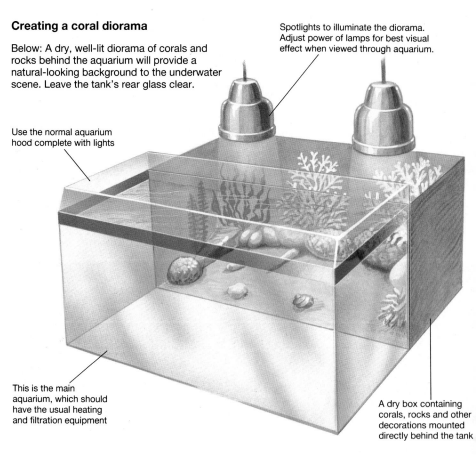

Use the normal aquarium hood complete with lights

This is the main aquarium, which should have the usual heating and filtration equipment

Spotlights to illuminate the diorama. Adjust power of lamps for best visual effect when viewed through aquarium.

A dry box containing corals, rocks and other decorations mounted directly behind the tank

Living corals
Some hobbyists cannot resist the challenge of keeping living corals and so-called 'living rocks'. Needless to say, these are expensive and not without their share of difficulties. For one thing, you must keep living coral or rocks clear of the tank base covering because polyps buried by the substrate will not survive. Another problem is choosing other animals to keep with them. Many fishes will devour the microscopic animals and polyps without any compunction. We do not know a great deal about keeping living corals and rocks, so probably the best chance of success is to set aside a separate specialist aquarium for these 'micro-living' organisms.

Marine algae
Many fishkeepers coming from freshwater to marine fishkeeping miss the 'greenery' of their previous aquariums. You could, of course, replace the living plants with plastic substitutes, but they would hardly recreate the natural appearance of a coral reef. Metal fixings or supporting wires would also cause problems. However, with the correct level of bright lighting, you can encourage the marine equivalent of freshwater plants to grow in the aquarium. These beneficial plants – primitive forms of seaweeds – are actually algae that not only bring colour to the tank but also provide grazing fishes and invertebrates with valuable vegetable food as well as absorbing minerals from the water. The algae derive much of their nourishment from the

waste products in the water, but you may have to supplement their needs by adding important trace elements, plant fertilizers and even extra carbon dioxide to the water. One drawback of any lush growth of algae is that it may suddenly die back without any warning and cause pollution in the tank. Always keep a close watch on it for any sign of deterioration.

The following species of marine algae are suitable for the aquarium.

Caulerpa prolifera (Sea-pen algae) is commonly used. It has elongated fleshy leaves and, like other members of the genus, a creeping stem that grows across the base of the aquarium. It is a good idea to obtain specimens still attached to rock; this will give them a good start in your aquarium. Marine algae is very brittle and cannot always support its own weight out of water, so handle it carefully. *Caulerpa sertularoides* is easily recognized by its narrower, alternate pine needle-type leaves. The leaves of *Caulerpa racemosa* are berry-shaped.

Enteromorpha spp. are more filamentous and may grow spontaneously on the walls of the aquarium. They provide excellent grazing for herbivorous fishes.

Chondrus sp. (Irish Moss), *Codium* sp. (Dead Man's Fingers), *Pencillus sp.* (Neptune's Shaving Brush) and *Ulva* spp. (Sea Lettuce) are all suitable types of saltwater algae for inclusion in a marine tank.

Above: Although it looks very much like a sea fan, this is a marine alga called *Udotea flabellatum*. It is fairly small in size (around 7cm/2.75in) and is ideal for the smaller tank.

Above: The marine alga *Caulerpa* provides several species which, given correct lighting conditions, thrive well in the aquarium. This is *Caulerpa racemosa*, with berry-like leaves.

Above: *Caulerpa prolifera*, the most common species in the genus. It has flat, lobe-shaped leaves and usually grows on rocks, but it may extend through the tank with its creeping stem.

Above: *Caulerpa cupressoides*, which has a more indented leaf pattern than *C. prolifera* and is a slightly paler green. Handle *Caulerpa* with care; it will collapse out of water.

Above: Another easily recognized species, *C. serptularoides*, with alternate leaves arranged 'herringbone' fashion from the main stem. The green shade may differ from other species.

Right: It is fairly unusual to encounter red algae as an aquarium decoration. This striking specimen is growing attached to a piece of rock and provides an excellent focal point.

SETTING UP THE AQUARIUM

These corals are the home of Damselfishes.

Siting the aquarium is important for practical reasons and, although a pleasant task in itself, you won't want to do it too often! Find a position for your tank that satisfies all the requirements outlined in this chapter, and remember that it will be there (hopefully) for a long time. Plan the decoration scheme well in advance and make sure you have everything you need close to hand. Write brief step-by-step notes if necessary, or even tape record a running schedule. Always ask for help with the electrics if in doubt; don't take risks or be caught out for the sake of a little pre-planning. Some people even forget to put the biological filter plate in first before adding the substrate – don't laugh, it could happen to you!

In this chapter we consider the stages involved in setting up a basic marine aquarium, using separate items of equipment. Even if you choose a 'total system', you will find that much of the information is relevant to you as long as you make the necessary allowances for the system you are using.

The tropical marine aquarium

A practical sequence of events to follow would be:

1 Preparing corals
2 Preparing the site and tank
3 Fitting a biological filtration system
4 Adding the substrate and decorations
5 Heating, aeration and other filtration equipment
6 Lighting
7 Preparing the water and filling the tank
8 Starting up and final checks
9 Maturing the biological filter bed

This may not seem the most obvious order of events, but there are good practical reasons for it, as you will learn. Before you start make sure that everything you need is within easy reach, even those items that you only use once. Put your tools and equipment on a table nearby and prepare a plan of action. Bearing in mind the probable size of a marine aquarium, it will have to be set up from scratch in its final chosen location. (See also page 15.)

Preparing corals

Decorative corals are the skeletal remains of millions of polyps that make up parts of the coral reef. Since the coral is dead when you buy it, you must ensure that it no longer contains the remains of the original animals (or other creatures that made their home in the coral) before you put it into the aquarium. Since it takes a relatively long time to ensure that the coral is sufficiently clean, preparing it for aquarium use is the first step in setting up. There are two ways to clean coral:

1 Soak the coral in a solution of household bleach (2 cups per 4.5 litres/1 gallon of water) for one or two weeks. During the next one to two weeks keep it in several changes of fresh water until all traces of the bleach smell have disappeared. Where the coral has a highly convoluted surface, you will need to repeat these cleaning operations. This method is quite popular, although sometimes it is very difficult to get rid of the smell of bleach once the coral is clean! Rinsing the coral under running water for 48 hours should do the trick.

2 Boil the coral for an hour or so and then rinse it thoroughly with a hose to remove any loose particles. Following an overnight soak, hose it down again and then leave the coral to bleach naturally in the sun for a few days before use.

These instructions for cleaning coral also apply to any seashells (be sure to wash the inside thoroughly) or other decorative materials that began life in the sea.

It is one of those unfortunate coincidences that the more attractive a piece of coral looks, the more brittle it is to handle and the more expensive it is to buy. Until you have some experience of handling corals, stay with pieces that are plainer and easier to handle. Of course, you can build up shapes from small pieces.

Cleaning corals for the aquarium

You can soak corals in a solution of household bleach until clean. Soak in fresh water to remove all traces of bleach

Use gloves as a protection against spiky corals and the effects of the bleach

You can clean small pieces by boiling them for at least an hour

Below: All signs of animal life must be removed from corals and shells intended for use in the aquarium. Deeply convoluted and indented corals are the hardest to clean thoroughly. You can clean coral either by soaking it in bleach or boiling it. In each case, be sure to rinse it thoroughly in clean water to avoid pollution.

Avoid using high water pressure that might damage delicate corals

An effective way of rinsing corals is with a hose – be sure to do it outdoors!

Preparing the site and tank

Choose a site for your tank that is near an electric power outlet and totally accessible, not only during the setting-up stage, but also to allow for easy maintenance afterwards. Place a slab of expanded polystyrene, or other suitable material, on the surface so that the tank sits on a firm, level cushioned surface.

Clear away any obstacles in your path that might cause you to fall – especially when carrying buckets of water or valuable corals. Make sure that you have enough airline and electric cable, together with connecting blocks, air valves and electrical plugs before you start.

A shelf above or below the tank will provide space on which to place some of the external equipment, which you can always box in afterwards.

New tanks should not leak but if you have any doubts, test yours (outdoors!) before you use it. Leaks can be simply repaired with aquarium silicone sealant; this is another outdoor job as the sealant gives off a heavy vapour. Once any necessary repairs have 'cured', remove all traces of excess sealant and wash the tank out thoroughly with salt water, using this opportunity to clean all the glass panels.

At this stage you can attach a cable tidy and a bank of ganged air valves to a convenient spot on the outside of the tank (but we will not be making use of them just yet.) If the tank is to stand against a wall, this is the time to paint the outside rear glass panel so that the room decor does not show through and spoil an artistic underwater picture. Alternatively, if there is room behind the tank, build up a dry 'aquascape' or diorama of corals and other suitable decorations. Illuminating this with a spotlight will appear to extend the visible 'depth' of the aquarium when viewed from the front. In this case, don't paint the back of the tank!

Fitting a biological filtration system

Always fit the biological filtration system into the aquarium before you add the substrate. The filter plate must cover the whole of the aquarium base to provide the maximum area of filtration and to ensure that there are no anaerobic pockets. It is vital that the water flows evenly through the substrate. To ensure that there are no gaps around the edges of the filter plate, you can seal it into position with aquarium sealant. If you do this, allow a further 24 hours for the sealant to cure before continuing the setting up sequence.

Fit the airlift tubes and make sure that they are firmly attached. On some air-operated filters the airline should be con-

Right: Substantial supporting piers are needed for these two corner-sited tanks. Check floor joist positions and make sure the aquarium's considerable weight is evenly distributed.

Siting the aquarium

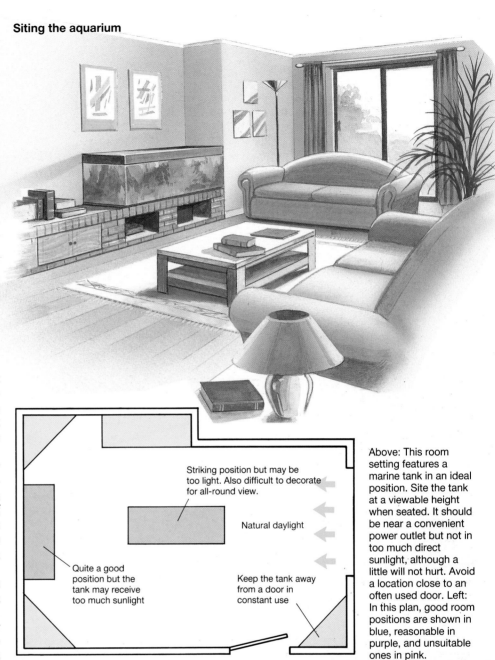

Striking position but may be too light. Also difficult to decorate for all-round view.

Natural daylight

Quite a good position but the tank may receive too much sunlight

Keep the tank away from a door in constant use

Above: This room setting features a marine tank in an ideal position. Site the tank at a viewable height when seated. It should be near a convenient power outlet but not in too much direct sunlight, although a little will not hurt. Avoid a location close to an often used door. Left: In this plan, good room positions are shown in blue, reasonable in purple, and unsuitable ones in pink.

nected right at the base of the airlift, so now is the time to fit it. Later on, the airline may well be under the surface of the substrate and much harder to get at. Connect the other end of the airline to an outlet on the ganged air valve block.

If you are using power-assisted biological filters, do not fit the heavy motor-impeller power head to the top of the return tube yet. Fitting it at this stage may inconvenience you, and there is always a risk that it may topple from the unsupported tubes and damage corals, or even the tank itself. Similarly, if you are using a 'reverse-flow' system, connect the flow

Above: To avoid water short circuiting around the biological filter plate, and to ensure that no sand gets beneath it, you can seal around the edges with aquarium silicone sealant.

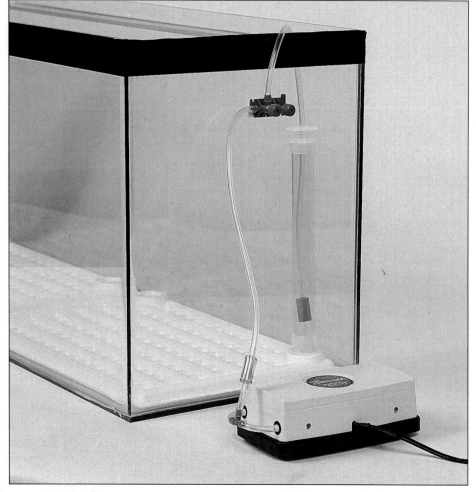

Above: Place the biological filter plate in the tank first. With large tanks, you may need to fit two separate plates, or cut to size, in order to cover the whole aquarium base.

Left: A powerful air pump will provide adequate 'down flow' through the filter. Note non-return valve in airline near pump, control valves and airstone in airlift tube for better efficiency.

Below: Increased water flow is provided by an electric pump mounted on the uplift tube. Reduce the height of the tube to accommodate this 'power head' below the glass ledge.

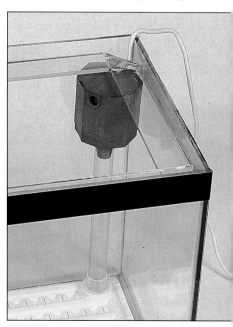

pipe from the external power filter to the top of the tube at a later stage. Although you may not be fitting these items together at this point, be sure to check that they *do* fit together; you may need to ask your dealer for different pipes.

Adding substrate and decorations

Before incorporating substrate materials, make sure they are thoroughly washed. This is particularly important if you are using crushed coral or coral sand as they may contain dead organisms. It is probably not worth the effort of testing it – by soaking some under water for a few days – your nose will tell you if it is clean! Just wash the material as a matter of course and at the same time you can also clean or bleach any rocks to be used.

Spread the coarsest substrate medium over the biological filter plate to an even depth of 5-7.5cm(2-3in). Place a plastic 'gravel-tidy' mesh on this layer of substrate before adding the finer top layers of coral sand. The mesh will prevent the filter plates being exposed by fishes digging or burying themselves in the substrate. Add more substrate towards the rear of the tank to raise the depth a further 5cm(2in) or so, using small rocks under the substrate to hold back the slope. Do not add the final rocks and corals until you have put all the 'technical equipment' into the tank.

Above: Add substrate (here, coral sand) above the biological filter plate to a depth of at least 5-7.5cm(2-3in). The uplift tube may need to be shortened to enable it to fit beneath the shelves around the tank. Although the pump is shown mounted on the uplift tube, you may care to remove it during decoration of the tank to lessen the risk of it falling off. Bank up the substrate at the rear to give a better effect from the front. This also encourages debris to fall forward.

Heating, aeration and other filtration equipment

Combined heater-thermostat units are best mounted at each end of the aquarium. (While separate heaters and thermostats function equally well, their use may be prohibited by electrical safety laws in some countries.) Make sure that combined units are mounted almost vertically and check whether they are designed for complete or only partial immersion in water. Ensure that heaters are mounted clear of the gravel – long heaters can be mounted diagonally on the rear panel – and ALWAYS use plastic mounting clips for all equipment. Connect the wires from the heater-thermostats as instructed by the manufacturer and wire both these and the air pump supply cables to the appropriate connections in the cable tidy. Cover any metal springclips attached to external thermostats with plas-

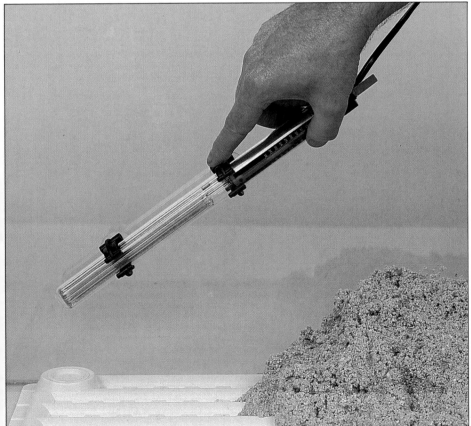

Above: Mount long thermostat-heater units diagonally on the rear wall using plastic clips. If the unit has a temperature scale, mount it so you can see and adjust it easily.

Right: Lighting, air pump and heating wiring should all be connected using a 'cable tidy' for neatness and safety. Dangling wires can be hazardous, especially near a wet aquarium.

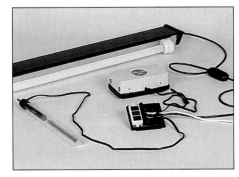

DO NOT CONNECT THE MAINS
SUPPLY AT THIS TIME.

tic airline. Install the thermometers last of all; you cannot use a floating thermometer until the tank is filled, but you can stick on external liquid-crystal models at any time.

Feed the output from the air pump into the air valve block. Ideally, mount the pump above the level of the water in the aquarium to prevent any possibility of water siphoning back into it should the electricity supply fail, or the pump stop for any other reason. Alternatively, using a 'one-way' check valve in the airline from the pump will serve the same purpose and allows the pump to be sited where most fishkeepers put it anyway – on a convenient shelf alongside or below the aquarium.

Place a long airstone along the back of the tank where it will be concealed by rocks or corals. Connect the airline tubing from the airstone to one of the air valves and bury the airline in the gravel. Remember that you may need to replace this airstone, so make it reasonably accessible for this purpose. Fill the body of the external filter (if used) with filter medium as required (see page 26). External filters and ultraviolet sterilizers can be situated away from the tank or hung on the side or rear of the tank. You will probably have to cut some of the hood away to make room for all the tubes to pass into the tank. Use a spray bar to distribute the returning water across the surface of the aquarium and thus prevent a powerful jet of water disturbing the tank decorations. It will also help to disperse carbon dioxide and provide additional aeration to the aquarium water.

Protein skimmers are best fitted as unobtrusively as possible inside the aquarium. A section of the cover glass should be easily removable to give access to the protein skimmer's collection cup for regular emptying. If you are using ozonized air, the supply to the skimmer should come *directly* from the ozonizer, which is in turn fed with

air from an outlet valve on the ganged air valve. Never feed ozonized air to the airlift of a biological filter, and protect the ozonizer against back siphoning of water in a similar way to the air pump.

Connect power supply cables from external power filters, power heads, sterilizers and ozonizers to the cable tidy. The sterilizer and ozonizer will not be required immediately and so you can connect them later if you wish.

Depending on the direction in which the water flow is to travel through the filter bed, fit the power heads (for downflow) or output tube from an external power filter (for reverse-flow) to the uplift tubes from the biological filter. Finally, add corals and further rocks if required. They can usefully hide the aquarium 'hardware', but be careful that they do not obstruct the water flow from the filter outlets. Remember that too much rockwork will reduce the fishes' swimming space and their choice of territories. You also risk obscuring some areas of the aquarium where a fish could become trapped, unseen by you.

Above: Place the decorative corals carefully to avoid damage and subsequent toppling. Position them to hide aquarium 'hardware' but avoid obstructing vital water flow.

Below: Trim plastic condensation trays so that they fit neatly. Two separate sliding pieces of glass may make feeding an easier task. Note the wires fed through cutouts in the corner.

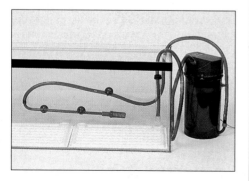

Above: A power filter is used to filter the aquarium water before pumping it through the biological filter plate in a reverse-flow direction, i.e. upwards through the substrate. Note the water intake near tank base.

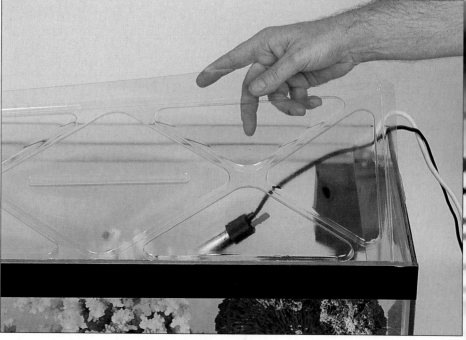

ght: Some hoods have fittings for fluorescent
bes built into them. If possible, mount the
arter gear away from the hood to avoid it
ecoming heavy and unbalanced. Note the
aterproof covers over the electrical
onnections to the fluorescent tube in the hood.

ighting

Jse waterproofed fittings to attach lamps
to the aquarium hood and be careful not to
rop the hood on the cover glass.

The associated starting gear for fluo-
escent lamps is very heavy and may unba-
nce the hood if it is fitted inside. For this
eason, you may opt to mount the starting
ear away from the hood, particularly when
sing several tubes.

Ensure that the hood is well ventilated to
llow the heat from the lamps – and carbon
ioxide from the tank – to escape. A close-
tting cover glass will also keep evapora-
ion losses to a minimum and prevent fishes
rom jumping out of the tank. Mount spot-
ghts over open-topped aquariums at least
0cm (12in) above the water surface, and
eep the cover glass spotlessly clean so as
ot to restrict the amount of light reaching
he aquarium.

Connect the lighting power lead to a
witched set of terminals in the cable tidy.

reparing the water

ou are now confronted with a practical
roblem – in what do you mix the sea
vater? Obviously, if this is your first aqua-
ium you can use the tank itself and on
alance, mixing the water in the tank after
he decorations and technical equipment
ave been put in is probably easier.

Add the fresh water to the tank carefully
o that you do not disturb the contoured
ase covering and the decorations. The
est way of doing this is to pour the water
nto a large plate or into a jug resting on the
ubstrate. In this way, the overflow will
ently fill the tank without causing any dis-
uption. Continue adding water until the
ank is full. Then add some salt. It is better
o underestimate the quantities needed at
his stage, since it is easier to add a little
nore salt than to dilute the final mix with
nore fresh water. (Note that you should
lways add salt to the water rather than the
ther way round.)

If you mix the sea salts in a separate con-
ainer, the main problem is calculating the
et amount of water needed to fill the fur-
ished aquarium. The best option is to
nake up sufficient sea water to fill the total
olume of the empty tank (easily calculated
rom the measurements or by referring to a
able of tank sizes and volumes) and be pre-
ared to waste some in the process.
emember to use a non-metallic container,
s outlined on page 21. (Also remember
hat you will need to prepare water in the
ame way before each regular partial water
hange.) Add the mixed sea water to the

furnished tank following the same precautions as described above.

Whichever method you have used to mix
the sea salts, there is no point in testing the
specific gravity of the water at this stage.
Wait until the water has reached the
required temperature, the filter systems
are running and the salts have fully dissolved before making final adjustments.

Right: Prepare synthetic sea water in a non-
metallic container, using a plastic or wooden
stirrer. Mark the outside of the bucket at a
known volume level, say 5 or 10 litres, for future
reference. Add the salt to the water and follow
the manufacturer's instructions carefully.

Below: When adding water to the decorated
tank (whether the water is fresh for mixing in the
tank, or already mixed), use a wide saucer or
plate to disperse the water flow evenly and to
avoid disturbing the substrate.

Filling the tank

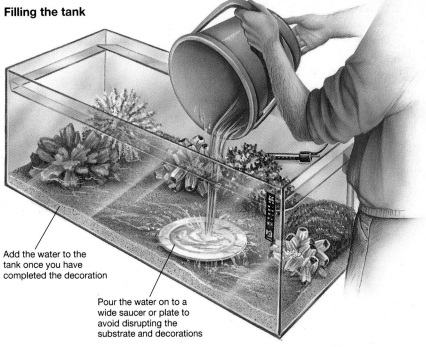

Add the water to the
tank once you have
completed the decoration

Pour the water on to a
wide saucer or plate to
avoid disrupting the
substrate and decorations

Starting up and final checks

You will have to prime the outside filter and UV sterilizer circuits with water. This is a simple process, best achieved by removing the return tube to the aquarium at the appliance end and sucking at the outlet from the filter or sterilizer. When water has filled each system, reconnect the return tubes, making sure that all water hose connections are tight.

Connect a supply cable from the cable tidy to a suitably fused plug, put the plug into the power socket and switch on.

Adjust the airflow from the individual air valves to operate the biological filter and airstone (if fitted). Water should be coming out of the power heads fitted to the uplift tubes, if this is the operating method you have chosen. Check that the water flow from the external filter is satisfactory. If there is an airlock in the system, you can usually remove it by rocking the filter gently to manoeuvre the trapped air round to the outlet.

A reading of the aquarium thermometer will tell you whether the heating apparatus is working. When the temperature has reached the pre-set level – approximately 24°C (75°F) – it is time to check the specific gravity of the water with a reliable hydrometer. (The plastic swing-needle type is sturdy and easy to use, but remember to knock any air bubbles off the needle to prevent it giving a misleadingly high reading.) If the specific gravity reading is too low, add some more salt and allow the water to circulate for a while before rechecking. Continue this procedure until the specific gravity is at the correct level. If it is too high, siphon out some sea water and replace it with *fresh* water to lower it. Continue either process as necessary until the specific gravity reaches the correct reading (see page 22 for recommended readings).

Maturing the biological filter bed

Once the tank has been set up, it will take some time for the nitrifying bacteria to become established. A build up of ammonia and nitrite will gradually diminish as the bacteria get to work in ever-increasing numbers. The maturation of the filter bed takes quite a long time – anything from two weeks to more than a month – depending on what materials the bacteria have to work on. There are several ways of speeding up maturation, all of which ensure that a steady supply of nitrogenous compounds is present to act as 'fuel' for the system.

You can add some substrate from an established marine aquarium, or seed the aquarium with special proprietary maturation preparations. You can allow small particles of food to rot away or (and this final method brings the added excitement of introducing livestock) you can put one or two relatively hardy fishes in the aquarium to provide the necessary organic waste materials themselves. Of course, you can combine any of these options.

Testing the water with an ammonia and nitrite test kit will show how the rate of maturation is progressing. During the first few days, the nitrite reading will increase but, after a while at its highest value, it will decrease to a stable minimum – hopefully to zero or less than 0.1mg/litre. At this stage it is safe to introduce some more livestock. Do not be tempted to add fishes up to the tank's maximum stocking level, however; the biological filtration system will simply not be able to cope with the immediate increase in ammonia and nitrite a large number of extra fishes would introduce. Build up the stock gradually so that the filter can increase its efficiency in step with the extra load.

Below: The newly set up aquarium. The printed seascape background is mounted externally on the rear glass. At this point the aquarium is not fully established; it will take some weeks before the biological filter has matured sufficiently for fishes to be added safely. Check the temperature, nitrite and pH levels regularly during this period. With adequate lighting, algae will grow on the corals, reducing their sterile look and providing food for herbivorous fishes.

Providing 'above-water' niches

Position a suitable platform and reduce the water level to encourage crabs to bask beneath the lights.

Ensure that any rock formations are stable. Use aquarium silicone sealant to glue pieces together if necessary

Above: The coldwater marine aquarium lacks the brilliant colours of the tropical tank but compensates in other ways; invertebrates are relatively easy to collect and keep. Anemones varying in size, shape and colour are ideal.

Left: A reduced water level gives animals the opportunity to leave the water and bask on rocks. Varying the direction of flow from filters also simulates more natural conditions for creatures used to currents in tidal zones.

The coldwater aquarium

Although you may be quite serious about setting up a coldwater marine aquarium, the fact that all the 'ingredients' will be fairly easy to obtain (and replace) probably means that you will not be quite so distraught if it does not turn out as successfully as you had hoped.

Most fishkeepers will find it impractical to transport large quantities of sea water regularly from the seashore to the home aquarium, unless there is a source of *unpolluted* sea water literally on the doorstep. To compensate for this most unlikely circumstance, most hobbyists bent on setting up a coldwater marine aquarium prepare a tank of synthetic sea water in advance of their collecting trips to the coast. (It is a good idea to take a sample of the natural sea water and measure its specific gravity

so that you can prepare the tank water to a similar quality.) Nevertheless, some natural sea water must be collected simply in order to carry the animals home. If you are determined to use natural sea water for the entire aquarium, however, be sure to follow the guidelines on page 196.

The main thing is to collect specimens sensibly, taking special care not to damage the animals' natural homes in the process. If you collect invertebrates, such as sea anemones, always gather them *together* with the rock on which they are sitting; prising them off may damage them. Many inhabitants of the coastal pools rely on rocks for living quarters or shelter, so always replace the rocks you remove with adequate substitutes. Do not overcrowd the fishes and other animals that you collect during the journey home. And do not use

the same container to transport fishes and invertebrates, since the one may eat the other – hardly the desired result!

The value of collecting seaweed is questionable, since its culture in the aquarium can be very much a hit-or-miss affair. Marine algae needs a great deal of light to thrive, and in providing sufficient light you risk raising the temperature of the aquarium above the relatively cool conditions that the other tank inmates require. For the same reason, you should not site the aquarium in direct sunlight.

To set up a coldwater aquarium, follow the same general principles described above for a tropical tank but, of course, you will not need any heating apparatus. It is better for filter-feeding animals not to incorporate powerful external filtration. A biological filter (perhaps combined with extra aeration) will suffice.

Many of the fishes will require hideaways, so you must incorporate these shelters in the furnishing design of the aquarium. You can always modify the aquarium layout, if necessary, to provide an area of 'land' above the water level where crabs can exercise – but be sure to use a close-fitting cover glass!

CHOOSING AND INTRODUCING FISHES

Lythrypnus dalli, a brilliantly coloured Goby.

The most vital choices you have to make start here. Ideally, allow the aquarium to mature before you introduce any livestock, but no doubt you will be keen to get going. Make haste slowly is the best advice; do not spoil your careful preparations by making an inconsidered choice of fishes. Always buy healthy stock from a reputable dealer and, using the second part of this book as a guide – do read it before you visit a dealer – choose fish that are suitable for the aquarium and compatible with other fishes. Remember to add new fishes to your collection gradually. Introduce the fish into the aquarium with care; a frightened, shocked fish will only decline in health in the days and weeks that follow.

Having taken all possible care to set up the tank and provide the ideal conditions, do not ruin your painstaking preparations by choosing unsuitable fish to put in the aquarium. Several factors must influence your choice of fishes: their compatibility, both with fishes of the same species and members of other families; their feeding requirements; their tolerance of artificial surroundings; their appearance and even their cost.

Buying healthy stock

Observe the fishes carefully in the dealer's tank before you buy them. They should not be thin, nor have a 'pinched-in' appearance. Freshwater fishkeepers are used to seeing their healthy fishes swim with erect fins, but remember that some marine fish naturally swim with their fins clamped shut, so this is not necessarily a sign of ill-health. Furthermore, some species of marines lack ventral, or pelvic, fins, an uncommon feature in freshwater fishes.

Since you are probably buying marine fishes for their dazzling colours, be sure to avoid any that look dull or have poorly defined markings. It should not be necessary to warn against buying fish with skin ulcerations, excessive skin mucus, protruding or clouded eyes. Look out for abnormal swimming or breathing actions; persistent scratching against rocks or corals; a failure to maintain a steady position in the water; a rapid respiration rate or a fish deliberately hanging in the bubbles from an airstone. Any of these signs may indicate fishes that are sick or distressed.

One of the major hurdles faced by the marine fishkeeper is how to accustom new fishes to feeding under aquarium conditions. Always ensure that fishes are feeding before you buy them. It may not be enough simply to see a fish take food; it is not unknown for fishes to regurgitate hastily eaten food on the journey home and die because of raised ammonia levels in the bag. Ideally, try to see the fish feeding and then say that you will leave a deposit and return in the next day or in a few days' time to pick up the fish. In the end, you must trust your dealer; good dealers will ensure that the fishes are feeding properly.

Before you buy fish for the first time, it may be a good idea to establish the specific gravity of the water in which the fish are currently held, so that you can prepare their future tank accordingly. Subsequently, unless you intend to buy all your future stock from the same dealer, you cannot be certain that the specific gravity will be the same as that in your aquarium once it is established. In most cases, however, any slight difference in specific gravity should not cause any problem, provided that you acclimatize new fishes as described later.

Shop around before you buy any fish. This will help you to judge the quality of fish in different stores. A store with a large turnover of fishes may be doing fantastic business, or it may be merely replacing losses of fish it cannot keep. Beware of unrealistically low prices. These might suggest that the fish have not been quarantined or that they have been collected by cheap and undesirable methods involving the use of cyanide or even explosives. Either way you risk buying unhealthy stock doomed to a short life in your aquarium.

Ideally, buy your aquarium and fishes from a reputable dealer, who will then be familiar with your set-up, its operation and likely fish-holding capacity. He will no mind advising you when you come back for stocks of fish and will discuss any problem that may arise. If your fish come from several different dealers, it may be difficult for you to pinpoint the source of any trouble with accuracy, and unfair to expect one dealer from a number to accept responsibility for any problem you might encounter.

The journey home

Once you have bought them, the fishes begin the final leg of their long journey from coral reef to home aquarium. Assuming they have survived all the traumas of capture, air travel and several changes of aquarium conditions, you must ensure that their introductory period into your aquarium is as stress free as possible. (See page 56 for stress and ill-health.)

Below: Buying fishes for your marine tank should be a pleasurable experience, but choose them with care. Colours should be intense and patterns well defined. Avoid fishes with skin blemishes, wounds, split fins, hollow-looking bodies or swimming difficulties, and ask to see the fishes feeding, if possible.

Always tell your dealer how long you will be getting home. If you have a journey of several hours ahead of you, he can use oxygen instead of air in the plastic bag or, if oxygen is not available, provide you with a larger bag. The dealer should enclose the plastic bag in a dark paper bag to reduce the light intensity for the fish. Even though you may be keen to inspect your purchase, do not take the plastic bag out in bright sunlight immediately outside the shop. This will inevitably stress the fish. The best option for the journey home is to use a darkened, well-insulated container. This will not only reduce stress from bright light but also cut down heat loss.

Introducing the fishes

Always unpack fishes in dimly lit conditions. Before releasing each fish, float the bag in the unlit aquarium for about fifteen minutes. Then open the bag and add a small quantity of water from the aquarium. Wait for five minutes and repeat the process. Doing this four times over a twenty-minute period will not only bring the temperature of the water inside the bag in line with that of the tank but also gradually acclimatize the fish to any slight variations in pH and specific gravity levels. If necessary, use an airstone to provide gentle aeration in the plastic bag. Since the fishes may already have been confined for several hours, it is not advisable to prolong this transfer process beyond about forty-five minutes.

If you quarantine new fishes in a separate aquarium, ensure that this is maintained at the same standard as the main tank. Holding fishes for a time in 'second-grade' conditions may cause more problems than trusting your dealer's quarantine arrangements and introducing new fishes directly into your main aquarium. Of course, any fishes in quarantine tanks will need to be acclimatized to the main tank in the same gradual way.

Despite the best of intentions, it may be argued (with some degree of logic) that any extra transference of fishes from one situation to another causes stress, no matter how slight. The extra quarantining stage may be an example of this. You must balance up all the pros and cons as they exist in your particular situation. Careful handling of healthy stock from a reliable commercial source will generally prove to be successful, but if any doubts arise then take any necessary precautions to protect your existing aquarium stock from health risks likely to be introduced by new additions. Quarantining in principle is fine – everyone agrees that it is the thing to do – but in practice things are often different, especially where impatience tempers even the highest ideals!

Do not worry if newly introduced fishes do not feed for the first day or two. After they have settled in, they should resume their normal feeding pattern.

If you are starting with a completely new aquarium, then add only one or two hardy (nitrite-tolerant) fishes to it. They will survive the rapid increase of nitrite as the biological filter bed matures and will provide additional 'ammonia-ammunition' for the bacteria to work on.

When adding new fishes to an established aquarium, you can reduce the likelihood of territorial squabbles by employing some 'fish psychology'. Feed the inhabitants of the main aquarium to take their minds off the newcomers, or even consider rearranging the coral/rockwork layout in the aquarium immediately before introducing new fishes so that all the fishes, old and new, are more preoccupied with home-finding than with quarrelling.

Compatibility

The aggressive behaviour of some fishes may be suppressed in a crowded display tank. Only when a fish has room to 'flex its muscles' in the comparative spaciousness of a home aquarium does it reveal its true nature. Very often this aggressiveness does not show itself when the tank is brightly lit. However, when the lights are turned off and the fishes settle down for the night, territorial squabbles may occur. This is another good reason for providing enough swimming space and a choice of refuges for all the fishes in the tank.

The table on pages 46-47 gives an indication of the compatibility between each family of fishes featured in Part Two of this

Above: Float the transportation bags in the aquarium for about 15 minutes before gradually allowing tank water in. This will help to reduce stress during the acclimatization period.

book. Using the table, the advice in Part Two and the guide to feeding requirements (see page 48), you can select those fishes that will suit your needs.

Lifespans

Our knowledge of marine fishkeeping is increasing all the time, but it is still difficult to give any accurate guidance to the projected lifespan of fishes kept in aquarium conditions. Nor has there been much research on the lifespan of species in the wild. Usually, lifespan is proportionate to size and the figures in the first panel below can only be approximate in the context of the hobby aquarium environment under the very best of conditions. The lifespan of fishes in conditions approximating more nearly to natural conditions, i.e. those in very large public aquariums, is understandably longer; a representative selection is featured in the second panel.

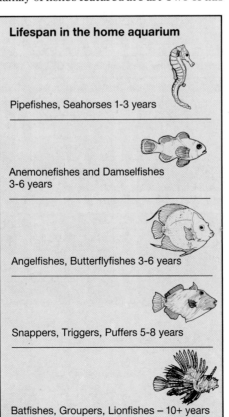

Lifespan in the home aquarium

Pipefishes, Seahorses 1-3 years

Anemonefishes and Damselfishes 3-6 years

Angelfishes, Butterflyfishes 3-6 years

Snappers, Triggers, Puffers 5-8 years

Batfishes, Groupers, Lionfishes – 10+ years

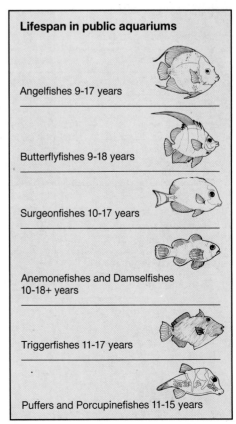

Lifespan in public aquariums

Angelfishes 9-17 years

Butterflyfishes 9-18 years

Surgeonfishes 10-17 years

Anemonefishes and Damselfishes 10-18+ years

Triggerfishes 11-17 years

Puffers and Porcupinefishes 11-15 years

Compatibility guide for tropical marine fishes and invertebrates

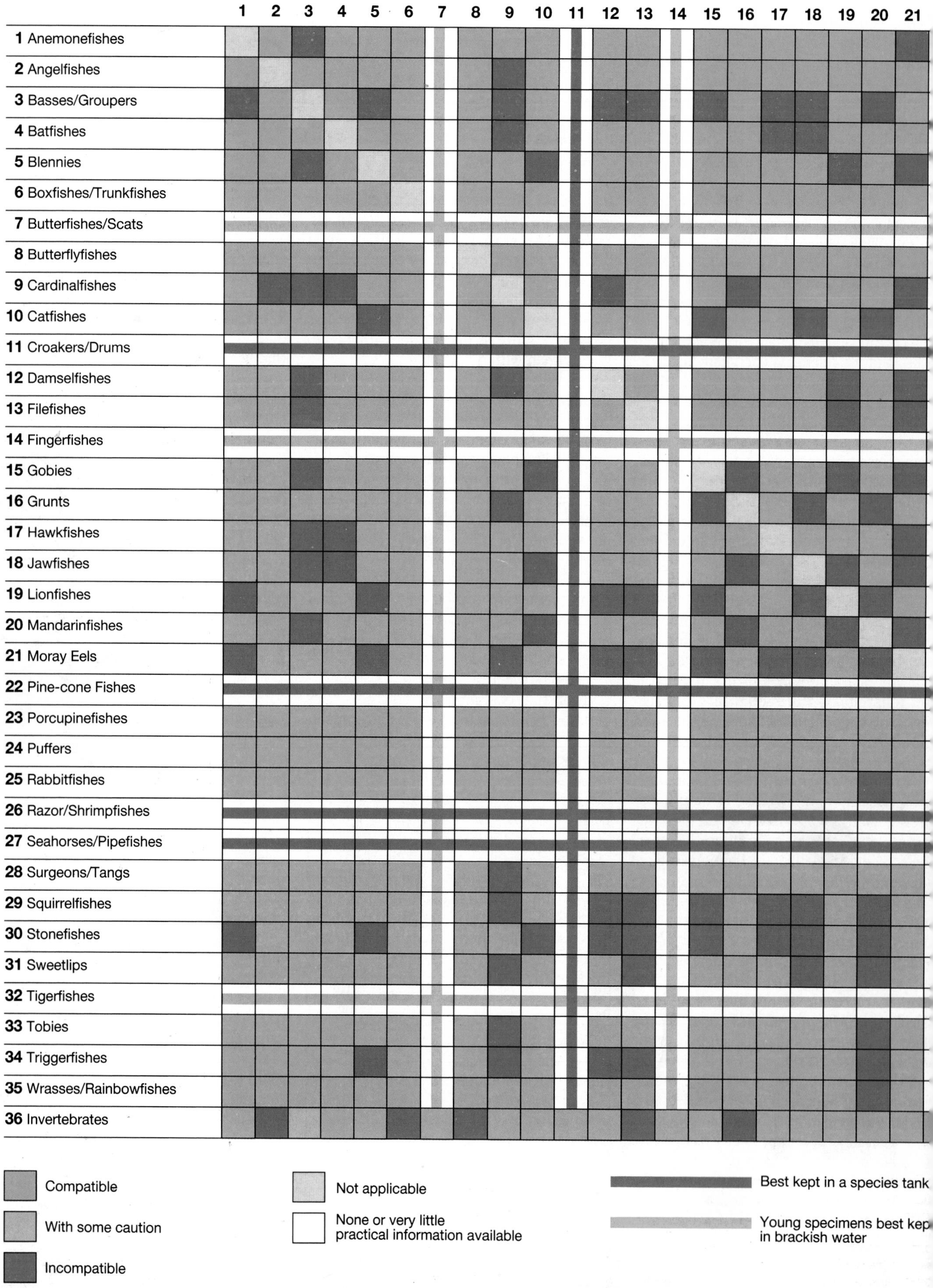

	1	2	3	4	5	6	7	8	9	10	11	12	13	14	15	16	17	18	19	20	21
1 Anemonefishes																					
2 Angelfishes																					
3 Basses/Groupers																					
4 Batfishes																					
5 Blennies																					
6 Boxfishes/Trunkfishes																					
7 Butterfishes/Scats																					
8 Butterflyfishes																					
9 Cardinalfishes																					
10 Catfishes																					
11 Croakers/Drums																					
12 Damselfishes																					
13 Filefishes																					
14 Fingerfishes																					
15 Gobies																					
16 Grunts																					
17 Hawkfishes																					
18 Jawfishes																					
19 Lionfishes																					
20 Mandarinfishes																					
21 Moray Eels																					
22 Pine-cone Fishes																					
23 Porcupinefishes																					
24 Puffers																					
25 Rabbitfishes																					
26 Razor/Shrimpfishes																					
27 Seahorses/Pipefishes																					
28 Surgeons/Tangs																					
29 Squirrelfishes																					
30 Stonefishes																					
31 Sweetlips																					
32 Tigerfishes																					
33 Tobies																					
34 Triggerfishes																					
35 Wrasses/Rainbowfishes																					
36 Invertebrates																					

Legend:

- Compatible
- With some caution
- Incompatible
- Not applicable
- None or very little practical information available
- Best kept in a species tank
- Young specimens best kept in brackish water

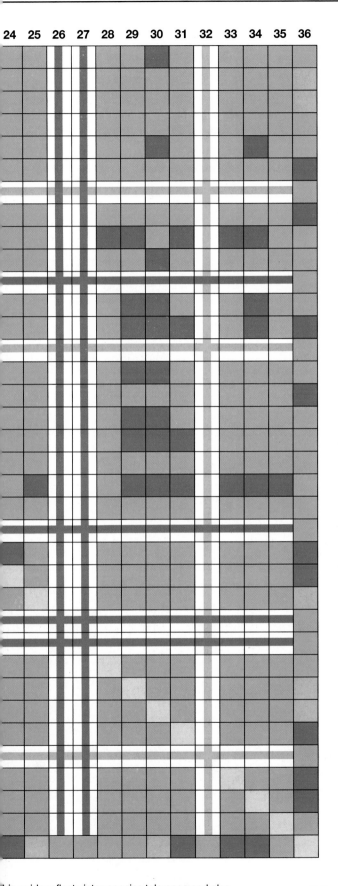

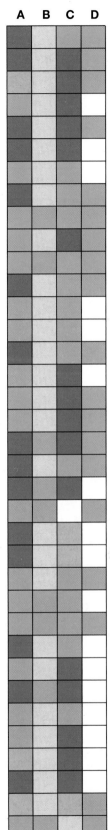

| | 24 | 25 | 26 | 27 | 28 | 29 | 30 | 31 | 32 | 33 | 34 | 35 | 36 | | A | B | C | D |

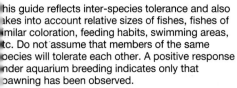

This guide reflects inter-species tolerance and also takes into account relative sizes of fishes, fishes of similar coloration, feeding habits, swimming areas, etc. Do not assume that members of the same species will tolerate each other. A positive response under aquarium breeding indicates only that spawning has been observed.

A Same or similar species

B Species tank

C Smaller fishes

D Aquarium breeding

Above: *Balistoides conspicillum*, the Clown Trigger; easily recognized by its coloration.

Above: The only marine Catfish, *Plotosus lineatus*, has smart markings when young.

Above: A teardrop-shaped colour patch covers the 'scalpels' in *Acanthurus achilles*.

Above: The starfish, *Protoreaster lincki*, uses bright colours to advertise its toxicity.

FEEDING

A long nose reaches food other fishes cannot.

Providing the correct food for your fishes is one thing, getting them to accept it in captivity may prove a little more difficult. Try to present the food to them in a manner that is as natural as possible; carnivorous fishe may begin with livefoods then be gradually tempted to eat dead food jerke about on a string. Supply greenfoods for herbivorous species and be prepared to keep a supply of cultured livefoods for finicky feeders. Study your fishes' feeding actions and habits and don't neglect the nocturnal feeders. You may have to use a little ingenuity when feeding invertebrates It is a good idea to use feeding time as an opportunity to count the inmate of your tank, and in the process draw closer to your cherished fishes.

The marine fishkeeper faces many challenges in his quest to maintain an aquarium of healthy contented fishes. Second only to the problems of controlling water quality is the question of how to feed the fishes. This means not only providing suitable foods but also, in some cases, teaching or persuading the fish to recognize and take them readily.

In nature, every animal is part of a food chain, living on or being eaten by the animals adjacent to it in the chain. Many marine fishes, for example, eat polyps from the living coral heads, take crustaceans, and scrape algae from surfaces of rocks. Small fishes are, in turn, the prey of larger fishes. This food chain is fine in the open ocean, where there is a continuous supply to keep it going. In the aquarium, the fishkeeper must provide suitable substitutes for the fishes and other tank occupants.

Marine fishes can be grouped into four feeding categories depending upon their requirements and how they feed. These groups can be summarized as open-water feeders, reef grazers, shy feeders and specialist feeders. Open-water feeders feed confidently, taking food in midwater or scouring the seabed debris. Reef grazers confine their feeding attentions to polyp and algae life on the coral reef and associated rocks. Shy feeders may hide in caves or burrow entrances waiting for feeding opportunities to present themselves. Another reason for feeding shyness can be the normal nocturnal habits, these species do not feel so confident enough to compete for food in the brightly lit aquarium. Specialist feeders, such as Seahorses and some Pipefishes, require food especially selected for them; these may be tiny live foods, or a liquidized emulsion. Many invertebrates, such as tubeworms, also require microscopic foods.

In the relative emptinesss of the coral reef, each fish can feed in its own way, occupying its natural place in the food chain. In the aquarium the fishes are forced to rub shoulders with each other; shy, hesitant feeders must take their chances alongside the more boisterous 'smash-and-grab' merchants. All these factors make up a complicated feeding puzzle for the fishkeeper to unravel.

Feeding types (in nature)

Open-water feeders: Blennies, Clownfishes, Damselfishes, Fingerfishes, some Gobies, Rabbitfishes, Lionfishes, Snappers, Squirrelfishes, Triggerfishes.

Reef grazers: Angelfishes, Butterflyfishes, Filefishes, Parrotfishes, Surgeons, Wrasses.

Shy feeders: Basslets, Cardinalfishes, Hawkfishes, Jawfishes.

Specialist feeders: Pipefishes, Seahorses, Razorfishes/Shrimpfishes.

Ease of feeding in the aquarium

Group	Easy	Reasonable once feeding	Difficult	Difficult, need live foods
Angels		●	●	
Basses	●			
Blennies	●	●		
Butterflyfishes (depending on species)	●	●	●	●
Cardinals		●		
Catfishes	●			
Clownfish	●	●		
Damsels	●			
Eels	●			
Filefish			●	
Gobies	●			
Jawfish		●		
Lionfishes		●		●
Seahorses			●	●
Squirrelfishes		●		●
Surgeons	●			
Tangs	●			
Triggers		●		
Wrasses	●			

Sources of food

Here we examine the advantages and disadvantages of a variety of foods available for marine fishes.

Prepared foods Many freshwater fish foods have been modified by their manufacturers to suit marine fishes. Research into foods specially formulated for marine fishes continues unabated and hopefully this will result in a wider range of acceptable foods that will simplify the job of the marine fishkeeper.

Prepared foods can be used in different ways. Flaked foods, marketed as either 'staple diet' or 'conditioning food' are easy to use. Large fish will accept them as they are, or they can be crumbled up for smaller species. Tablet foods can be offered in a variety of ways depending on the feeding manner of the recipient. Sometimes they are snapped up as they 'free-fall' through the water; they may be stuck to the aquarium glass to be pecked at by grazing species; or they can lie on the tank floor for invertebrates to feed on. A liquid suspension, made by grinding up tablet food and mixing it with some *aquarium* water, is ideal for filter-feeding animals, such as corals and tubeworms, etc.

Fresh meat foods As the staple diet of fishes in nature comes from the sea, it should be possible to buy supplies from the fishmonger for your fish. Shellfish meat, such as mussels and crab meat, etc. are usually accepted by bold feeders, although there is always a strong risk of introducing disease from these sources and also fouling the water. The main advantage of feeding 'like to like' is that the natural foods will contain valuable trace elements. Specially formulated prepared foods and gamma-irradiated foods are safer.

Frozen foods Many types of frozen foods are produced commercially specifically for fishkeepers and these provide the bulk of the diet for many marine fishes. These foods will keep for several months in a suitable freezer and 'meal-size' portions can be thawed out as required. Ideal frozen foods for marine fishes include *Mysis* and other shrimps, krill, squid, clam, crab and lobster eggs. The commercial suppliers of frozen food for aquarium use treat it with gamma rays to ensure that it is free from disease organisms. Use the wide range of frozen foods with complete confidence.

Right: A variety of dried foods is available from your aquatic store. These will provide a wide range of diets and allow for different feeding methods. The foods shown here are (clockwise from bottom left): tablet foods, floating foodsticks, large flakes, small flakes, and freeze-dried krill (centre). Use these with live, frozen and freeze-dried foods for a balanced diet.

Setting up an algae farm

To culture algae for herbivorous fishes, simply set up a small aquarium in a sunny position and allow natural growth to take place. Take out algae-covered rocks and put them in the main aquarium for the fishes.

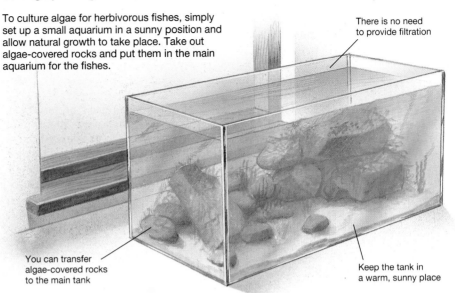

There is no need to provide filtration

You can transfer algae-covered rocks to the main tank

Keep the tank in a warm, sunny place

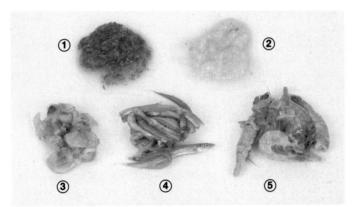

Left: A selection of natural fish foods which are suitable for the marine aquarium:

1 *Mysis* shrimps.
2 Lobster eggs.
3 Cockles.
4 Lancefish.
5 Prawns (*Cerastoderma*).

These foods may be stored in the freezer until required, but ensure that they are thoroughly thawed.

Freeze-dried foods The freeze-drying process has made it possible to preserve many natural foods for fish in captivity. Small aquatic animals, such as *Tubifex* worms, bloodworms, brineshrimps and krill (marine crustaceans), are available in freeze-dried form. Meats, such as beef, heart and liver, can all be freeze-dried and provide an excellent alternative to flaked food. They help to vary the diet and prevent the fishes from becoming bored with a monotonous feeding regime.

Live foods Many live foods fed to freshwater fishes can also be used in the marine system. Marine fishes will accept *Daphnia* (small freshwater crustaceans) and well-cleaned *Tubifex* worms or chopped earthworms. (Many fishkeepers prefer not to use *Tubifex* worms, considering that their muddy, often-polluted freshwater origins make them a bad health risk.) You can culture whiteworms and grindalworms yourself, but only offer these in moderation.

Brineshrimps (*Artemia salina*) are an excellent disease-free and nutritious living food for marine fishes. The eggs of these saltwater shrimps are readily available from aquatic dealers and are easy to hatch in a well-aerated saline solution. The newly hatched nauplii stages are ideal for filter-feeding invertebrates and are relished by Butterflyfishes in particular. Both newly hatched brineshrimps and the larger adult forms provide food for Butterflyfishes, but obviously there is more nutritional value in the larger forms. Be sure to organize a continuous supply or else wean such fishes off brineshrimps and on to a more practicable diet. Raising the tiny brineshrimps with yeast-based foods over several weeks will produce a stock of fully grown shrimps suitable for larger fishes. Live *Mysis* shrimp, often available from aquatic stores, provide yet another tasty snack. You can also culture marine rotifers. These are tiny planktonic animals, half to one-third the size of newly hatched brineshrimps, whose dormant eggs can be hatched and raised in a micro-algae liquid to provide food for the larval stages of fishes and for filter-feeders.

Live freshwater fish fry can be a good starter with which to tempt difficult feeders, but do not allow them to become too dependent on these delicacies, otherwise you will be making a rod for your own back. The fish might well starve should your plans for breeding 'fish for food' go awry. Remember that freshwater animals do not normally live very long in sea water, although Mollies, which live in brackish water in the wild, survive longer than the average livebearer. Inexpensive goldfish fry are a suitable food source for large fishes, such as Lionfishes.

However tempted you may be to offer surplus or specially bred fishes as livefood,

never dispose of sick or ailing fishes by this method; it is a sure way of passing on disease to the fish in your aquarium.

Fresh vegetable foods It is essential to provide vegetable materials in the marine diet, since many marine fishes are naturally herbivorous. Algae provide the most natural form of vegetable food for marine fishes. You can grow algae in the main aquarium or, should the number of herbivorous fishes exceed the supply, you can set up a spare tank as an 'algae farm'. Simply furnish the tank with a few rocks and corals, fill it with sea water and stand it in a sunny position. You can scrape algae from the rocks, or transfer the entire algae-covered rocks into the main aquarium for the benefit of grazing fishes. Lettuce and spinach leaves (possibly crushed and pre-cooked a little to soften them) or pre-soaked rolled oats can also be effective sources of vegetable matter.

A balanced diet

Understandably, most of the research on fish nutrition has been centred upon species raised in captivity for conservation purposes or for food – trout bred on fish farms, for example. It seems logical, however, that these findings also apply to other fishes maintained in captivity, including ornamental marine fishes.

Such research has shown how vital it is to provide a diet containing the right balance of carbohydrates, proteins and fats to provide energy and build body tissue. This has lead to the production of high-quality prepared foods for a wide range of fishes, as we have seen, and should underly all our decisions about suitable diets. It is clear, for example, that fishes need a ready supply of so-called 'essential' amino acids (the building blocks of proteins) for normal growth and healthy development. These requirements are species dependent and vary with the age of individual fishes. Deficiency in any particular essential amino acid produces characteristic symptoms, ranging from a reduced growth rate to death. Although it is possible to add these amino acids to the diet in a 'free' form, some fishes cannot make use of them in this form; hence the need for a well-balanced and varied diet.

Nutritional research also shows that fishes need highly unsaturated fatty acids for good health. Once vital reason for this is that such fats enable the delicate membranes throughout the body of a fish to remain flexible and fluid at relatively low temperatures. It is particularly important to protect fats in fish foods from becoming rancid, i.e. oxidized, since rancid fats in the diet can cause specific health problems.

It is also important to remember the vital role that minerals and vitamins play in

Vitamin sources in foods	
FOOD	**VITAMIN**
Algae	A, B$_{12}$, C, E
Beef	A, B$_2$, B$_6$, B$_{12}$, C, K
Crustaceans	A, B$_2$, B$_6$, D, K
Daphnia	D, K
Earthworms	D
Egg yolk	A, B$_{12}$, D, E
Fish meat	B$_2$, B$_6$
Fish eggs	C
Fish liver	A, D
Lettuce	A, C, B$_2$, B$_6$, B$_{12}$, C, E, K
Mealworms	D
Mussels	B$_2$, B$_6$, B$_{12}$
Shrimps	D, K
Snails	D
Spinach	A, B$_2$, B$_6$, C, E, K
Tubifex	D
Water plants	A, C, K
Wheat germ	E
Yeast	A, B

Making a brineshrimp hatchery

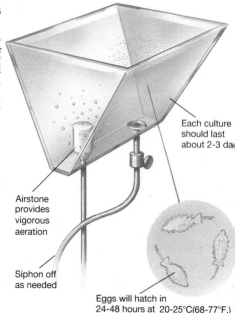

Each culture should last about 2-3 da[ys]

Airstone provides vigorous aeration

Siphon off as needed

Eggs will hatch in 24-48 hours at 20-25°C(68-77°F.)

Above: You can make your own brineshrimp hatchery with five pieces of glass as shown here. A heater-thermostat may be needed to keep water at the optimum temperature. Vigorous aeration will speed the hatching.

Right: Young fishes and invertebrates require small particle food. Immediate foods or culturing compounds shown here are (clockwise from top left): liquid marine food, algae-encouraging culture, brineshrimp foods, rotifers and their culturing foods, brineshrimp eggs.

he diet. Although needed in only very small amounts, vitamins act as 'catalysts' to activate the nutritional processes. Some vitamins are manufactured in the fish's body; others must be constantly available in the food. No single food provides all the essential vitamins, but all foods contain some vitamins. Thus, part of the bonus of providing a varied and balanced diet is that the fish receives all the vitamins from a variety of sources. Vitamin groups may be fat soluble (A,D,E and K) or water soluble (B and C). Vitamin B is a collective name for a group of vitamins known by individual names and/or numbers, such as B_1 (Thiamine), B_2 (Riboflavin), B_6 and B_{12}. The vitamin table shown opposite is not a recipe for a balanced diet, it simply shows the vitamin content of some common aquarium foods.

Feeding methods

The well-tried formula of feeding 'a little and often' applies equally well to marine fishes, with one very important proviso: to prevent pollution of the aquarium, always clear away any remains of food once the fish have lost interest in it. (A check on the nitrite level will indicate any evidence of overfeeding, or perhaps the presence of a decaying fish body, or an inefficient biological filter.) One exception to this practice of removing uneaten food very promptly is to dangle a chunk of food in the water for a period of time for the benefit of bold nibbling fishes. However, this method is not suitable for a community of fishes containing both bold and shy fishes, since the latter will lose out in the competition for food.

Invertebrates, such as sea anemones, need not be fed as frequently as fish; they may take in food when it is offered, but sometimes they spit out any surplus food or digest and then eject the entire contents of the stomach, almost as soon as your back is turned. This can also pollute the aquarium. (See also 'Tropical Invertebrates' and 'Coldwater Fishes and Invertebrates', pages 187-199).

One way of encouraging new arrivals to eat is to use a 'teacher fish', i.e. one that has no qualms at all about dashing out and snapping up food. Damselfishes are excellent in this respect. Bear in mind also that merely casting flakes on the water surface will not satisfy every fish in the aquarium. Some fishes are not physically adapted for surface feeding anyway, and many others may not care to feed in the bright glare of a fully lit aquarium.

Grazing fishes can be accustomed to the taste of dried foods by painting a liquidized emulsion of meat and algae foods onto a rock; when dry, place the rock into the tank for browsing fish to peck at.

Fishes that normally prey on live foods can be taught to accept dead food by attaching it to a short thread and jiggling it in front of their noses until they learn to take it.

Observe the habits of the fishes and note your own successes and failures when feeding them. By collating the results you will gradually work out a feeding routine that suits both you and the fish. Some of the larger fish become hand tame after a time, but it is still a wise precaution to impale food on a cocktail stick before offering it, in order to avoid being bitten by sharp teeth.

Feeding fish during holiday periods may cause some concern, but it is not a difficult problem to overcome. You cannot leave marine fishes to their own devices for as long as freshwater species, so the best arrangement is probably for someone to feed the fish in your absence. A fellow hobbyist or reliable neighbour may be willing to help out, but to avoid any risk of overfeeding, make up small packets containing the exact amount of food for each meal, stipulating that on no account should additional supplies be given. This is much safer than allowing a well-intentioned but inexperienced enthusiast to look after your fish, since they always overestimate the amount of food required. It is better to come home to a tank of hungry living fishes than to a tank of overfed dead ones.

Tempting a difficult feeder

Above: Once marine fishes begin to feed readily in captivity, your prospects of future success will have increased greatly. Many of the larger fishes will become tame and take food from your hand, but beware – many have very sharp teeth and so it is safer to offer food on a stick or with tweezers. Feed sedentary invertebrates, such as sea anemones, using tweezers to place suitable morsels of food into their tentacles.

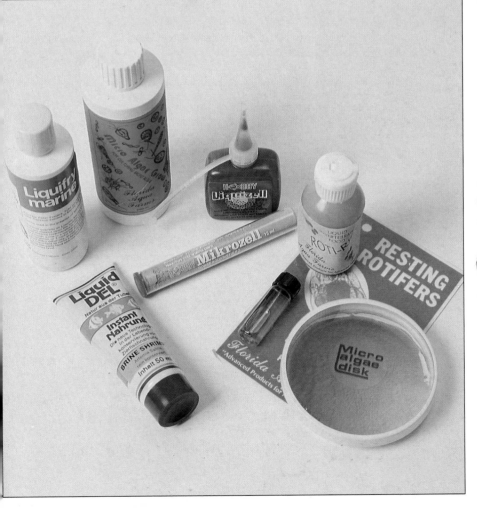

REGULAR MAINTENANCE

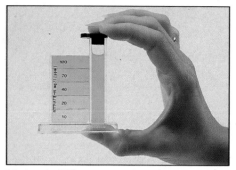

Modern test kits are accurate and easy to use.

You may feel you have enough to remember, do, look out for and worry about, but learning to spot signs of impending problems is better than trying to deal with them later on! Methodical routine maintenance need not take longer than a few minutes each day or an hour or two once a week or fortnight. Again, as when setting up, you may find listing the maintenance tasks helps you to develop a workable system; certainly written records are useful to establish what went wrong (or right!). Naturally there will be more to do in the early days, but enthusiasm will carry you over that period and, once the aquarium has settled down, you should find the time spent a pleasure rather than a chore.

One of the chief pleasures of fishkeeping is the relatively short amount of time you need to devote to routine maintenance compared to the rewards it will bring you. How much time you actually spend in front of the tank enjoying the result of your labours is up to you.

Routine checks

There are a number of checks that you should make on a daily and weekly basis.

First and foremost is a daily temperature check, together with a 'head count' of the fishes. Counting fish is best done at feeding time, when they usually congregate in one spot. Locate any absentees and search carefully for a missing fish: it may simply not be feeling hungry or sociable, but if it continues to behave this way, or seems off-colour, then you must assume something is wrong and begin further checks. If the fish is dead, remove the body before it decomposes and pollutes the aquarium and before other fishes become infected with any disease that may have caused its demise. Of course, the dead fish may not have succumbed to any disease; it may have been harrassed to death by other fishes – in which case, be sure to check the compatibility of species before replacing. Nevertheless, it is still vital to remove its body as soon as you discover it, to prevent fouling of the aquarium. Marine fishes are sensitive to any stress or disturbance, so try to use your eyes more than your hands and keep your physical intrusions into the tank to the absolute minimum. If you do not find a fish in the tank, look on the floor, since some marine fish are expert escapers!

As the marine aquarium gradually becomes established, the fish will settle down into their natural behavioural patterns. If you observe the fishes' normal activities, you will soon be able to recognize any irregularities that may be early indications of trouble.

Check pH, ammonia, nitrite and nitrate levels in established tanks at fortnightly intervals. The pH level should remain between 7.9 and 8.3. In a newly set up aquarium, it is a good idea to test the pH level more frequently. Stabilize the pH level by adding buffering materials, but if it falls again soon after being adjusted then some water renewal is needed.

As mentioned on page 42, be sure that the nitrite level has fallen to a minimum before introducing the first fishes, and keep it low by adding new stock gradually. In this way, you can avoid overloading the biological filtration system. Nitrate levels will continue to rise unless held in check by regular partial water changes. Many fishe

Hints and tips for a healthy aquarium

☐ Choose healthy stock and quarantine *all* new additions, provided that you keep the quarantine tank up to the standard of your main tank. Avoid stressing the fish in any way.

☐ Do not hope to keep all the fishes that you like the look of; bear in mind the feeding habits of different species, their compatibility with fish of the same or different species and their eventual mature size.

☐ Do not use any metal objects in the aquarium. Purists even remove the inside half of magnetic algae-scrapers when they are not using them.

☐ Remove uneaten food at the earliest opportunity; any water siphoned off during this process can be filtered through a fine cloth and returned to the aquarium. Acclimatize fish to any new food over a period of time.

☐ Learn to recognize symptoms of impending water problems: frothy, cloudy, yellowing and smelly water are all signs of deteriorating conditions.

☐ Do not neglect regular partial water changes. Changing 20-25% of the water in the aquarium each month is an average guide, but an invertebrate tank may require more frequent changes.

☐ Top up evaporation losses with *fresh* water.

☐ Make all changes to the water *gradually*. For example, after siphoning off 20-25% of the tank water for a water change, add the new water slowly over a period of at least half an hour. Remember to turn off power heads or other motorized filters that may be left 'high and dry' when the water level is low.

☐ Keep cover glasses clean. Salt spray soon renders them opaque, which prevents the full light intensity reaching right down into the water.

☐ Check that the water flow rate from filters remains high. Clean external mechanical filters and replace both the filter medium and activated carbon frequently – at least once a week if necessary. Wash filter media in tank water to avoid killing any bacterial colonies.

☐ You can check the efficiency of activated carbon by adding a few drops of a dye, such as methylene blue, next to the filter inlet. If clear water emerges from the outlet, the carbon is still working; if blue emerges, the carbon needs replacing.

re tolerant of higher levels of nitrate than are invertebrates. Practical experience of marine fishkeepers shows that up to 40mg/ litre is normal for fishes, with a maximum of mg/litre for invertebrates.

When topping up evaporation losses (with *fresh* water) check the specific gravity; readings of 1.020-1.023 is the normal range for the marine aquarium, even though some species come from natural waters with a higher specific gravity.

Emergency measures

If a heater fails, causing a drastic drop in temperature, carefully re-heat some of the aquarium water in an enamelled pan and gently return it to the aquarium. Standing bottles of hot water in the aquarium will also help to restore warmth, but be careful

not to let the bottles' displacement cause an overflow. In the meantime, replace the faulty heater. (Always keep a spare!).

Should the electricity supply fail, the large volume of water in the aquarium will act as a heat reserve until the power is restored, unless the break in supply is very long. Heat some tapwater by alternative means and put bottles of hot water in the tank as described above. During winter emergencies, lag the aquarium with expanded polystyrene sheets to conserve heat, or wrap it in blankets or layers of newspaper if a serious heat loss seems imminent. In the event of a prolonged

Right: Scrape algae from the front glass with an abrasive plastic scourer. Leave algae on all remaining surfaces for grazing fishes.

power failure, the lack of aeration and the interruption of water movement through the aquarium – possibly causing a failure of the biological filter system – may pose a greater danger to the fishes than a gradual heat loss. For these circumstances, a battery-powered standby air pump would be a good investment and could be used to maintain water movement and the filter system until the power is restored.

If the thermostat sticks in the 'on' position, switch off the heating circuit, increase the aeration rate to create more turbulence and even consider immersing the external filter return tube in a bucket of cold water. This will gradually reduce the temperature of the water returning to the aquarium. Floating plastic bags filled with ice cubes will help to lower the temperature. Once the temperature has reached normal levels again, do not forget to switch the heating back on again – having corrected the fault in the meantime.

With such valuable animals as marine fishes, you may wish to consider incorporating back-up systems, or at least having spare heater-thermostats, pumps, power filters, etc. An additional, separate thermostat to control the electrical supply to the main heater-thermostat unit(s) can be fitted and set a few degrees *above* the required water temperature. Then, if the main thermostat sticks 'on', the supply will be interrupted before the aquarium overheats. A further refinement could be a buzzer alarm to indicate trouble; battery-operated buzzer alarms are available to indicate power failures.

Look on the bright side

Finally, do not look on routine tasks as chores to be avoided; most of them should be part of the pleasurable task of providing your fishes with the care and attention that they undoubtedly deserve. They will repay you in the best manner possible – with a living picture of beauty and colour.

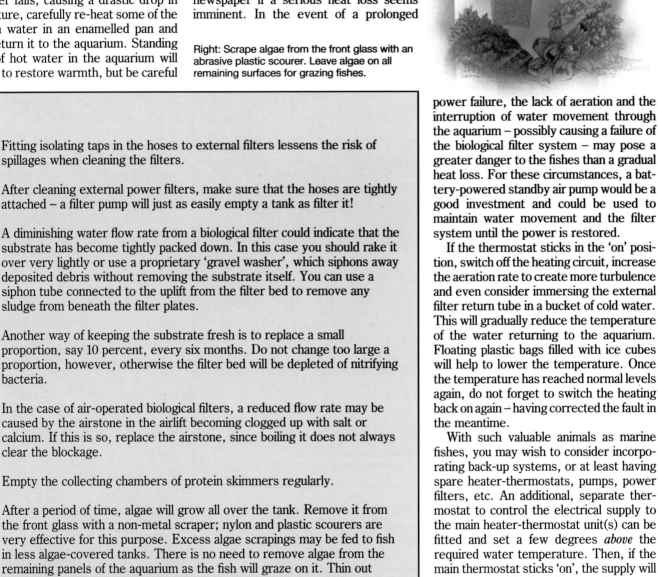

☐ Fitting isolating taps in the hoses to external filters lessens the risk of spillages when cleaning the filters.

☐ After cleaning external power filters, make sure that the hoses are tightly attached – a filter pump will just as easily empty a tank as filter it!

☐ A diminishing water flow rate from a biological filter could indicate that the substrate has become tightly packed down. In this case you should rake it over very lightly or use a proprietary 'gravel washer', which siphons away deposited debris without removing the substrate itself. You can use a siphon tube connected to the uplift from the filter bed to remove any sludge from beneath the filter plates.

☐ Another way of keeping the substrate fresh is to replace a small proportion, say 10 percent, every six months. Do not change too large a proportion, however, otherwise the filter bed will be depleted of nitrifying bacteria.

☐ In the case of air-operated biological filters, a reduced flow rate may be caused by the airstone in the airlift becoming clogged up with salt or calcium. If this is so, replace the airstone, since boiling it does not always clear the blockage.

☐ Empty the collecting chambers of protein skimmers regularly.

☐ After a period of time, algae will grow all over the tank. Remove it from the front glass with a non-metal scraper; nylon and plastic scourers are very effective for this purpose. Excess algae scrapings may be fed to fish in less algae-covered tanks. There is no need to remove algae from the remaining panels of the aquarium as the fish will graze on it. Thin out excessive growths, as a sudden 'algae death' could cause pollution.

☐ When treating fishes with disease remedies, follow the manufacturer's recommendations. Most treatments are designed to be added to the whole aquarium, but remember that copper-based cures will kill most invertebrates in the tank. (Which is one reason why it is more difficult to keep fishes and invertebrates together. A practical ratio would be 80 percent invertebrates to 20 percent, or even less, fishes.) If necessary, remove sick fishes and treat them separately from the main tank. Do not mix medications. Sterilize all equipment after use and do not share a net between two tanks.

BREEDING MARINE FISHES

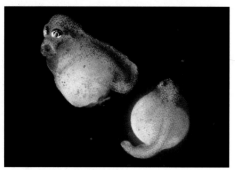

Young seahorses developing from embryos.

Little is known about the reproduction of marine fishes. In the first place, it is difficult to observe fishes spawning in the wild, for obvious reasons. When studying potential reproductive activities, you may miss a spawning entirely unless you know what to look for. Even if reproduction occurs in captivity, the chances of any recorded information reaching the light of da depends on how, and where, such information is published. Not all authors have access to a wide range of journals, and not all successful aquarists publish in the recognized scientific papers, limiting their knowledge to airings in museum, university and other relatively low-circulation publications. Perhaps you can add to our knowledge?

The majority of marine fishes kept in aquariums are juveniles. This is a situation forced upon hobbyists by commercial choice, smaller fish being easier and cheaper to airlift around the world. Thus, many species are never seen in their true adult forms or colours.

However, as research and experience reveal more information about the requirements of fishes in the marine aquarium, it is possible to improve their conditions and diet, and so increase their life expectancy. Today, more marines are reaching maturity in captivity and this in turn increases the chances of successful breeding.

This brief section reflects the current situation on breeding marines and offers a few helpful hints.

Spawning methods

Marine fishes employ various methods of spawning, in much the same way as do freshwater species. There are egg-scattering species, egg-depositors, mouth-brooders and pouch-brooders. The egg-depositors include the Clownfishes, Damselfishes and Neon Gobies, whose spawning behaviour is similar to freshwater Cichlids. The Jawfish incubates eggs in its mouth, while the male Seahorse assumes a similar role with eggs in his abdominal pouch. Within the framework of differing spawning methods, there is also a diversity of breeding behaviour. Fishes may, for instance, form longterm partnerships; a male may set up an attendant harem of females; shoals of fishes may seasonally congregate for a mass spawning; or a male and female may spontaneously spawn as and when the opportunity occurs.

Seasonal conditions can also affect spawning activity. There is little point in spawning, for example, if the young fry from demersal eggs (i.e. ones that settle on the bottom) are swept away from the haven of the reef (in terms of food and safety) by offshore water currents. On the other hand, the same offshore currents might be of benefit to pelagic (floating) eggs, removing them from the danger of being eaten by surface-feeding reef fishes.

Of the species that have been recorded as having spawned in captivity, the major-

Fishes spawned in captivity

This table shows a selection of marine fishes that have spawned in captivity. No detailed information is available on the exact size of aquarium used, however, or whether the fry were raised successfully.

Egg-scatterers
Angelfishes: *Centropyge* sp., *Holacanthus* sp., *Pomacanthus* sp.
Butterflyfishes: *Chaetodon* sp.
Croakers and Drums: *Equetus* sp.
Mandarinfishes: *Synchiropus* sp.
Wrasses: *Thalassoma* sp.

Egg-depositors
Anemonefishes: *Amphiprion* sp.
Damselfishes: *Abudefduf* sp., *Dascyllus* sp.
Gobies: *Gobiosoma oceanops*
Hawkfishes: *Oxycirrhites* sp.

Mouth-brooders
Jawfishes: *Opisthognathus* sp.

Pouch-brooders
Seahorses: *Hippocampus* sp.

ity are relatively small, so there is no need to plan a home extension to accommodate spacious breeding aquariums.

Basic requirements for breeding

There are just three essentials for successful spawning: pairs of fishes, space and the right conditions to encourage spawning. You might think that there should be more to it than that, but once you have fulfilled these three requirements you should be well on the way to success. The problems arise in doing just that.

Identifying pairs of fishes

Identifying a likely pair of parent fishes from the inmates of your tank is not easy. So little work has been done to identify the differences between the sexes that it might

be easier to let the fish decide for then selves! However, most fishkeepers wou' begin by making some commonsens assumptions; you could expect a female t become stockier at breeding time; a mal might have intensified and more sharpl defined colours or elongated fins, etc.

In Clownfishes, colour intensity and pattern definition seem to favour the male sex The problem is simpler to solve in on Damselfish, *Pomacentrus coeruleus* where the male has a blue tail and deepe blue coloration with pale patches, while th female's tail is colourless. Male Angel fishes are generally larger than adu females and may develop a dorsal filament Male Seahorses have a recognizable abd(minal pouch, and male Pipefishes have visible slit on the ventral surface.

The best clues to sexual differences ar found by close observation of the fishes; two fish have similar markings but fight then you can assume that these are tw males engaged in a territorial dispute. two fish of the same species have slightl different markings but seem to get on we together, then you could well have a pai Further observation may reveal which se is which. Of course, once you see one (them laying eggs then you are halfwa there!

Providing space for breeding

Space is important when attempting t breed fishes, for two reasons: space t establish spawning territories and spac for the spawning act itself. You must allo sufficient space for several fishes from th same species to be kept together withou squabbling while they sort out natur partners within a group. Clownfishes an Neon Gobies, among the first species to b successfully spawned, need less room tha the larger Butterflyfishes or Angelfishes.

Once the fishes have paired up, th physical act of breeding can be quite local ized in some species, although other require some extra vertical space. Man larger egg-scattering fishes, for example spawn after an upward-swimming court ship display and pairing action. This 'launc of fertilized eggs well above the fishes normal living level is thought to occur fo

Above: Like many marine fishes, the Mandarinfish (*Synchiropus sp.*) spawns in midwater after an ascending swimming courtship pattern. It places the fertilized, floating eggs into surface water currents well away from other fishes on the reef. Here, the female fish appears to be riding 'piggy-back' on the male.

Above: Anemonefishes (*Amphiprion sp.*) have a spawning method very similar to that of freshwater Cichlids. A pair of fishes will first select and clean a suitable site (often in the close vicinity of their home sea anemone) Here, the eggs are laid and fertilized, and then guarded carefully until they hatch.

two reasons: to allow the adult fishes to spawn in comparative safety away from predators and also to place the floating fertilized eggs in a food-filled environment to sustain the newly hatched fry. Egg-depositors, on the other hand, do not require such extra space, since they spawn and guard their eggs in a smaller area.

Let us suppose that two fish in your aquarium pair up. What do you do next? Ideally, they need a home of their own in which to spawn, but it is always possible that the stress of being moved will put them off the idea. The stress of moving all the other fish out of the tank could have the same effect (and stress the other fish too!). Perhaps the best solution, if the tank is big enough, is to let the pair choose their own territory and then separate this area from the rest of the tank using a tank divider. A sheet of opaque glass is ideal for this purpose. Even though such a divider isolates both parts of the tank – extending slightly above the water surface, too – there is no need to be concerned that the water temperature will be affected because the heater-thermostat is confined to one half. If you are using an undergravel biological filter system, the water is circulated around the tank through the filter plate, which extends below the partition. However, do not forget to feed both parts of the tank!

If you do set up a separate spawning/hatching aquarium, it should not contain an external power filter, or any filtration system which could trap the young fry. If a biological system is fitted, it should be slow running. It need not even be operated until the fry are two to three weeks old, as there will be no nitrogenous waste materials to nitrify until then. In the absence of a biological filter to control the build up of ammonia, make a partial water change of about ten percent every other day. Use an airstone to maintain water circulation, and this will duplicate the water currents that pelagic eggs are subjected to in nature.

Conditions to encourage spawning

If you have been following the correct routine maintenance procedures outlined on pages 52-53, the right conditions for spawning will prevail in the aquarium at all times. Obviously the fish should be in excellent physical condition, having been well fed on all their favourite foods.

It may also be important to know when the fish spawn in nature, particularly for those species that range outside the tropical zones. Day length may vary according to the season or geographic locality and you should adjust the aquarium lighting to reflect these natural variations. For example, spring and summer days are longer than autumnal or winter days, and fish that spawn in spring and summer will expect higher water temperatures than at other times. Simulating the equatorial day for strictly tropical species is relatively easy, simply turn the aquarium lights on for 12 hours and off for 12 hours.

Salinity could also affect spawning in the aquarium, even though it does not necessarily vary in nature. Reducing the specific gravity slightly to 1.020 – or even lower – has been known to trigger off spawning activity in some Damselfishes. Be sure to adjust the specific gravity over a period of days, however, so that the fish are not stressed. If you are lucky and the fish do spawn, then raise the fry at this lower salinity and gradually acclimatize them to the main aquarium's higher specific gravity before transferring them. If lowering the specific gravity does not work, then readjust it to normal, again over a period of days, before transferring the potential spawners back to the main aquarium.

Feeding fry

Feeding the young is the next big task. Although brineshrimp might seem to be an obvious first food, even the newly hatched nauplii could prove too large to be acceptable to marine fry. Fortunately, a recent development in food cultures should alleviate the problem: it is now possible to culture rotifers in an algal suspension and these tiny animals together with the algae are the most suitable first foods.

Meeting the challenge

If you wish to try breeding marines, Clownfishes and the Neon Goby may offer a good chance of success. Some American hobbyists prefer to breed the Seahorse, since pairs – complete with a pregnant female – are often commercially available in the USA. The theory is that, since the fry emerge from the male's pouch free swimming and functional, they stand a better chance of survival than the tiny and extremely delicate fry born to other species of marine fishes.

As you can see, the list of marine species bred in captivity is quite short compared with freshwater breeding successes, but it represents no mean achievement by those fortunate enough to have been involved. It also holds out more than just a ray of hope for future marine fishkeepers. Perhaps you, emboldened by these early triumphs, can hope for even greater success. Eventually, the problems will be solved by dedicated fishkeepers making careful observations and keeping detailed records of their findings. If you feel that you are up to the challenge, the rest of the marine fishkeeping world awaits your findings and results with bated breath.

BASIC HEALTH CARE

Fin rot is clearly visible on this Angelfish.

It is never too late to repeat the adage 'prevention is better than cure'. Setting up the best environmental conditions, careful buying and introduction of healthy compatible stock, correct feeding and regular aquarium maintenance are essential for good health. However, marine fishes are less tolerant to abuse than their freshwater relatives and there is always some risk of disease. Fortunately, there is adequate help at hand from your dealer or veterinarian. Your best weapon against disease is common sense coupled with sound aquarium management. Supplement these with all the information you can find on your fishes and avoid reckless diagnoses or excessive methods of treatment.

It is probably true that most marine fishes die as a result of bad aquarium management, be it overfeeding, underfeeding, the wrong diet, bad handling, induced stress or bad water conditions. However, an outbreak of disease can also cause fatalities among fish and is a worry to the fishkeeper.

In their natural habitats, marine fishes live in permanently ideal conditions. In the comparatively claustrophobic aquarium, where there is no escape from poor conditions, the fish are more likely to succumb to parasitic attacks or microbial disease. Marine fish will always be at risk until they have recovered from the stresses imposed by their capture and transportation. It is not so much a question of 'if disease breaks out' but 'when', and every marine fishkeeper should be prepared for the inevitable. Many authorities combine remedial treatment with the quarantine period as a matter of course.

Minimizing the risks

The two main causes of fish disease, apart from direct exposure to infection, are stress and poor water conditions, both of which are, or should be, under the direct control of the hobbyist. We have discussed ways of minimizing the stresses of transportation and introducing fishes to the new aquarium (see pages 44-45) and maintaining the correct water conditions (see pages 20-31). Now we come to the last possible safeguard – quarantining – which you must apply, especially if an established collection of fish is awaiting new arrivals.

The value of quarantining

All new fishes *must* be thoroughly screened for disease. Initial screening has already been carried out in the store, otherwise you would not have bought the fish in the first place. However, stress is quite likely to trigger the symptoms of disease and these will probably become apparent within a short space of time.

By keeping new purchases in a separate tank for two to three weeks you not only confirm their freedom from disease, or improve your chances of treating it, but you will also protect your main collection from the risk of introducing disease along

with the new fish. A further advantage of quarantining is that it allows a new fish to regain its composure and build up its strength before it faces the other occupants of the main aquarium.

The quarantine tank can also double as a treatment tank. Apart from a few flowerpots and slates against the walls to provide temporary refuges, it will need little in the way of furnishings. Besides heating, two other life-support systems are necessary: aeration, because medications may deplete the dissolved oxygen in the water, and a suitable but essentially simple filtration medium, since activated carbon and other chemically active media may remove medications from the water. Be sure to monitor the water chemistry carefully.

While they are in the quarantine aquarium, inspect the fish for any external skin damage or lesions. Also check on the fishes' feeding habits. If they take food readily then feed them often, but avoid the temptation to overfeed and be sure to remove any excess uneaten food. Inspect the fish regularly for visible signs of parasitic attack; raising the water temperature by a few degrees will accelerate the life cycle of any parasites present so that they become apparent more quickly.

Adding a prophylactic agent, such as a proprietary remedy for *Oodinium*, is usual, whether parasites are visible or not. When there is no sign of disease, the medication in the water can be removed, or reduced,

using activated carbon in the filter body. the remedy colours the water, this wi gradually fade as the medication i removed. Gradually reduce the water tem perature and adjust the pH level to that c the main aquarium before attempting t transfer 'clean' fishes to their new home Be sure to follow the procedures outline on page 45 when introducing fishes to th quarantine tank, or when transferring ther between different aquariums.

You may be concerned about providin efficient filtration in the quarantine tan during the isolation period, which should b long enough for any latent disease t appear. If you use a reasonably spaciou tank, the build-up of ammonia, nitrite an nitrate should not become a problem, sinc you are unlikely to quarantine a large num ber of fish at any one time. A sponge filte should be able to cope: in these circum stances, the sponge cartridge will act pri marily as a mechanical filter, for tw reasons: there may not be sufficient nitro genous waste products to sustain a viabl colony of nitrifying bacteria, and som remedies – often used as a background pre ventative treatment during the isolatio period – may adversely affect any bacteria colonies that do develop.

Below: The treatment aquarium for sick fishes need not be as sumptuously furnished as the main aquarium. A good external power filter and extra aeration are especially recommended. Such a set-up can also be a quarantine tank.

A basic treatment tank

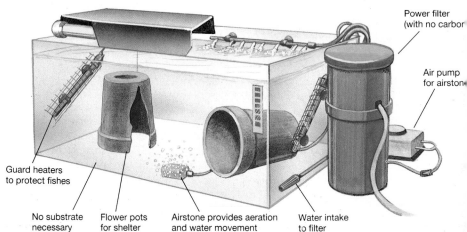

Power filter (with no carbor

Air pump for airston

Guard heaters to protect fishes

No substrate necessary

Flower pots for shelter

Airstone provides aeration and water movement

Water intake to filter

Although everyone acknowledges the theory of quarantining, putting it into practice may have its pitfalls. There is no point in quarantining fish if the conditions in the quarantine tank leave something to be desired, for example. The isolation tank must be as scrupulously maintained as the display aquarium; there is positive danger in introducing fishes into sub-standard conditions. Of course, this immediately poses the question of whether you are prepared to run a second tank – which will be uninhabited for much of the time – in anticipation of acquiring new stock.

An alternative strategy to maintaining a quarantine tank in parallel to the display aquarium is to provide a temporary holding area for new fishes for a relatively short period. If you time the introduction of new fishes to tie in with a regular partial water change, you can use the discarded water from the main aquarium to fill a small tank of, say, 45 litres(about 10 gallons) and equip this with a heater-thermostat, aerator and a sponge filter. Hold the new fish in this secondary tank for 24 hours or so without feeding them, and add a light dose of a copper-based cure the following day. Before transferring the fish to the main aquarium, give them a *freshwater* bath for 10-15 minutes (or until they become disturbed, whichever is the sooner). Set up the freshwater bath using tapwater in a small tank of 4.5 litres (1 gallon), for example. This should eliminate most problems. (See below for more information on freshwater baths.)

A further option is not to provide quarantine facilities and to simply trust to luck. Of course, it makes sense to ensure that the luck is heavily weighted in your favour by using an experienced dealer and listening to his advice.

Recognizing disease

The feeding habits of marine fishes are a sure indication of their state of health, and the first sign of illness is usually a loss of appetite. This is why you should ask your dealer if you can see a fish feeding. Fish caught and/or transported under anaesthetics may have been irreparably harmed and, although they may look fit and healthy in the store, they may never regain their appetites and slowly starve to death.

Once the fishes are in the aquarium, you can judge their state of health by following the same guidelines that you applied in the shop before you bought them. Watch out for signs of parasitic attack, such as fish scratching themselves against rocks and corals. Also look for abnormal reddening in specific areas, such as the bases of the pectoral, pelvic and other fins; this can be a clear sign of a bacterial infection, which usually responds well if treated promptly with antibiotics or medicated foods. An

Telltale signs of health problems

Fins: Damaged or torn fins invite infection, especially if tank conditions are below standard; red areas at fin base indicate bacterial infection.

Loss of weight: Weight loss may be caused by tuberculosis, or the fish may not be feeding.

Eyes: Look for protrusion or cloudiness.

Skin: Covering of dustlike spots, extra mucus, 'cotton wool' growths or more easily visible spots indicate possible parasitic infection.

Mouth: 'Fungus' around the mouth may be a bacterial, not a fungal attack, and so may not respond to fungus treatments.

Abnormal swimming: This may be due to digestive or swimbladder disorders, abrupt changes in pH or specific gravity, poisoning or stress.

Faeces: Long, white and stringy faeces and/or inflamed vent are generally due to poor diet lacking in roughage or greenstuffs.

Scales: Scales standing out from the body may indicate bacterial infection causing 'dropsy'.

Colours: Faded colour patterns usually indicate a stressed fish.

Gills: Extended, inflamed gills and/or increased breathing rate indicates parasitic attack.

Above: Early accurate diagnosis of illness is vital if treatment is to be successful. Observe the fishes closely for symptoms and signs of abnormal behaviour, such as fishes which are 'off-colour' or not feeding, listlessness, exterior parasites, unnatural breathing rates, etc.

excessive breathing rate, or a tendency for the fish to hang in the stream of bubbles from an airstone are both indications that something is wrong.

A word of caution, however. Do not be too quick to jump to the wrong conclusions. Check all the aquarium conditions before diagnosing a specific disease. Once you know that the environmental conditions are not to blame, you can begin other investigative measures.

The freshwater fish's way of signalling impending ailments by clamping its fins shut is not a sign of disease in marine fishes. On the contrary, very often the reverse is true. Only those conditions that produce external symptoms can be identified positively at an early stage. It is usually possible to diagnose internal disorders only following a post mortem, since once the symptoms become apparent it is too late to effect a remedy. In these cases, it is kinder to destroy the fish humanely. One method is to place it into a dish of ice cubes and put the dish into the deep freeze. (Do not freeze fish before a post mortem, however; it disrupts the tissues.)

Treatment of disease

At the onset of disease, you must take several factors into consideration. The first decision is whether to treat the whole aquarium or whether to isolate the sick fish. This decision may be affected by the nature of the disease itself. Another important factor is whether there are invertebrates, or even algae, in the aquarium, since doses of medication strong enough to cure fish will almost certainly be fatal to invertebrates and algae. Some remedies, although not entirely harmful, will set back the nitrifying bacteria in the filtration system – another good reason for treating fish in a hospital tank rather than in the main aquarium. The hospital tank can be equipped and furnished in the same way as the quarantine tank. Remember to follow

the acclimatization procedures when transferring fishes to or from it.

Numerous reliable remedies are available nowadays; they are the result of prolonged research programmes. Be sure to follow the manufacturer's directions for their use as closely as possible. The most widely used remedies are based on copper in some form. The effectiveness of copper-based remedies can be nullified, however, by some of the water-treatment additives, which will eliminate nonchelated copper from the water (chelated metallic ions are bound up with an organic molecule). The power of copper-based remedies will also be diminished by calcareous substances in the water. In 'standard' set-up aquariums with a deep layer of substrate, additional doses may be needed. In 'total systems', which may contain relatively little substrate, less medication will be needed to provide the same effective dose. (It is worth checking with the system's manufacturers on this point.) In either case, be sure to use a copper test kit to monitor the exact amount of remedy in the water.

Modern remedy dispensers seems to be standardizing on their measuring caps, which are easier and more accurate to use than the 'number of drops per litre' approach, especially since the drop size may vary from one remedy to another!

As a general rule, use only one remedy at a time. Although it is true that some chemicals work better in combination than alone, it is also possible that the ingredients of some treatments may prove toxic when mixed together. If in doubt, ask your dealer for advice. At any rate, always restore normal water conditions before beginning a second remedy if the first has not worked.

Freshwater baths

A freshwater bath is a useful immediate measure when dealing with parasitic attacks. This may sound a peculiar, or even drastic, treatment for saltwater fishes, but it merely reverses the familiar treatment used to remove parasites in freshwater aquariums, i.e. exposing fishes to totally different conditions for a brief period of time. The fresh water exerts a different osmotic pressure on the parasites, causing them to swell up and, hopefully, drop away from the host fish.

Ensure that the temperature and pH level of the fresh water closely matches that of the marine aquarium water to prevent shocking the fish. Although these baths are described as 'freshwater baths', it is usual to add enough salt to the water to make it slightly brackish (one part sea water, nine parts fresh water, for example).

Obviously, you should not leave a fish in a freshwater bath once it shows any signs of distress. Some fishes react in different ways to being immersed in fresh water. An Angelfish, for example, may show immediate signs of distress by laying on its side and then recover just as quickly to complete the period of treatment in the bath. A Wrasse, on the other hand, may turn on its side and die if not removed as soon as possible. To check on the condition of a fish, simply place your hand near the container; if it shows no response by moving, remove the fish straight away.

Antibiotics

Antibiotics are obtainable on prescription from your veterinarian. They can effect a cure but are not without drawbacks. Most are broad-spectrum antibiotics and so it is difficult to assess which remedy is the most useful against any one disease. Their use in an established aquarium is not recommended, as they will destroy the bacterial filter bed. A possible way of giving antibiotics is to soak some food in the medication, although it does tend to come out again. Ask your veterinarian for advice or use a medicated food.

Sterilizers

Exposure to UV light may kill some very small parasitic organisms, or keep their numbers to a minimum, but larger organisms must be exposed to much higher doses of radiation. Sterilizers of a size sufficient to eliminate these parasites would be impractical. Using ozone to kill parasites, or diatomaceous earth filters to screen them out physically, may be partially successful, but there is insufficient evidence to provide reliable guidance on their effectiveness.

Sudden deaths in the aquarium

Every now and then, fishkeepers may experience a setback for which there appears to be no apparent cause or obvious reason. In the marine aquarium, the worst of these is the dreaded 'wipe out'. This phrase is singularly descriptive: one day all is progressing well and the next everything is dead. So swift is this disaster that there is little opportunity to spot any signs of impending catastrophe. Authorities who have made a prolonged study of the phenomenon report that, before it occurs, fish behave slightly oddly – hiding, breathing differently or darting erratically around the aquarium. Extra foaming action at the water surface has also been observed. Furthermore, it seems that a fish from the problem tank can be confined in a container in the same tank and continue to live, while its unconfined tankmates die around it. Consider all these observations and you have the makings of a real mystery.

There are two kinds of wipe out, one of which can be more easily explained than the other. We have seen that the biological filtration system in any newly set up marine aquarium must be allowed to mature before animals can be added with absolute safety. It has also been suggested that one or two hardy, nitrite-tolerant fishes can be put in the tank to accelerate this maturation process. Only too often, the beginner notices the hoped-for minimum nitrite reading and then promptly adds too many fishes, which overloads the system and causes deaths to occur in this 'new tank syndrome'.

Possible causes of a wipe out which can occur in a well-established aquarium, on the other hand, are more difficult to pin down. The sudden loss has been attributed to various possibilities: accelerated bacterial action producing toxic materials (particularly those involved in the ammonia waste product conversion process); excessive algal spores; and excessive quantities of waste products and protein in the water, all resulting in a drop in the oxygen level. The continuous use of protein skimmers, ozone and UV sterilization has been suggested as deterrents, but an efficient biological filtration system allied to protein skimming should allay most fears, until further research reveals the actual cause.

Above: The cauliflower-like growths affecting the base of the pectoral fins on this Clubnosed Wrasse (*Gomphosus* sp.) is due to a viral ailment, lymphocystis. This may disappear with time and improved aquarium conditions, but treatment is still an uncertain business.

Above: The cloudy area between the spines of this Spiny Boxfish is due to the parasite *Chilodonella*. If it spreads to the gills, breathing will become adversely affected. However, *Chilodonella* cannot exist without a host and will die within 3-5 days in a fish-free tank.

Above: A Red Emperor Snapper, *Lutjanus sebae*, attacked by *Cryptocaryon irritans*. The white spots can be seen around the head and on the fins. Effective treatment, although often resisted, is usually by means of copper-based remedies or other anti-parasite treatments.

Disease table

Symptoms	Cause	Treatment
Gills affected, breathing difficulties, mouth kept open. Fish listless, not eating. Eyes may become cloudy. Triangular spots on body (with apex towards rear of fish).	*Benedenia*, a trematode parasite similar to *Dactylogyrus* gill fluke.	Proprietary remedies and anti-parasite treatments are effective. Be sure to follow instructions and check for incompatibility with invertebrates. Also consider giving the affected fish a freshwater bath – with extreme care.
Body swellings that may be either localized or spread over larger areas. Secondary infections may occur if swellings burst. (See also 'dropsy' if swellings accompanied by scale protrusion.)	Bacterial infection. This may be caused by various bacteria. Other bacterial conditions are described below.	Use copper-based remedies and then medicated food. Follow veterinarian's or manufacturer's instructions for use when giving medicated foods.
Opaque areas on the skin, especially on the dorsal surface of the body.	*Chilodonella*, a single-celled parasite that attacks skin around a wound or ulcer. May spread to the gills and cause asphyxia.	Anti-parasite treatments are effective. Requires a host fish, so an uninhabited aquarium will be free of the parasite within about 5 days.
White spots 2mm (0.08in) in diameter appear on body and fins. Fish scratch themselves energetically against rocks and corals. Breathing may become rapid if gills are affected.	*Cryptocaryon irritans*, parasite, causing 'salt water itch.' The one-celled parasites penetrate the outer layer of skin. Secondary infection may follow.	Proprietary remedies containing copper or other anti-parasite remedies are effective; follow instructions carefully and check for incompatibility with invertebrates, corals etc.
Thin white slimy faeces. Rear part of body may be swollen.	Diarrhoea. Generally poor diet, insufficient roughage or rotten, unclean fish meat given as food.	Raise tank temperature to 28°C (82°F). Do not feed for two days then give plenty of roughage foods such as shrimp, water fleas, etc.
Pronounced swellings of body accompanied by erect scales.	'Dropsy' often resulting from a bacterial infection. Similar to dropsy in freshwater fishes, hence use of the same name.	Consult your veterinarian for advice. If caught in time, the most effective treatment will involve giving suitable antibiotics to the affected fish and its contacts.
One or both eyes protrude from the socket. Disorders of the eye are also connected with other ailments.	Exophthalmus or 'pop-eye'. In one eye, the cause may be TB; in both eyes, it may result from chronic or acute bacterial infection. Possibly parasites as well.	No definite remedy, but anti-bacterial and anti-parasite treatments may prove effective. A small consolation is that the victim does not appear to be too distressed by the condition.
Edges of fins ragged; tissue between rays gradually disintegrates.	Fin rot. Bacterial infection often aggravated by poor water conditions.	Copper-based remedies and antibiotics may be effective if used early enough, otherwise surgical trimming may be necessary. Be sure to improve aquarium conditions.
White tufts of cotton-wool-like or thread-like growths on the body. (See also *Chilodonella*.)	*Saprolegnia* – a fungus. Usually affects fish with mucus deficiencies, open wounds or other skin ailments. Encouraged by excessive organic matter in the water.	Immediate partial water changes can be effective, as are malachite green remedies, temporary 'freshwater baths' and antibiotic treatment. Wipe away fungal growth with cotton wool if possible.
Rapid breathing rates and gaping gills, but without other external signs as found in *Oodinium* and *Cryptocaryon*.	Gill trematode parasites, such as *Dactylogyrus* and other species. Tiny worm-like 1mm (0.04in) flukes grip with disc of hooks.	A brief formalin bath (3cc per 4.5 litres/gallon of 37% formaldehyde solution) for 15-30 minutes, followed by treatment as for *Oodinium* and *Cryptocaryon*.
Fish becomes emaciated, although it may still be eating normally. Fins become ragged, the scales are raised in groups. Colours fade, eyes may protrude. Problems with balance develop. The symptoms can be very similar to tuberculosis.	Ichthyosporidium, an internal fungal disease. Complex infection cycle may involve direct spread of fungal spores or through eating copepod crustaceans carrying spores. Infection spreads through body and damages internal organs.	No effective cure known, but raising the temperature to 28-30°C (82-86°F) and feeding medicated foods may help.
Cauliflower-like growths appear on the body and fins. These may develop over a period of several weeks.	Lymphocystis, a viral infection. Affected fishes may eventually waste away or recover spontaneously.	Improving aquarium conditions often induces self-healing. Treatment of viral infections is always uncertain.
Tiny, dust-like white spots on body and fins. Fish scratch against rocks and corals. Gills may be inflamed; affected fishes typically show rapid gill movements. Breathing becomes affected.	An infection by the single-celled parasite *Oodinium ocellatum* – known as coral fish disease. Infection cycle involves formation of cysts on tank floor that release new batches of free-swimming parasites.	Proprietary remedies and anti-parasite treatments are effective, but follow instructions carefully and check for incompatibility with invertebrates, corals etc.
Dull eyes and rapid breathing. Fish suddenly dash and whirl about the tank and usually die from exhaustion.	Poisoning by external paint fumes, tobacco smoke, metals in water, poisons secreted by other fishes.	Immediate partial water changes, with a total water change as a last resort, or in the event of undergravel filter bacterial failure.
Fish cannot control its position in the water.	Swimbladder trouble, often caused by chilling.	Isolate fish in warmer conditions and consider using medicated foods.
Fish becomes emaciated, although it may still be eating normally. Fins ragged, scales raised in groups, colours fade, eyes may protrude. Symptoms similar to Ichthyosporidium. Usually only individual fishes affected, although others may succumb over a longer period.	Tuberculosis. Bacterial infection. Difficult to diagnose accurately because the collective symptoms include some seen in other diseases.	Antibiotics may bring temporary relief. Isolate sick and dying fish; otherwise cannibalism will occur and may spread the disease to other fishes in the aquarium.
Discoloured skin, loss of appetite, open ulcers, vent and junction of body and fins inflamed.	Ulcer disease, an infection with *Vibrio* bacteria.	Consult your veterinarian, who may treat the affected fish with antibiotics. Also consider using medicated foods.
Wounds	Perhaps caused by bullying in the aquarium, accidental damage or mishandling when transferring fishes, etc.	Apply povidone iodine or mercurochrome (2%) with a cotton bud to the affected area. For delicate fish, dilute the stock solution even further before application.

PART TWO
SPECIES GUIDE

In this part of the book we present a photographic survey of some of the many species of both tropical and coldwater marine fishes and invertebrates that you may consider keeping.

Which species to include in a book – and which to leave out – is not a simple matter. Apart from the limitations imposed by space and the availability of pictures and information, there is always the question of why some species are included at the expense of other, maybe even more deserving species. Personal preference naturally exerts a subconscious influence, but we have tried to take a wider view by including not only those species that have stood the test of time, but also the more exotic fishes that are known to be delicate. They are available to you, the fishkeeper, and only by encouraging you to persevere in your endeavours (and warning of the possible difficulties) will any progress be made in this young, but rapidly expanding branch of fishkeeping.

Relatively few marine fishes reach their natural adult size in captivity. Most of the research into the size of adult fish has been carried out by ichthyologists studying the fish in the wild. Do not be disheartened if your fishes do not attain the same size, or take it as a sign that you are not looking after them properly. Wherever possible, the sizes of species kept in captivity have been provided. If the fish are given the best water conditions and space to grow, it should soon be possible to narrow the gap.

If you are thinking of including any of the species in this book in your aquarium, be guided by the amount of information provided; the more information there is, the longer the species has been kept in aquariums and the more likely it is to thrive in captivity. Such species may be considered suitable for the beginner to keep. This is the first step; with experience you will acquire the confidence to keep some of the less well documented species and, maybe, extend the frontiers of knowledge yourself.

A shoal of Green Chromis (Chromis caerulea).

TROPICAL MARINE FISHES

Right: *Although it is fantastically beautiful, the Blue-faced Angelfish (Euxiphipops xanthometapon) is one fish that you should graduate to keeping only after a long period of time; surely you would not want to lose such an attractive fish through your own inexperience?*

Although nearly three-quarters of the earth's surface is covered by salt water, relatively few marine fishes are kept in the aquarium. And of these, by far the most are tropical species. Nevertheless, such is the appeal of this small group of fishes that the marine fishkeeping hobby has flourished and continues to attract more hobbyists around the world.

The most striking tropical marine fishes are native to the coral reefs and coastal waters, where collection is quite easy. Fishes from the deepest waters usually grow too large for the aquarium, and also present too many collection and transportation problems. The majority of suitable fishes come from the Indo-Pacific Oceans, the Caribbean area of the Northern Atlantic Ocean, and the Red Sea.

The water conditions on a tropical reef are extremely stable – the water is well oxygenated and almost completely free from waste products due to the constant cleansing action of the sea. The water is relatively shallow and this means that the fishes are quite used to fairly high light levels. One distinct advantage of simulating these brightly lit conditions in the aquarium is that growths of green algae (usually shunned by freshwater fishkeepers) can be encouraged, much to the appreciation of the fishes, many of which are herbivorous by nature.

Coral reef fishes are extremely territorial, each fish's chosen 'living space' in nature being much larger than that possible in the average indoor aquarium. This makes keeping shoals difficult in many cases because the fishes are intolerant of other members of the same species, although they rarely regard different 'neighbours' as a threat.

These are the challenges facing the tropical marine fishkeeper: maintaining clean, stable conditions; providing enough space; and choosing compatible species. Achieve these successfully and you can then sit back and admire these truly wonderful 'living jewels' of the sea.

Left: *If you could tear yourself away from this beach paradise and don a face mask and snorkel, you could soon be sharing the underwater delights of the fishes' natural home. With patience, a little practical knowledge and plenty of understanding, you can gradually simulate the tropical coral reef in your home aquarium.*

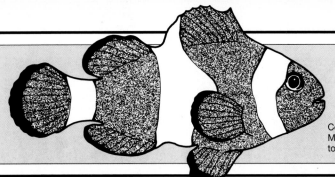

Common Clown (*Amphiprion ocellaris*)
Mature at 80mm (3.2in) and shown as a guide
to the maximum wild size of each species.

Family: ACANTHURIDAE
Surgeons and Tangs

Family characteristics
Members of this Family are characterized by their high profile and
laterally compressed, oval bodies. In addition, they have very
sharp 'scalpel-like' erectile spines on the caudal peduncle (hence
the name 'surgeons'), which are used during inter-territorial
disputes and in defence. The dorsal and anal fins are long based
and the eyes are set high on the head. The scales often end in a
small protruberance, giving a rough feel to the skin. In their natural
habitat these fishes may grow up to 400mm (16in), but aquarium
specimens usually attain only half the size, if that, of their wild
counterparts.

Although there are no drastic colour changes between juveniles
and adults in most species, the Caribbean Blue Tang (*Acanthurus
coeruleus*) has a yellow juvenile form. Since the adult colour occurs
at no predetermined age or size, small fishes can show adult
coloration while larger specimens retain their immature colours.
When the change occurs, the body is the first area to show the
blue adult colour, followed by the caudal fin. Thus, for a period
there is an intermediate stage which has a blue body with a yellow
caudal fin.

Although external differences between the sexes are normally
rare, some darkening of the male's colours during breeding is quite
usual. Size is not a reliable indication of the sex of the fishes;
sometimes the male is larger, sometimes the female. The pelagic
(free floating) eggs that result from the typical ascending spawning
actions of two fishes (or a group of fishes) take a long time –
possibly months – to pass through the planktonic stage. This
means that, although spawning in captivity may occur under
favourable conditions, rearing the fry may prove to be much more
difficult. (See pages 54-55 for general advice on breeding.)

Diet and feeding
Surgeons and Tangs need to be fed several times each day,
especially if there is insufficient algal growth for them to browse
upon. In fact, algae are such an important element of their diet that
you should not introduce them into an algae-free aquarium.

Young fishes grow very quickly and will starve if denied ready
nourishment. Although many species are herbivorous, others will
eat small animals too, which means that once they have become
accustomed to feeding in captivity they will take many of the
established dried, frozen and live foods.

Aquarium behaviour
Surgeons and Tangs live in shoals around the coral reefs of the
world. In the aquarium, however, they forsake this gregariousness
and will quarrel among themselves, unless you provide a suitably
spacious tank. Established species often resent new fishes
introduced into the aquarium; smaller fishes may well get off with a
warning but similarly sized fishes can suffer attacks. Young
specimens, whose scalpels are not as dangerous as those of
adults, mount threatening motions against newcomers, but these
displays are generally shortlived. Once settled in, they are quite
hardy fishes.

Above: **Acanthurus achilles**
*Members of the Acanthuridae
Family are easily distinguished by
their oval shape. Apart from one or
two species, many – like this
Achilles Tang – are brilliantly
coloured, with beautiful body
patterns. These fishes graze on
growths of algae (the high
forehead makes it easy), which
constitute a vital part of their diet.
Keep them in a well-lit aquarium
with an abundant supply of
vegetable matter.*

Acanthurus coeruleus
Blue Tang
● **Distribution:** Western Atlantic.
● **Length:** 300mm/12in (wild),
150mm/6in (aquarium).
● **Diet and feeding:** Mainly algae.
Bold grazer.
● **Aquarium behaviour:** Small
species may become bullies if
established in the aquarium ahead
of other fishes, but this tendency
generally decreases with time.

Young fishes are yellow with blue
markings around the eye. As they
age, the fish develop narrow blue
lines, the adult fish being darker
blue than the 'almost adult' fish.
The scalpels on the caudal
peduncle are ringed with yellow or
white in adult fishes.

Acanthurus achilles
Achilles Tang; Red-tailed Surgeon
● **Distribution:** Pacific.
● **Length:** 250mm/10in (wild),
180-200mm/7-8in (aquarium).
● **Diet and feeding:** Will accept
the usual protein foods, such as
gamma-irradiated frozen foods
(*Mysis* shrimp, plankton, krill, etc.)
and live brineshrimp, plus algae
and other greenstuff. Shy grazer.
● **Aquarium behaviour:** Normally
peaceful, but very delicate.
Compatible with most fish, but

may fight at first with other
members of its own Family. Do not
add to tank until the first fish are
established.

The brown body is offset by
yellow-red baselines to the dorsal
and anal fins. The white marking
on the gill cover behind the eye
and the dull white patch on the
chest are shared by other
members of the Family, but the
feature that positively identifies this
fish is the teardrop-shaped

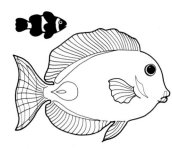

orange-red area on the caudal
peduncle, in which the scalpels are
set. Young specimens do not have
nearly as many red markings as
the adult fish.

A practical reminder
You will get maximum enjoyment from
fishkeeping by providing your fishes
with the very best conditions. Only then
will they be able to repay your efforts
with a healthy appearance and long life.

Above right:
Acanthurus coeruleus
*The juvenile form of the Blue Tang
differs in two significant respects
from the adult: firstly, the young
fish is bright yellow with blue-
rimmed eyes, whereas the adult is
blue overall. (Do not confuse the
juvenile Blue Tang with Zebrasoma
flavescens, see page 70).
Secondly, the strongly territorial
nature of the juvenile generally
lessens with age and the adult fish
becomes more sociable.*

Right: **Acanthurus coeruleus**
*As you might expect, the adult
Blue Tang is a uniform blue all over
(here shown at a sub-adult stage),
except for some yellow or white
coloration around the scalpels on
the caudal peduncle region. It is
not possible to say at exactly what
age or size a fish will change into
adult coloration. As a result, there
have been many instances of
confusion when fishkeepers have
tried to identify different species.*

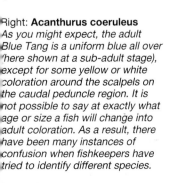

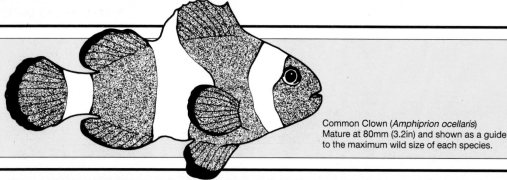

Common Clown (*Amphiprion ocellaris*)
Mature at 80mm (3.2in) and shown as a guide
to the maximum wild size of each species.

Acanthurus glaucopareius

Goldrim Tang; Powder Brown
● **Distribution:** Mainly the Pacific Ocean, but is sometimes found in the eastern Indian Ocean.
● **Length:** 200mm/8in (wild).
● **Diet and feeding:** Algae. Bold grazer.
● **Aquarium behaviour:** Normally peaceful.

It is fairly easy to identify this fish by the white area on the cheeks. Yellow zones along the base of blue-edged dorsal and anal fins may extend into the base of the caudal fin. A yellow vertical bar extends across the caudal fin. Another name for this attractive species is *Acanthurus aliala*.

Acanthurus leucosternon

Powder Blue Surgeon
● **Distribution:** Indo-Pacific.
● **Length:** 250mm/10in (wild), 180-200mm/7-8in (aquarium)
● **Diet and feeding:** Protein foods and vegetable matter. Bold grazer.
● **Aquarium behaviour:** Keep only one in the aquarium. Dealers usually segregate juveniles to prevent quarrels developing.

This is a favourite Surgeon among aquarists. The oval-shaped body is a delicate blue; the black of the head is separated from the body by a white area beneath the jawline. The dorsal fin is bright yellow, as is the caudal peduncle. The white-edged black caudal fin carries a vertical white crescent. The female is larger than the male. In common with all Surgeonfishes, it requires plenty of space and well-aerated water.

Acanthurus lineatus

Clown Surgeonfish; Blue-lined Surgeonfish; Pyjama Tang
● **Distribution:** Indo-Pacific.
● **Length:** 280mm/11in (wild), rarely above 150mm/6in in the aquarium.
● **Diet and feeding:** Algae. Bold grazer.
● **Aquarium behaviour:** Small specimens can be quarrelsome. Keep only one per tank or, alternatively, try keeping several together on the assumption that there is safety in numbers – rather than a mischievous two or three.

The yellow ground colour of the body is covered with longitudinal dark-edged, light blue lines. The pelvic fins are yellow.

Above: **Acanthurus glaucopareius**
The alternative common names of White-cheeked Surgeon and Lipstick Surgeon (see also Naso lituratus*) are equally apt, for the markings on this fish are extremely fine. There is some justification in defining it as a Powder Brown as the colour patterning is similar to that of the Powder Blue Surgeon. It is fairly easy to keep in the aquarium, being quite peaceful.*

Above right:
Acanthurus leucosternon
One of the most familiar of all Surgeonfishes, the Powder Blue Surgeon is a firm favourite with hobbyists. When first captured and during transportation, dealers keep them separated to prevent fights breaking out. Given room and sufficient vegetable matter, it makes a welcome contribution to the marine collection.

Right: **Acanthurus lineatus**
This is one of the fishes in the Family with a split level of coloration; there is a lighter area to the lower body with decorative parallel longitudinal lines above. Acanthurus sohal (page 68) has a similar body pattern. Like other Surgeonfishes, it appreciates some coral or rockwork to provide welcome sheltering places.

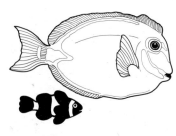

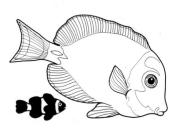

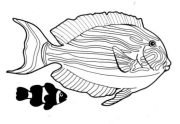

A practical reminder
Select the biggest tank you can afford
(or find room for); a large surface area is
more important than overall capacity.
This will ensure more stable water
conditions, vital to marine fishes.

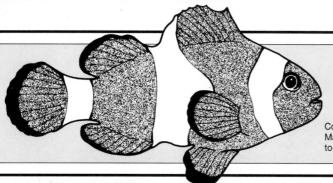

Common Clown (*Amphiprion ocellaris*)
Mature at 80mm (3.2in) and shown as a guide
to the maximum wild size of each species.

Above: **Acanthurus sohal**
*This striking fish is not a common
sight in aquatic dealers' tanks, but
its smart lines make it readily
noticeable when it does appear.*

Acanthurus sohal
Zebra Surgeon; Majestic Surgeon
● **Distribution:** Red Sea.
● **Length:** 250mm/10in (wild),
180mm/7in (aquarium).
● **Diet and feeding:** Algae. Bold
grazer.
● **Aquarium behaviour:** Small
specimens can be quarrelsome;
keep only one per tank.

This smart fish is similar in body
shape to *A.lineatus*. Its blue-
edged, blue-black fins add an
outline to the pale body, and the
scalpels are marked with a vivid
orange stripe. The upper part of
the body and head are covered
with a series of parallel dark lines.
A rare but beautiful fish.

Naso lituratus
Lipstick Tang; Lipstick Surgeon
● **Distribution:** Indo-Pacific.
● **Length:** 500mm/20in (wild),
200mm/8in (aquarium).
● **Diet and feeding:** Protein foods
and greenstuff. Bold grazer.
● **Aquarium behaviour:** Normally
peaceful.

The facial 'make-up' of this fish is
quite remarkable; the lips are red
or orange and a yellow-edged,
dark brown-grey mask covers the
snout and eyes. The front of the
narrow dorsal fin is also bright
yellow. The basic colour of the
dorsal fin varies according to
geographical origin of the fishes;
Hawaiian specimens have a black
dorsal, in those from the Indian
Ocean the dorsal is orange. The
two immovable, forward-pointing
'scalpels' on each side of the
caudal peduncle are set in yellow
patches. The male fish is larger
than the female.

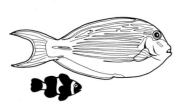

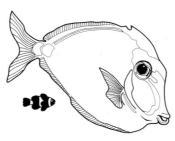

Above: **Naso lituratus**
*The extremely well-defined facial
markings of the Lipstick Tang are
quite remarkable, worthy of any
beautician's salon.*

Right: **Naso lituratus**
*The remainder of the streamlined
fish is no less attractive, with a
lyre-shaped caudal fin and double
scalpels set in vivid patches.*

A practical reminder
The aquarium will be very heavy when completely furnished. Ensure that its foundation is firm and level. You will need an electrical outlet nearby and adequate access for maintenance.

Paracanthurus hepatus
Regal Tang
● **Distribution:** Indo-Pacific.
● **Length:** 250mm/10in (wild), 100-150mm/4-6in (aquarium).
● **Diet and feeding:** Algae. Bold grazer.
● **Aquarium behaviour:** May occasionally be agressive towards members of the same species.

The brilliant blue body has a black 'painter's palette' shape marking, but the most striking feature of this species is the bright yellow wedge section in the caudal fin. The dorsal and anal fins are black-edged, and the pectoral fin is yellow-tipped. This fish was once called *P.theuthis.*

Left: **Paracanthurus hepatus**
This fish's black markings and yellow caudal fin make positive identification very easy.

69

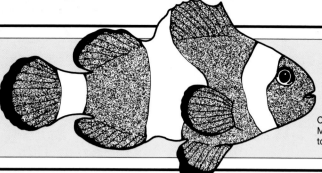

Common Clown (*Amphiprion ocellaris*)
Mature at 80mm (3.2in) and shown as a guide
to the maximum wild size of each species.

Zebrasoma flavescens
Yellow Tang
● **Distribution:** Pacific Ocean.
● **Length:** 200mm/8in (wild),
100-150mm/4-6in (aquarium).
● **Diet and feeding:** Algae. Bold
grazer.
● **Aquarium behaviour:** Highly
territorial. Keep either a single fish
or a group of six or more per tank;
never keep two or three together.

It is unusual to find a marine fish of
a single colour, but the vividness
of the bright yellow makes up for
any lack of pattern. This species
can be distinguished from juvenile
forms of *A. coeruleus* by the
absence of blue around the eyes,
although a more obvious guide is
the difference in shape of the head
and mouth.

Right: **Zebrasoma flavescens**
*Many such Surgeonfish and Tangs
are quarrelsome, but keeping them
in larger numbers may reduce
friction between individuals.*

Below: **Zebrasoma flavescens**
*The long snout of this species
enables it to graze effortlessly on
luxuriant growths of algae.*

A practical reminder
All-glass tanks are best for marine
fishes as the salt water cannot damage
them. Make sure that the glass is thick
enough to withstand the pressure of
water in the size of tank recommended.

Below: **Zebrasoma veliferum**
*This is an extremely variable
species. In this adult, the pale
brown vertical stripes extend into
the large dorsal and anal fins.*

Right: **Zebrasoma veliferum**
*A juvenile specimen, with a
different body pattern and no facial
markings. The typical Tang body
shape is clearly visible.*

Zebrasoma veliferum
Striped Sailfin Tang
● **Distribution:** Indo-Pacific,
Red Sea.
● **Length:** 380mm/15in (wild),
180-200mm/7-8in (aquarium).
● **Diet and feeding:** Protein foods
and greenstuff. Bold grazer.
● **Aquarium behaviour:** Normally
peaceful, but may be aggressive
with large fish. Young specimens
do better in captivity.

The main feature of this species is
the large sail-like dorsal fin and
almost matching anal fin; both are
patterned. Coloration of both fins
and body may be variable in
shades of brown overlaid with
several vertical bands. The female
fish is larger than the male.

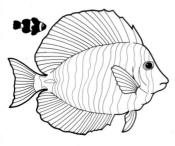

Zebrasoma xanthurum
Purple Sailfin Tang; Emperor Tang
● **Distribution:** Indo-Pacific,
Red Sea.
● **Length:** 200mm/8in (wild).
● **Diet and feeding:** Protein foods
and greenstuff. Bold grazer.
● **Aquarium behaviour:** Normally
peaceful.

The body colour may vary from
purplish blue to brown, depending
on the fish's natural habitat. A
number of dark spots cover the
head and front part of the body.
The caudal fin is bright yellow.

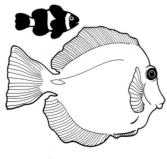

Right: **Zebrasoma xanthurum**
*The specific name, xanthurum,
refers to the yellow caudal fin.*

71

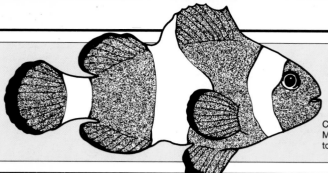

Common Clown (*Amphiprion ocellaris*)
Mature at 80mm (3.2in) and shown as a guide
to the maximum wild size of each species.

Family: APOGONIDAE
Cardinalfishes

Family characteristics
Cardinal fishes are generally slow-moving, often nocturnal fishes that hide among coral heads during the day. However, at the approach of a net, they can move very fast! They are usually found on coral reefs, but some frequent tidal pools and one species enters fresh water.

Unusually for a marine fish, the two separate dorsal fins are carried erect. This feature, together with the large head, mouth and eyes, is a characteristic of the Family.

Reproduction is by mouthbrooding. The male generally incubates the eggs, although in some species this task is undertaken by the female. In other species within the Family, both sexes share the responsibility.

Diet and feeding
Once acclimatized to aquarium conditions, Cardinalfishes will eat most live and dried foods (but never flake food). Do not keep them with fast-swimming boisterous fishes or they will lose out in the competition for food. It is a good idea to feed Cardinalfishes late in the evening, since this will suit their nocturnal lifestyle and may result in a greater willingness to accept new foods.

Aquarium behaviour
Hardy fishes that should be acclimatized gradually to the bright lights of the main aquarium. During the quarantine period, slowly increase the lighting level from dim to full strength.

Above:
Sphaeramia nematopterus
The body shape of this fish might be reminiscent of the freshwater tetras, although it boasts an extra dorsal fin and much larger eyes.

Right: **Apogon maculatus**
Much slimmer than the more common Pyjama Cardinalfish, the Flamefish is also a nocturnal species by nature, and prefers to share its aquarium with less boisterous fishes.

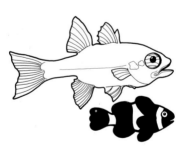

Apogon maculatus
Flamefish
● **Distribution:** Western Atlantic.
● **Length:** 150mm/6in (wild), 750mm/3in (aquarium).
● **Diet and feeding:** All foods. Shy.
● **Aquarium behaviour:** Prefers a quiet aquarium with fishes of a similar disposition.

This bright red fish with two white horizontal lines through the eye is very easy to identify. It has two dark spots on the body, one below the second dorsal fin and the other on the caudal peduncle (although faint at times). It is a nocturnal feeder and, although shy, usually settles down well in captivity.

Sphaeramia (Apogon) nematopterus
Pyjama Cardinalfish; Spotted Cardinalfish
● **Distribution:** Indo-Pacific.
● **Length:** 100mm/4in (wild), rarely seen above 75mm/3in in the aquarium.
● **Diet and feeding:** All foods. Keen.
● **Aquarium behaviour:** Do not keep with larger boisterous species.

This fish has three distinct colour sections to its striking body, each dissimilar to the next, almost as if it had been assembled like an 'identikit'. The large head section, back to the first of the two dorsal fins, is yellow-brown in colour. A dark brown vertical band joins the first dorsal fin to the pelvic fins. A spotted paler area covers the rear of the fish. The large eyes indicate a naturally nocturnal behaviour. It may be necessary to acclimatize this species with live foods, but once settled in the aquarium it will eat well. However, do not offer flake food. This fish was formerly known as *Apogon orbicularis*.

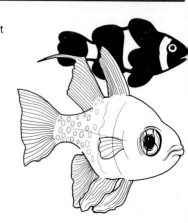

A practical reminder
If you intend 'upgrading' your system at a later date, be sure to allow enough room in your tank to house new equipment. Protein skimmers and similar systems need extra height.

Family: BALISTIDAE
Triggerfishes

Family characteristics
Members of this Family have acquired their common name from the characteristic locking and unlocking mechanism of the first dorsal fin. This fin is normally carried flat in a groove, but it can be locked into position by a third ray and prevents the fish from being eaten or withdrawn from a crevice in which it has taken refuge.

Triggerfishes are relatively poor swimmers. They achieve propulsion by undulating wave motions of the dorsal and anal fins, the caudal fin being saved for emergency accelerations when required. The pelvic, or ventral, fins are absent in most species, or are restricted to a single spine or knoblike protruberances.

Body coloration can range from the dull to the psychedelic. The patterning around the mouth is typically exaggerated, probably to deter rivals or predators. The teeth are very strong and often protrusive – ideal for eating shelled invertebrates and sea urchins. Needless to say, you should not keep Triggerfishes with invertebrates in the home aquarium. Also take care that they do not nip your fingers!

Reproduction takes place in pits dug in the sand within the territory of one of the female fish. These terrritories, in turn, are all enclosed within the dominant male's greater territory. The eggs, presumed to be demersal (i.e. heavier than water), are released either in an ascending swimming action or over a preselected site.

Some species guard the eggs, but others do not.

In the sea, Triggerfishes live alone and are intolerant of similar species in the aquarium. They may adopt peculiar resting positions, headstanding or even lying on their sides.

Diet and feeding
Triggerfishes are greedy feeders, accepting anything that is offered. Natural foods taken by the bottom-feeding species of the Family include echinoderms such as starfishes and sea urchins, which they devour complete with the spines. Triggerfishes consume the Crown of Thorns Starfish in a specific manner – they first blow the starfish over so that its spines are out of the way and then eat the soft unprotected underbelly. Species that occupy the middle and upper waters of the tank take plankton and green foods. Suitable aquarium foods include dried foods, chopped earthworms and small fishes (Guppies, *Gambusia* and other livebearing fry).

Aquarium behaviour
The behaviour of Triggerfishes in the aquarium varies from peaceful to unaccommodatingly aggressive, depending on the species. Fishes rest at night in crevices or caves, and so it is avisable to aquascape the aquarium to allow for this. Do not be surprised, however, if the fish take advantage of your thoughtfully provided refuges when you try to net them! In nature, they favour underwater cliff faces, especially the Caribbean species.

Balistapus undulatus
Undulate Triggerfish; Orange-green Trigger; Red-lined Triggerfish
- **Distribution:** Indo-Pacific.
- **Length:** 300mm/12in (wild), 200mm/8in (aquarium).
- **Diet and feeding:** Corals, crustaceans, molluscs, sea urchins. Bold grazer.
- **Aquarium behaviour:** The most aggressive Trigger of all. Keep out of aquariums that contain invertebrates and most fish. Using its powerful jaws, *B.undulatus* is in the habit of picking up lumps of coral and distributing them elsewhere in the aquarium. Despite its aggressive behaviour and potential size – in a large tank it will grow to about 300mm/12in – it is a rewarding fish to keep, becoming quite tame and enjoying a lot of fuss from its owner.

This species was first discovered in 1797 by the Scottish explorer Mungo Park. In the wild, it is found over a wide area of the Indo-Pacific, although not around Hawaii. The body coloration can vary quite markedly, as its common names suggest. Indian Ocean variants have orange tails,

while Pacific specimens have orange-rayed green caudal fins. Males are larger, with no orange banding on the head. Several large spines are arranged in two rows on the caudal peduncle.

Above: **Balistapus undulatus**
It is more than 190 years since this fish was first discovered and described for science and it is not difficult to understand why it might be regarded as an asset to the marine aquarium. However, its striking coloration, and the fact that it can become hand-tame must be taken into consideration along with another of its traits – it's a very aggressive fish.

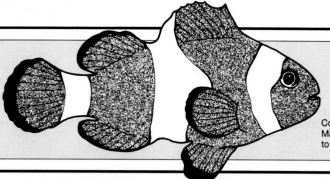

Common Clown (*Amphiprion ocellaris*)
Mature at 80mm (3.2in) and shown as a guide
to the maximum wild size of each species.

Above: **Balistes bursa**
*The coloration around the mouth,
together with the lighter body
colours, accentuates and
apparently enlarges the actual size
of the mouth, a good deterrent
against would-be predators. Like
all Triggerfishes, the head appears
disproportionately large compared
to the rest of the body. Note the
almost non-existent pelvic fins.*

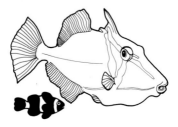

Balistes (Hemibalistes) bursa

*White-lined Triggerfish;
Bursa Trigger*
● **Distribution:** Indo-Pacific.
● **Length:** 250mm/10in (wild),
150mm/6in (aquarium).
● **Diet and feeding:** All foods.
Bold.
● **Aquarium behaviour:**
Unsociable towards other
Triggerfishes. Aggressive in
general to other fishes.

The red and yellow lines on the
head joining the eye to the pectoral
fin and the snout to the pectoral
fin are the principal clues to the
identification of this fish. An area of
light blue runs below the horizontal
line from snout to vent. The fins are
practically colourless. Males are
larger and more colourful than
females. This fish is also known as
Sufflamen bursa.

Balistes vetula

*Queen Triggerfish; Conchino;
Peja Puerco*
● **Distribution:** Tropical western
Atlantic.
● **Length:** 500mm/20in (wild),
250mm/10in (aquarium).
● **Diet and feeding:** Crustaceans,
molluscs, small fishes, usual frozen
foods, etc. Bold; will take good-
sized pieces.
● **Aquarium behaviour:** Do not
keep with small fishes. Although
peaceful with other species, it will
quarrel with its own kind.

Dark lines radiate from around the
eyes and there are striking blue
facial markings. The tips of the
dorsal fin and caudal fins become
filamentous with age, especially in
the male, which is larger and more
colourful than the female. This
beautifully marked species may
become hand-tame in captivity.

Right: **Balistes vetula**
*A characteristic of Triggerfishes is
that many will become hand-tame
in time. You should exercise care
when hand-feeding, however, for
their slightly protrusive teeth are
very sharp. Impaling pieces of food
on a cocktail stick before offering
to the fish will be a safer method of
hand-feeding, and the fish will not
know the difference anyway.*

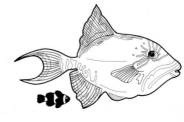

A practical reminder
Choose the correct size heater; allow
about 2 watts per litre of water. Large
tanks need two heaters. Do not test
heaters out of water and always switch
off power before adjusting thermostats.

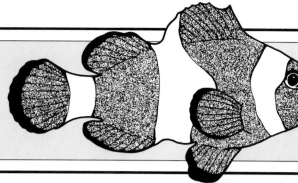

Common Clown (*Amphiprion ocellaris*)
Mature at 80mm (3.2in) and shown as a guide
to the maximum wild size of each species.

Balistoides conspicillum

*Clown Trigger; Big-spotted
Triggerfish*
● **Distribution:** Indo-Pacific.
● **Length:** 500mm/20in (wild);
250mm/10in (aquarium).
● **Diet and feeding:** Crustaceans,
molluscs. Bold.
● **Aquarium behaviour:**
Aggressive. Do not keep with small
fishes.

An easily recognizable species,
with its large white-spotted lower
body. The 'brightly painted' yellow
mouth may deter enemies, while
the disruptive camouflage assists
species recognition. Both the
dorsal and anal fin are basically
pale yellow and the caudal fin is
dark edged. This fish is also known
as *Balistoides niger*.

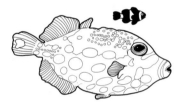

Right: **Balistoides conspicillum**
*With its spectacular coloration, the
Clown Trigger is an unmistakable
fish. An aggressive species.*

Below: **Melichthys ringens**
*A peaceful Indo-Pacific species
that is very similarly marked to
M.niger from the Caribbean.*

Melichthys ringens

Black-finned Triggerfish
● **Distribution:** Indo-Pacific.
● **Length:** 500mm/20in (wild),
250mm/10in (aquarium).
● **Diet and feeding:** All foods.
Bold grazer.
● **Aquarium behaviour:** Peaceful.
A very gentle Triggerfish.

The body is brownish and the fins
are black, but it is the white lines at
the base of the dorsal and anal fins
and the white-edged caudal fin
that distinguish this species.

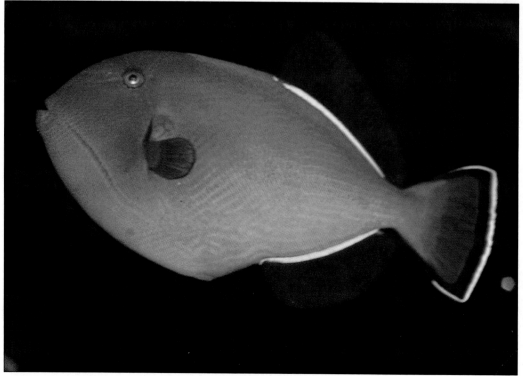

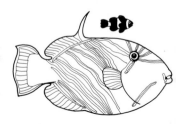

A practical reminder
The marine aquarium needs bright light.
Avoid using tungsten lamps. Either fit
fluorescent tubes inside the hood, or
suspend mercury vapour or metal halide
lamps above the aquarium.

Odonus niger
Black Triggerfish
● **Distribution:** Indo-Pacific and
Red Sea.
● **Length:** 500mm/20in (wild),
250mm/10in (aquarium).
● **Diet and feeding:** All foods.
Bold.
● **Aquarium compatibility:** Fairly
sociable and peaceful.

The body coloration of *O. niger*
can vary from blue to green from
day to day. The red teeth are often
quite conspicuous. Propulsion is
achieved by undulations of the
dorsal, anal and caudal fins rather
than by body movements. Red Sea
specimens require a higher
specific gravity than those
from the Indo-Pacific Ocean.

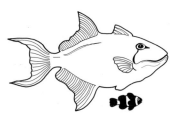

Below: **Odonus niger**
*Maybe the photographer
frightened the fish into erecting its
first dorsal fin, in anticipation of
perhaps capture or worse! Whilst
Triggerfishes have apparently less
means of manouevrability, by
lacking pelvic fins, they manage
very well by using dorsal and anal
fins to equally good effect.*

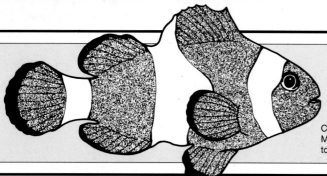

Common Clown (*Amphiprion ocellaris*)
Mature at 80mm (3.2in) and shown as a guide
to the maximum wild size of each species.

Rhinecanthus aculeatus

Picasso Trigger
● **Distribution:** Indo-Pacific,
Red Sea.
● **Length:** 300mm/12in (wild),
230mm/9in (aquarium).
● **Diet and feeding:** Crustaceans,
molluscs, sea meat foods. Bold.
● **Aquarium behaviour:**
Aggressive towards members of
the same species and towards
other fish of the same size.

The 'avant garde' colours of this
fish make it a popular species. A
number of diagonal white bars
slant upwards and forwards from
the anal fin. The mouth and jawline
are accentuated with colour and a
blue and yellow-brown stripe
across the head connects the eye
with the pectoral fin base. This fish
may emit a distinctive whirring
sound when startled.

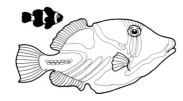

Family: BLENNIIDAE
Blennies

Family characteristics
Bluntheaded, elongate and constantly active, Blennies make a
cheerful addition to the aquarium, although they should be kept in
a species tank rather than in a community collection. They
naturally frequent inshore waters, hiding in any handy cave or
crevice, not always bothering to follow the tide out to sea. Provide
suitable living quarters in the aquarium using short lengths of
plastic piping, either laid on the aquarium floor or stacked up in
small piles to form 'apartments'.
   The dorsal fin is long and there are cirri (hairy, bristle-like
growths) above the high-set eyes. The skin is slimy, hence the
alternative name of Slimefishes.
   Male Blennies tend to be larger and more colourful than females.
During breeding, the male may undergo changes in colour during
both the pre- and post-spawning periods. One member of the
Family, the False Cleanerfish, lays its eggs in any handy shelter –
empty shells are particularly acceptable – and the eggs are
guarded by the male.

Diet and feeding
Blennies are completely omnivorous, eating everything from algae
to small fishes and bits of large ones! They will even take dried
foods with apparent relish.

Aquarium behaviour
Some Blennies are very aggressive to any other fishes;
Ophioblennius is a typical case that should not be kept with any
fish less than twice its size.

Above: **Rhinecanthus aculeatus**
*Whether used for camouflage,
species recognition or as a
deterrent, the exaggerated
patterns make the Picasso Trigger
instantly distinguishable from other
members of the Family. Here, the
front dorsal fin is being carried flat.*

Aspidontus taeniatus

*False Cleanerfish; Sabre-toothed
Blenny; Cleaner Mimic*
● **Distribution:** Indo-Pacific.
● **Length:** 100mm/4in (wild).
● **Diet and feeding:** Skin, scales
and flesh – preferably from living,
unsuspecting victims! Sly and
devious.
● **Aquarium behaviour:** Do not
keep with other fishes.

Using its similarity in size, shape
and colour to the true Cleanerfish,
Labroides dimidiatus, this fish
approaches its victims who expect
the usual 'cleaning services';
instead they end up with a very
nasty wound and a little bit wiser.
Easily distinguished by its
underslung mouth, which gives it a
shark-like appearance. Because of
its predatory nature, this species is

A practical reminder
Three things help maintain the correct light levels in the aquarium: well-filtered water, a spotlessly clean cover glass and the regular renewal of lamps, especially fluorescent tubes.

Above: **Ecsenius bicolor**
The rearmost body colour of this fish is often hidden from view, since it spends much of the time in the many hiding places carefully provided by the hobbyist. It is ironical – make a fish comfortable and it promptly hides from view!

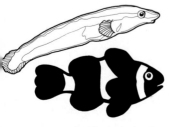

not recommended for inclusion in the home marine aquarium under any circumstances. It is featured here primarily as a warning, so that you can avoid it.

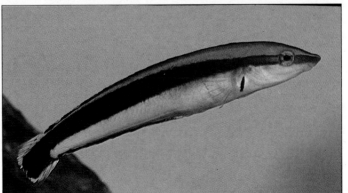

Above: **Aspidontus taeniatus**
Familiarize yourself thoroughly with this fish, for it is one you should avoid at all costs. It uses its coloration to mimic the true Cleanerfish, Labroides dimidiatus, *and denude its unsuspecting victims of large lumps of flesh!*

● **Aquarium behaviour:** Shy with larger fishes; provide plenty of hiding places.

The front half of this fish is brown, but the rear half is orange-red. During spawning, the male turns red with white bars. The female's breeding colours are light brown and yellow-orange. After spawning, the male changes colour again, becoming dark blue with light patches on each side of the body.

Ecsenius (Blennius) bicolor
Bicolor Blenny
● **Distribution:** Indo-Pacific.
● **Length:** 100mm/4in (wild).
● **Diet and feeding:** Meat foods and algae. Bottom-feeding grazer.

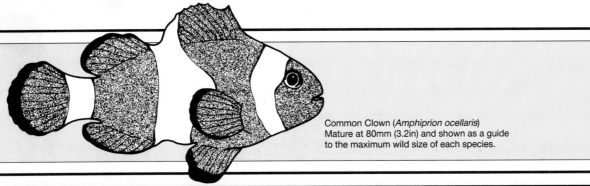

Common Clown (*Amphiprion ocellaris*)
Mature at 80mm (3.2in) and shown as a guide
to the maximum wild size of each species.

A practical reminder
It is more convenient to make up synthetic sea water than to use the real thing, which is not only inconvenient to collect, but also may be unsafe to use because of pollution and disease.

Above: **Salaria fasciatus**
It is a pity that Blennies are so keen on hiding away in caves and under rocks, for it is only when they emerge into more open areas that you can see their body colour patterns, long finnage and cirri – crestlike growths above the eyes.

Above left:
Ophioblennius atlanticus
A member of the combtooth Blennies group, the Redlip Blenny varies in colour from very dark to almost white. It is a very territorial fish and often perches on coral outcrops apparently on 'sentry duty' on the lookout for potential intruders.

Left: **Petroscirtes temmincki**
Striped Slimefish is hardly an attractive name, but Blennies in the aquarium often reveal endearing characteristics as they scurry around their territories. This highly camouflaged species lacks the usual cirri on the head.

Ophioblennius atlanticus
Redlip Blenny
● **Distribution:** Tropical western Atlantic.
● **Length:** 120mm/4.7in (wild).
● **Diet and feeding:** Meat foods and algae. Bottom-feeding grazer.
● **Aquarium behaviour:** Territorial, and it chases everything.

Keep this rare species in a community of small fishes and provide plenty of hiding places; lengths of plastic pipe are particularly suitable.

Petroscirtes temmincki
Striped Slimefish
● **Distribution:** Indo-Pacific.
● **Length:** 100mm/4in (wild).
● **Diet and feeding:** Algae, small animals. Bottom grazer.
● **Aquarium behaviour:** Can be kept in small groups of the same species.

The body shape is that of a typical Blenny, with the eyes set up high on the head. There are no cirri. The coloration is black with white blotches, plus bright blue spots on the head region.

Salaria fasciatus
Banded Blenny
● **Distribution:** Indo-Pacific.
● **Length:** 100mm/4in (wild).
● **Diet and feeding:** Small animal foods and algae. Bottom grazer.
● **Aquarium behaviour:** Requires plenty of hiding places.

The elongate body is covered with mottled light and dark brown vertical bands, extending into the long-based dorsal fin. The eye patterning – radiating stripes around the rim – is a particular feature.

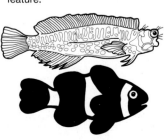

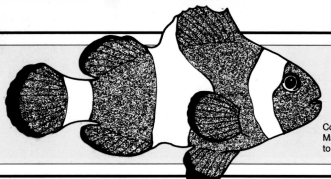

Common Clown (*Amphiprion ocellaris*)
Mature at 80mm (3.2in) and shown as a guide
to the maximum wild size of each species.

Family: CALLIONYMIDAE
Mandarinfishes

Family characteristics
Mandarinfishes and the related Dragonets are small, mainly bottom-dwelling species that often bury themselves in the sand during the day. Sometimes they will perch on a firm surface not too far away from the aquarium floor.

Sexing these fish is fairly straightforward, males having longer dorsal and anal fin extensions and brighter colours than females. Reproduction is by internal fertilization, often following a ritualistic courtship display and a clasping together of the two fishes. The eggs are scattered in open water, and are normally described as pelagic. (In contrast to so-called demersal eggs, which are deposited on a surface). Although this behaviour has been observed in aquariums, no fry have yet been raised in captivity.

Diet and feeding
Members of this Family feed predominantly on small marine animals, such as crustaceans, that live among the debris on the seabed. Provide the commercially available shrimps in the aquarium.

Aquarium behaviour
Mandarinfishes should be kept singly or in matched pairs. They are ideally suited to a quiet aquarium containing fishes of a similar disposition. Seahorses make suitable companions.

Synchiropus picturatus
Psychedelic Fish
● **Distribution:** Pacific.
● **Length:** 100mm/4in (wild).
● **Diet and feeding:** Small crustaceans and algae. Shy bottom-feeding grazer.
● **Aquarium behaviour:** Likely to be intolerant of their own kind. May be better able to cope with livelier tankmates than *Synchiropus splendidus*.

The basically green body is adorned with lemon-edged, darker green red-ringed patches. This species is found in the Philippines and Melanesia. It is less common than *S. splendidus*.

Synchiropus splendidus
Mandarinfish
● **Distribution:** Pacific.
● **Length:** 100mm/4in (wild).
● **Diet and feeding:** Small crustaceans and algae. Shy bottom-feeding grazer.
● **Aquarium behaviour:** It is best kept in a quiet aquarium away from larger, more lively fishes.

This fish has much more red in its coloration, in random streaks around the body and fins. Males usually develop a longer dorsal spine. It is said that the skin mucus of this and the previous species is poisonous, a fact often signalled in gaudily patterned fishes.

Below: **Synchiropus picturatus**
Not quite so gaudily coloured as the following species, the bottom-dwelling, less common

Psychedelic Fish has bold patterns clearly outlined against the subdued green of its body. An attractive subject for a quiet tank.

A practical reminder
When checking the specific gravity or the pH value of the water, ensure that it is at the correct temperature; otherwise you will obtain false readings. Make adjustments gradually.

Below:
Synchiropus splendidus
The long extension to the dorsal fin of the male fish is well illustrated here. The fish may be showing off its vivid colours to a nearby female before joining her in a vertical courtship ascent in the water, prior to the release and fertilization of eggs during spawning.

Family: CENTRISCIDAE
Razorfishes/Shrimpfishes

Family characteristics
The Shrimpfish, the principal member of this Family, has a completely straight top to its body. This is because the first ray of the dorsal fin projects horizontally past the rear end of the body like a protective cover. This forces the dorsal and caudal fin to be bent downwards, below the horizontal line. The word 'horizontal' becomes meaningless, however, because these fishes typically swim in a head-down position. The mouth is very small and tubular.

Diet and feeding
Razorfishes need a diet of small live foods, such as brineshrimp and finely chopped shrimps, and dried food.

Aquarium behaviour
These are delicate fishes to transport, and can be difficult to keep, but they often make rewarding aquarium subjects because of their distinctive appearance and curious behaviour. They are ideal fishes for an invertebrate aquarium.

Aeoliscus strigatus
Razorfish; Shrimpfish
● **Distribution:** Indo-Pacific.
● **Length:** 125mm/5in (wild).
● **Diet and feeding:** Very small animal foods. Bottom grazer.
● **Aquarium behaviour:** Usually thrive best in a species aquarium of their own, but will live peacefully with Seahorses.

Their habit of feeding and resting in a head-down position makes these interesting fishes to observe. The longitudinal (turned vertical) black stripe provides perfect camouflage, especially when they hide among long-spined sea urchins. They are susceptible to the effects of copper, so accurate dosage when treating disease is vital. (See page 57 for guidance on using copper-based remedies in the marine aquarium.)

Above: **Aeoliscus strigatus**
No, the picture isn't printed the wrong way round, this is the normal swimming attitude of these fishes. Spot them among the long spines of sea urchins if you can!

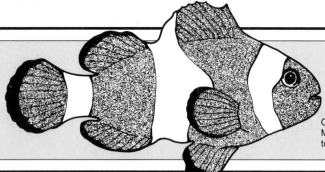

Common Clown (*Amphiprion ocellaris*)
Mature at 80mm (3.2in) and shown as a guide
to the maximum wild size of each species.

Family: CHAETODONTIDAE (including POMACANTHIDAE)
Angelfishes and Butterflyfishes

Family characteristics
This Family contains two very important groups of aquarium fishes: the Angelfishes and the Butterflyfishes, both favourites with the fishkeeper. The two groups are now classified separately as Chaetodontidae (Butterflyfishes) and Pomacanthidae (Angelfishes), but such is their similarity in appearance and aquarium requirements that it is more practical to treat them as one for the purposes of this book.

The body form is oval and laterally compressed. These features, together with the terminal mouth, provide a strong clue as to the their natural habitat: coral heads, where their thin-sectioned bodies can pass easily between the branches. Their amazing colour patterns camouflage and protect vulnerable parts of their bodies, and assist species identification. Juvenile Angelfishes have a different coloration pattern to the adults and it is not always possible to identify a young Angelfish with certainty; many species are similar at this stage – blue with white markings.

Of the two groups, Angelfishes are the most numerous. The surest way of distinguishing between the two groups is to look for the spine found on the gill cover of Angelfishes but not on Butterflyfishes.

There appear to be no external differences between the sexes, although at breeding times the females may become noticeably swollen with eggs. Both groups of fishes spawn in a similar manner, ascending in the water to release eggs and sperm. Once fertilized, the eggs float briefly until they hatch. The larvae then feed on plankton for some time before sinking to the bottom. One or two reports of aquarium spawnings indicate that demersal (i.e. non-floating) eggs were laid on a site, but these occurrences are presumed to be isolated incidents brought on by confinement and not typical of the Family as a whole.

Diet and feeding
Most members of the Chaetodontidae are grazing fishes that feed on algae, sponges and corals; some are omnivorous, however, and include small and planktonic animals in their diet. You will need to feed young fishes several times a day with live brineshrimp. Larger fish should be offered cultured worm foods (whiteworm, grindalworm, chopped earthworms, etc.) as well as dried foods. It is a good idea to get a new Angelfish feeding readily while in the quarantine tank, before introducing it into the main aquarium. Living corals, sea anemones and invertebrates will not last long in the same aquarium with Butterflyfishes, although Angels are less likely to prey on them. One or two species have evolved long snouts for reaching even further into crevices for food.

Aquarium behaviour
Although very attractive, these fishes are not really suitable for inexperienced fishkeepers. They can be difficult to maintain in captivity, particularly the algae- and sponge-eating species, while the polyp-eating species are practically impossible to sustain. These species are easily upset by changes in water conditions, usually showing any dissatisfaction with aquarium life by going on hunger strike; one day they are quite content with the diet you provide and the next day they will simply not touch it.

They are fairly territorial and Angels may be intolerant of their own kind, although most of the Butterflyfishes are compatible. Angelfishes are generally relatively tolerant of dissimilarly-sized fishes; smaller fishes do not alarm them, and they do not feel especially threatened by larger ones. However, when faced with a fish of the same proportions, quarrelling may occur. In a large aquarium with a good number of retreats, you can expect better results. Both Butterflyfishes and Angelfishes need refuges in which to shelter at night. Bear this in mind when decorating the tank; use rockwork and suitable pieces of coral – glue fragments together with sealant if necessary – to create hiding places.

ANGELFISHES

Apolemichthys arcuatus
Bandit Angelfish; Banded Angelfish
● **Distribution:** Pacific.
● **Length:** 180mm/7in (wild).
● **Diet and feeding:** Mainly sponges and algae, but freeze-dried foods can be offered. Grazer.
● **Aquarium behaviour:** Little information.

The diagonal white-edged dark stripe that runs from the eye to the rear of the dorsal fin gives this fish its apt common name. The anal and caudal fins are similarly dark with white edging and the dorsal fin is yellow-gold.

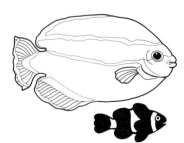

Right: **Apolemichthys arcuatus**
Whether the two common names are merely corruptions of one another or not, they both seem to suit this fish most aptly.

84

A practical reminder
Keep a close check on the nitrite content of the water, especially during the early weeks. It is safest to wait until it has fallen to a stable minimum before you introduce livestock.

Apolemichthys trimaculatus

Three-spot Angelfish

● **Habitat:** Indo-Pacific.
● **Length:** 250mm/10in (wild).
● **Diet and feeding:** Mainly algae, but offer freeze-dried foods and greenstuff. Grazer.
● **Aquarium behaviour:** Territorial, keep individual species only. This is not the easiest Angel to maintain in captivity.

The three 'spots' that give the fish its common name are around its head – one on top and one on each side of the body behind the gill covers. The lips are bright blue, and the anal fin is black with a broad white area immediately next to the body.

This species is fussy about water conditions and may also be difficult to acclimatize to aquarium life. Provide a variety of foods.

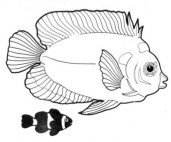

Above:
Apolemichthys trimaculatus
The specific name of this fish refers to the three prominent spots on the body, immediately behind the gill covers and on the top of the head. Note the contrasting band of black on the edge of the anal fin and the pale area close to the body. Needs care in captivity.

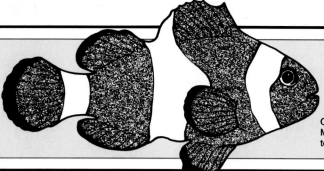

Common Clown (*Amphiprion ocellaris*)
Mature at 80mm (3.2in) and shown as a guide
to the maximum wild size of each species.

Arusetta asfur

Purple Moon Angel

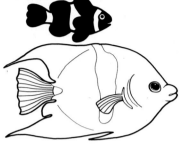

● **Distribution:** Indian Ocean, Persian Gulf and Red Sea.
● **Length:** 150mm/6in (wild).
● **Diet and feeding:** Meat foods and plenty of greenstuff. Grazer.
● **Aquarium behaviour:** Territorial.

This species has a yellow vertical bar across the blue body in front of the anal fin. In this respect it differs from a similar-looking species, *Pomacanthus maculosus*, whose yellow bar begins well into the anal fin. The dorsal and anal fins are elongated and the yellow colour is repeated on the caudal fin.

Right: **Arusetta asfur**
Compare the extended dorsal and anal fin outlines of this Indo-Pacific Angelfish with those of the smaller 'dwarf' Centropyge species shown below and on following pages.

A practical reminder
To help mature the biological filter, add some sand from an established marine aquarium, use a maturing agent or introduce a pair of hardy nitrite-tolerant fishes, such as Damselfishes.

Genus Centropyge – DWARF ANGELFISHES
Species in the genus *Centropyge* deserve a special introduction, although we have maintained their position in the A-Z sequence of the Angelfish section.

These are ideal aquarium fishes, principally because they are miniature versions of the larger Angelfishes. An obvious bonus is that you can keep a greater number of fishes in the same relative space, and they may be less expensive too! In the wild, they are found more commonly at the base of the reef rather than among the coral polyps, although they are never far away from a safe retreat. Unlike some other Angelfishes, *Centropyge* species more often than not associate in pairs, with several pairs sharing the same area. Their main diet appears to be algae, which they graze from the reef surfaces. Should treatment be required, these fishes will accept lower doses of a copper-based remedy for a longer time than normal, but may not tolerate the higher doses given to larger related species.

Centropyge argi
Pygmy Angelfish; Cherubfish; Purple Fireball
● **Distribution:** Western Atlantic.
● **Length:** 75mm/3in (wild).
● **Diet and feeding:** Meat foods and plenty of greenstuff. Grazer.
● **Aquarium behaviour:** Often happier if kept in pairs.

A deeper water fish, which lives around the base of the reef rather than at the top. The colour patterns around the head may vary in detail from one species to another and there is no difference in the juvenile colour form, as in other Angelfishes. It is possible to keep compatible pairs in the

aquarium, since natural territories are not particularly large.

Above: **Centropyge bicolor**
Literally, a two colour Angelfish. Juveniles are found in shallower waters than the adults. Despite its wide distribution in the Pacific, C.bicolor is not found in Hawaii.

Left: **Centropyge argi**
If two fishes of this attractive species appear to keep each other's company consistently, the result may be a spontaneous spawning in the aquarium.

Centropyge bicolor
Bicolor Cherub; Oriole Angel
● **Distribution:** Pacific.
● **Length:** 125mm/5in (wild).
● **Diet and feeding:** Meat foods and plenty of greenstuff. Grazer.
● **Aquarium behaviour:** Peaceful, providing plenty of hiding places are available.

The rear part of the body, from behind the head as far as the caudal fin, is bright purple-blue.

The small bar across the head over the eye is the same bright shade, while the head and caudal fin are yellow. In groups, a solitary male will dominate a 'harem' of females. If the male is removed from the group or – as in nature – dies, then one of the females will change sex to replace him. This procedure occurs every time the group becomes 'male-less'. This species is susceptible to disease. Use copper remedies with care.

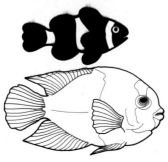

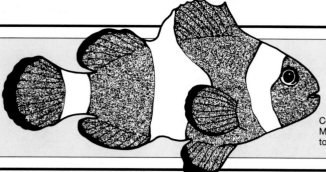

Common Clown (*Amphiprion ocellaris*)
Mature at 80mm (3.2in) and shown as a guide
to the maximum wild size of each species.

Centropyge bispinosus
Coral Beauty
● **Distribution:** Indo-Pacific.
● **Length:** 120mm/4.7in (wild).
● **Diet and feeding:** Meat foods
and plenty of greenstuff. Grazer.
● **Aquarium behaviour:** Will settle
down if retreats are close at hand.

In young specimens, the head and
body are outlined in deep purple;
red flanks are vertically crossed by
many thin purple lines. The adult
fish has much larger areas of gold/
yellow on the flanks, again crossed
by dark vertical stripes. The
pattern is very variable, however;
specimens from the Philippines,
for example, have more purple and
red coloration than those from
Australasian waters.

Below: **Centropyge bispinosus**
*The colour patterns of this species
vary according to its native home.*

A practical reminder
Biological filtration is vital in the marine aquarium; along with regular partial water changes, it is the most convenient and efficient way of reducing nitrogenous toxic wastes.

Centropyge eibli
Eibl's Angelfish
● **Distribution:** Indo-Pacific.
● **Length:** 150mm/6in (wild), 100mm/4in (aquarium)
● **Diet and feeding:** Most foods. Grazer.
● **Aquarium behaviour:** Peaceful.

The pale grey-gold body is crossed with gold and black lines, and some gold patterning appears in the anal fin. The rear part of the dorsal fin, the caudal peduncle and caudal fin are black, edged in pale blue. The eye is ringed with gold.

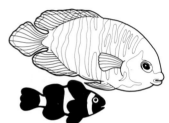

Centropyge acanthops
African Pygmy Angelfish
● **Distribution:** Indian Ocean, along the eastern seaboard of Africa.
● **Length:** 75mm/3in (wild).
● **Diet and feeding:** Meat foods and plenty of greenstuff. Grazer.
● **Aquarium behaviour:** Peaceful.

A blue fish with a yellow head and dorsal area, plus a pale yellow caudal fin. An ideal, peaceful aquarium subject. It is similar to *C. aurantonotus* (Flame-backed Angelfish) from the West Indies.

Left: **Centropyge eibli**
The combination of subtle colours of this fish come as a surprise – and very nearly a disappointment – when compared to the more vivid, even gaudy, hues of its relatives.

Below: **Centropyge acanthops**
The telltale spine on the gill cover distinguishes this species as an Angelfish, despite having a body shape more like a Damselfish. It is also often confused with C.fisheri.

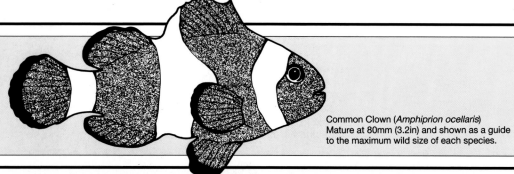

Common Clown (*Amphiprion ocellaris*)
Mature at 80mm (3.2in) and shown as a guide
to the maximum wild size of each species.

Centropyge flavissimus
Lemonpeel Angelfish
● **Distribution:** Indo-Pacific.
● **Length:** 100mm/4in (wild).
● **Diet and feeding:**
Predominantly greenstuff, but
might be persuaded to take meaty
foods. Grazer.
● **Aquarium behaviour:** Peaceful.

A plain yellow fish except for the
blue outlines around the eye,
bottom lip and gill cover edge.

A practical reminder
Water flow through biological filters, using the sand bed as the nitrifying bacterial colony, can be either downward or upward. Reverse-flow systems keep the sand cleaner.

Above left:
Centropyge flavissimus
A yellow fish with blue-ringed eyes.

Left: **Centropyge heraldi**
Unlike C.flavissimus, *this fish must be content with being plain yellow.*

Centropyge heraldi
Herald's Angelfish
● **Distribution:** Indo-Pacific.
● **Length:** 100mm/4in (wild).
● **Diet and feeding:** Mainly greenstuff, but also takes meaty foods. Grazer.
● **Aquarium behaviour:** Peaceful.

C.heraldi is also plain yellow, lacking even the blue details of *C.flavissimus.* Specimens collected from around Fiji have a black edge to the dorsal fin.

Centropyge loriculus
Flame Angelfish
● **Distribution:** Pacific.
● **Length:** 100mm/4in (wild).
● **Diet and feeding:** Meat foods and plenty of greenstuff. Grazer.
● **Aquarium behaviour:** Peaceful.

The fiery red-orange body has a central yellow area crossed by vertical dark bars. The dorsal and anal fins are similarly dark-tipped. The Flame Angelfish (often erroneously referred to as *C.flammeus*) is a hardy species and usually settles down quite well. Because of its peaceful disposition it may be kept in fairly small aquariums.

Above: **Centropyge loriculus**
There is no doubt at all about the identification of this species. Its vivid coloration distinguishes it from any other dwarf Angelfish.

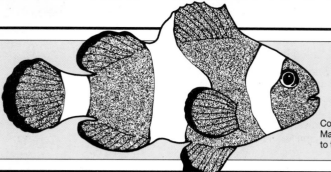

Common Clown (*Amphiprion ocellaris*)
Mature at 80mm (3.2in) and shown as a guide
to the maximum wild size of each species.

Centropyge multifasciatus

Multibarred Angelfish
● **Distribution:** Pacific.
● **Length:** 120mm/4.7in (wild).
● **Diet and feeding:** Mainly greenstuff. Grazer.
● **Aquarium behaviour:** Not known, but probably peaceful.

A rare fish, deeper bodied than the usual shape for the Family. The pale body is crossed by several vertical black bars that extend into the dorsal and anal fins, those on the anal fin turning yellow. The caudal fin is also black barred. The mouth and pelvic fins are yellow.

Centropyge vroliki

Pearl-scaled Angelfish
● **Habitat:** Pacific.
● **Length:** 120mm/4.7in (wild).
● **Diet and feeding:** Meat foods and plenty of greenstuff. Grazer.
● **Aquarium behaviour:** Territorial.

At first glance this species could be confused with *C.eibli*, but it lacks the vertical lines. The pale body is edged with dusky black dorsal, anal and caudal fins. The eye is ringed in gold, and the rear edge of the gill cover and the base of the pectoral fin are also gold. This species has hybridized with *C.flavissimus*.

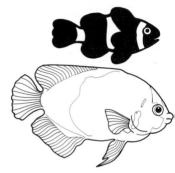

Although widely available, this species may be less popular with fishkeepers simply because of its muted colours.

A practical reminder
Always use plastic tubing with ozone as rubber (especially air pump diaphragms) will be destroyed. Excessive levels will make even some plastics brittle and you may experience headaches or nausea.

Far left:
Centropyge multifasciatus
Another rare fish from the Pacific. Its patterning of vertical stripes should make it a popular variety.

Above: **Centropyge vroliki**
Like its relative, C.eibli, the Pearl-scaled Angelfish is not endowed with striking colours, but it deserves to be more popular.

Left:
Chaetodonplus conspicillatus
If you see one of these fishes, and are experienced enough to keep it successfully, be sure to snap it up.

Chaetodonplus conspicillatus
Conspicuous Angelfish
● **Distribution:** Pacific.
● **Length:** 250mm/10in (wild).
● **Diet and feeding:** Crustaceans, coral polyps, algae. Grazer.
● **Aquarium behaviour:** Little is known about how well this species adapts to life in the aquarium.

The brown body is ringed by blue-edged dorsal and anal fins. The clearly defined eyes are a 'conspicuous' feature of the vivid yellow face; the mouth is a contrasting blue. Further areas of bright yellow appear at the base of the pectoral and caudal fins; the pelvic fins are blue.
   This rare species – considered by many marine fishkeepers to be the 'Jewel of the Angelfishes' – is found mainly around Lord Howe Island, about 640km(400 miles) off the east coast of Australia.

93

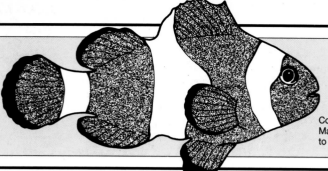

Common Clown (*Amphiprion ocellaris*)
Mature at 80mm (3.2in) and shown as a guide
to the maximum wild size of each species.

Chaetodonplus duboulayi

Scribbled Angelfish
● **Distribution:** Pacific.
● **Length:** 220mm/8.5in (wild).
● **Diet and feeding:** Crustaceans, coral polyps, algae. Grazer.
● **Aquarium behaviour:** Not known.

The rear portion of the body from the gills, together with the anal and dorsal fins, is dark blue with scribbled markings. A vertical yellow bar immediately behind the white gill cover is connected to the yellow caudal fin by a narrow yellow stripe along the top of the body. A dark bar covers the eye, and the mouth is yellow. A nitrate-free, but algae covered tank is ideal. Imported specimens are rarely available.

Chaetodonplus septentrionalis

Blue Striped Angelfish
● **Distribution:** Western Pacific.
● **Length:** 210mm/8.25in (wild).
● **Diet and feeding:** Crustaceans, coral polyps, algae. Grazer.
● **Aquarium behaviour:** Not known.

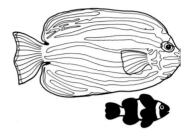

The brown body, dorsal and anal fins are covered with horizontal wavy blue lines. All the other fins are yellow. Juveniles are differently marked, being black with a yellow black-based caudal, and yellow margins to the dorsal and anal fins.

Below: **Chaetodonplus duboulayi**
Not a great deal is known about this recently introduced Angelfish. Provide it with the best of conditions and in time hobbyists will be able to find out more.

A practical reminder
Be careful when using ultraviolet lamps
in sterilizers. Never remove the lamp
from its casing when lit; it is dangerous
to look directly at the lamp unless you
have adequate eye protection.

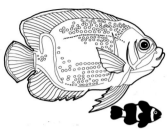

Euxiphipops navarchus
*Blue-girdled Angelfish; Majestic
Angelfish*
● **Distribution:** Pacific.
● **Length:** 250mm/10in (wild).
● **Diet and feeding:** Meat foods
and greenstuff. Grazer.
● **Aquarium behaviour:** Young
specimens adapt better to
aquarium life.

Left:
Chaetodonplus septentrionalis
*The brown body of this Angelfish
makes a contrasting background
for the wavy blue stripes.*

Below: **Euxiphipops navarchus**
*When seen underwater, the dark
blue areas, yellow saddle-back
patch and yellow caudal fin help to
confuse the 'fish shape' outline.*

Blue-edged dark areas on the
head and caudal peduncle of this
fish are connected by a dark
ventral surface. The rest of the
body is rich orange flecked with
fine blue iridescent spots. The
plain orange anal and blue dorsal
fins are both edged in pale blue, as
are the dark pelvic fins. Like other
large Angelfishes, the juvenile form
is dark blue with vertical white
stripes. (See pages 100 and 102.)

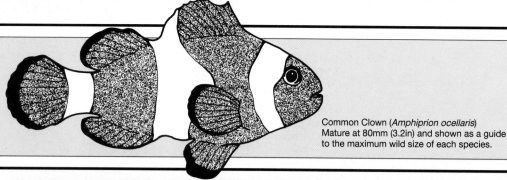

Common Clown (*Amphiprion ocellaris*)
Mature at 80mm (3.2in) and shown as a guide
to the maximum wild size of each species.

Euxiphipops
xanthometapon

*Blue-faced Angelfish; Yellow-faced
Angelfish; Blue-masked Angelfish*
● **Distribution:** Indo-Pacific.
● **Length:** 380mm/15in (wild),
300mm/12in (aquarium)
● **Diet and feeding:** Meat foods
and greenstuff. Grazer.
● **Aquarium behaviour:** Young
specimens adapt better to
aquarium life.

Despite the inclusion of 'xantho'
(the Greek word for yellow) in the
specific name, this fish is usually
known as the Blue-faced
Angelfish. Obviously, some people
feel that a greater part of the face

is coloured blue, rather than
yellow. Do not allow the attractive
colouring and majestic appearance
of this fish to tempt you unless you
are an experienced fishkeeper; it
needs special care. Juveniles are
dark blue with white markings.

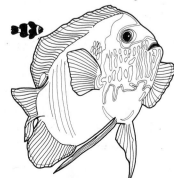

Holacanthus
bermudensis
(H.isabelita)

Blue Angelfish
● **Distribution:** Western Atlantic.
● **Length:** 450mm/18in (wild).
● **Diet and feeding:** Meat foods
and greenstuff. Grazer.
● **Aquarium behaviour:**
Aggressive when young; grows
large.

When adult, these fish are blue-
grey in colour with yellow tips to
the dorsal and anal fins. The
juveniles of this striking species
can be distinguished from those of
H.ciliaris by the straight blue
vertical lines on dark blue bodies.

Above:
Euxiphipops xanthometapon
*If any marine fish is capable of
exhibiting sheer arrogance, then
this spectacular species must be a
front-running candidate. The eye is
highlighted in yellow but a false
eye on the dorsal fin makes an
alternative, albeit false target.*

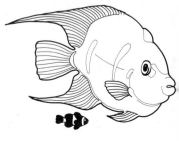

A practical reminder
Switch off power filters for a short time when feeding invertebrates; this will prevent their food (made by liquidizing usual aquarium foods) being extracted by the filtration system.

Above: **Holacanthus ciliaris**
When faced with this fish, who could deny its claim to be the Queen Angelfish? Young fish have royal blue vertical markings on a dark blue, gold-finned body. The body hues also appear to change under varying lighting conditions.

Left: **Holocanthus bermudensis**
This Blue Angelfish is nearly reaching full adulthood; the body stripe has yet to fade completely and in maturity the overall colour will become a delicate blue.

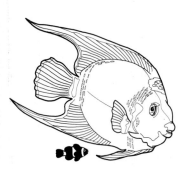

Holacanthus ciliaris
Queen Angelfish
● **Distribution:** Western Atlantic.
● **Length:** 450mm/18in (wild).
● **Diet and feeding:** Meat foods and greenstuff. Grazer.
● **Aquarium behaviour:** Aggressive when young; grows large.

A very beautiful fish in the aquarium. Variations in colour pattern occur, but generally this species has more yellow than *H.bermudensis*. Hybrids between this species and *H.bermudensis* are classified as *'H.townsendi'* but this is a non-valid name. Young specimens of *H.ciliaris* have more curving blue vertical lines on the dark blue body than the young of *H.bermudensis*.
  Queen Angelfish are reported to be prone to outbreaks of white spot disease, but can be successfully treated with copper-based remedies. They are quite resistant to such treatment and may even withstand some degree of overdosing without ill effects.

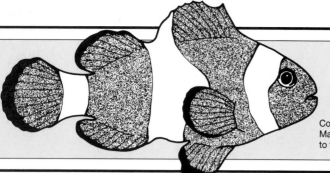

Common Clown (*Amphiprion ocellaris*)
Mature at 80mm (3.2in) and shown as a guide
to the maximum wild size of each species.

Holacanthus passer
King Angelfish
● **Distribution:** Pacific.
● **Length:** 450mm/18in (wild).
● **Diet and feeding:** Mainly greenstuff. Grazer.
● **Aquarium behaviour:** Aggressive; grows large.

The body is a dark brownish gold colour with a single vertical white stripe. The caudal fin is yellow. The dorsal and anal fins show gold patterning and edging. Young specimens have extra blue stripes on the rear of the body.

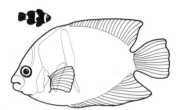

Below: **Holacanthus passer**
Only the yellow caudal fin and white stripe remain from the gold juvenile coloration. Blue stripes, previously separated, now merge.

Holacanthus (Apolemichthys) tricolor
Rock Beauty
● **Distribution:** Western Atlantic.
● **Length:** 600mm/24in (wild), 300mm/12in (aquarium).
● **Diet and feeding:** In nature, sponges. Will eat meat foods and algae but may not thrive. Grazer.
● **Aquarium behaviour:** Aggressive.

Juvenile forms of this fish are yellow with perhaps just a blue-edged dark spot on the body, but this enlarges to cover two-thirds of the body as the fish matures.

This good looking but very aggressive species will offer a challenge to the experienced fishkeeper with a spacious aquarium. Feeding can be a problem, requiring patience and care; even when they appear to be feeding well, these fishes miss their normal diet of marine sponges. If the aquarium conditions are good, however, and you feed good-quality frozen foods, then you may well achieve success with this fish.

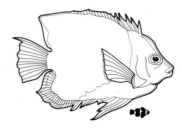

Pomacanthus (Pomacanthodes) annularis
Blue Ring Angelfish
● **Distribution:** Indo-Pacific.
● **Length:** 400mm/16in (wild), 250mm/10in (aquarium).
● **Diet and feeding:** Meat foods and greenstuff. Grazer.
● **Aquarium behaviour:** Territorial.

Blue lines run from either side of the eye diagonally across the brown body. The lines rejoin at the top of the rear portion of the body. A dominant blue ring lies behind the gill cover. Juveniles are blue with a distinctive pattern of almost straight transverse white lines.

Right: **Holacanthus tricolor**
The Rock Beauty is an extremely attractive fish. Before buying one, however, you should make sure it is eating readily; these fish feed naturally on sponges and can be hard to acclimatize to aquarium diets. Tends to be aggressive.

Below right:
Pomacanthus annularis
This head shot shows clearly how the common name of 'Blue Ring Angelfish' was inspired. Again, juveniles are blue with horizontal white markings, which turn blue and slant up more diagonally with approaching maturity.

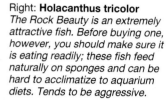

A practical reminder
Make regular use of a 'gravel-washer' to clean the substrate. Use it when making regular partial water changes; it will remove substrate dirt along with a portion of the aquarium water.

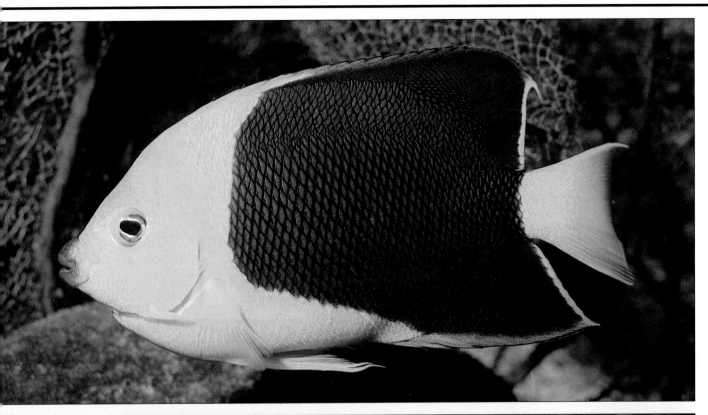

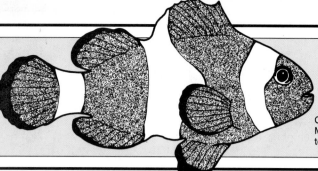

Common Clown (*Amphiprion ocellaris*)
Mature at 80mm (3.2in) and shown as a guide
to the maximum wild size of each species.

Pomacanthus imperator
Emperor Angelfish
● **Distribution:** Indo-Pacific.
● **Length:** 400mm/16in (wild),
300mm/12in (aquarium).
● **Diet and feeding:** Animal foods
and greenstuff. Grazer.
● **Aquarium behaviour:** Very
inquisitive towards new additions
to the aquarium.

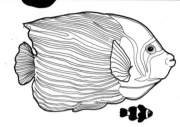

The yellow body is crossed with
diagonal blue lines. The dark blue
of the anal fin extends into a
vertical wedge behind the gill
cover. The eye is hidden in a blue-
edged dark band. The caudal fin is
yellow. Juveniles are dark blue
with white semicircular or oval
markings. Like all Angels, this
species requires the very best
water conditions possible. Many
fishkeepers have grown this
species on from juvenile to adult.

Right: **Pomacanthus imperator**
*Clearly a juvenile, with the
distinctive white markings on a
blue background. Such patterns
provide excellent disruptive
camouflage for the young fishes in
the dappled light of the coral reefs.*

Below: **Pomacanthus imperator**
*Despite the colour changes
apparent in this adult, the eye
remains hidden beneath a dark bar,
giving protection against attack.*

A practical reminder
Avoid building up coral structures too
elaborately; you will find it difficult to
reposition them without breaking and
makes netting fish a frustrating task.
Clean corals thoroughly before use.

Pomacanthus paru
French Angelfish
● **Distribution:** Western Atlantic.
● **Length:** 300mm/12in (wild).
● **Diet and feeding:** Meat foods
and greenstuff. Grazer.
● **Aquarium behaviour:** Young
specimens may be 'nippy', since
they act as cleaner fishes.

The young fish is black with bright
yellow vertical bands. The adult
fish is predominantly grey with
bright speckles. Juvenile members
of the Atlantic Pomacanthids
exhibit cleaning tendencies
towards other fishes, and each
Angel's territory is recognized as a
cleaning station.

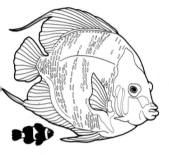

Right: **Pomacanthus paru**
*This is the juvenile stage, with a
pattern of yellow stripes on a black
background. As the fish develops
into a sub-adult (below) the stripes
begin to fade and the adult
coloration appears (seen fully
developed at below right).*

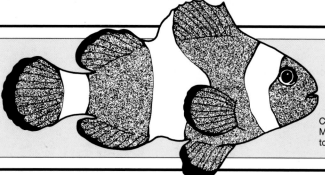

Common Clown (*Amphiprion ocellaris*)
Mature at 80mm (3.2in) and shown as a guide
to the maximum wild size of each species.

Pomacanthus
semicirculatus
Koran Angelfish
● **Distribution:** Indo-Pacific,
Red Sea.
● **Length:** 400mm/16in (wild),
380mm/15in (aquarium).
● **Diet and feeding:** Meat foods
and greenstuff. Grazer.
● **Aquarium behaviour:** Territorial.

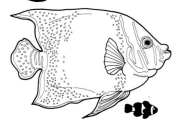

The body is golden brown with
blue speckles and the fins are
outlined in blue. There are vertical
blue lines on the head. The white
markings on the juvenile are in the
shape of semicircles rather than
straight lines. During the colour
change to adulthood, the markings
on the caudal fin often resemble
Arabic characters in the Koran –
hence the common name.

Right and below:
Pomacanthus semicirculatus
*Like most Angelfishes, the juvenile
form (right) is differently coloured
to the adult. Again, the usual dark
blue background is apparent and
only the way in which the white
markings are curved gives a clue
to the species' indentity. The near-
adult form (below) has almost lost
the juvenile white markings.*

A practical reminder
Marine algae, especially of the genus
Caulerpa, bring welcome greenery to
the marine tank and make fine
substitutes for freshwater plants.
Be sure to provide bright lighting.

Pygoplites diacanthus
*Regal Angelfish; Royal Empress
Angelfish*
● **Distribution:** Indo-Pacific and
Red Sea.
● **Length:** 250mm/10in (wild),
180mm/7in (aquarium).
● **Diet and feeding:** Sponges and
algae in nature. In the tank, they
will take frozen bloodworm, frozen
Mysis shrimp, mussel meat, etc;
even flake sometimes. Grazer.
● **Aquarium behaviour:** Shy,
requires plenty of hiding places.

Dark-edged, bright orange slanting
bands cross the body and extend
into the dorsal and anal fins. The
caudal fin is plain yellow. Feeding
can be a problem, and may make
it difficult to acclimatize this
species to aquarium life. It requires
a low nitrate level in the tank.
Specimens from the Philippines
are relatively pale in colour, and
consequently less desirable, and
are virtually impossible to feed.
Those from Sri Lanka, the
Maldives and the Red Sea will eat

in good water conditions and are
brighter in colour. As some
encouragement, one specimen of
this species has grown 125mm (5in)
during seven years in captivity.

Below: **Pygoplites diacanthus**
*If you can keep this Regal
Angelfish in the very best of
conditions and provide it with just
the right diet, then over a period of
years it will repay you by
displaying amazing colours and,
indeed, a truly regal manner.*

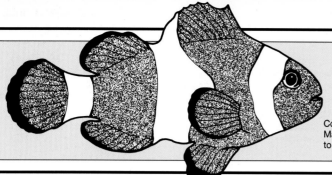

Common Clown (*Amphiprion ocellaris*)
Mature at 80mm (3.2in) and shown as a guide
to the maximum wild size of each species.

BUTTERFLYFISHES

Family characteristics
Butterflyfishes are colourful and attractive, but if they are not confident in the aquarium they will hide away from suspected dangers and provide you with little opportunity to appreciate them. Like many freshwater fishes, Butterflyfishes may undergo colour changes at night; the usual transformation is the appearance of darker splodges over parts of the body.

Diet and feeding
Feeding is of paramount importance to these mostly timid fishes, which may lose out in the rush for food. The result is that many Butterflyfishes may starve to death in a short space of time. Offer cultured worm foods (whiteworm, grindalworm, small earthworms etc.), dried foods and algae. A good alternative to worm foods – or any other terrestrial and/or freshwater aquatic live foods, which tend to stop wriggling very rapidly in sea water – are the many good-quality frozen foods available from your dealer. Live foods such as *Mysis* shrimp and brineshrimp will also be much appreciated by these elegant, if difficult, fishes.

Aquarium behaviour
Ensure that the aquarium has sufficient retreats and hideaways to give the fishes some form of security. Unfortunately, the most exotically coloured (and hence most desirable) Butterflyfishes often prove to be the most difficult to acclimatize to aquarium life. Although we feature some of these especially beautiful fishes in this section, they may prove to be expensive, shortlived disappointments in the aquarium. In this respect, many should simply be left in the sea. The tragedy is that in order to learn how to keep them successfully, so many die in the attempt.

Chaetodon (Anisochaetodon) auriga
Threadfin Butterflyfish
● **Distribution:** Indo-Pacific, Red Sea.
● **Length:** 200mm/8in (wild), 150mm/6in (aquarium).
● **Diet and feeding:** Crustaceans, coral polyps and algae in the wild. Offer suitable live and frozen foods in the aquarium. Grazer.
● **Aquarium behaviour:** Peaceful, but shy.

A black bar crosses the eye, and the mainly white flanks are decorated with a 'herring-bone' pattern of grey lines. The anal, dorsal and front part of the caudal fin are yellow, and there is a dark 'eye-spot' in the rear part of the dorsal fin. The common name refers to a threadlike extension to the dorsal fin. *C.auriga* is a hardy species that can be weaned on to food of your choice by gradual substitution.

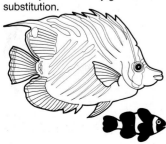

A practical reminder
Of the artificial decorations available, moulded logs look the most natural, but be sure that they are suitable for the marine aquarium. Plastic plants may have toxic supporting wires or fixings.

Left, below left: **Chaetodon auriga** *Juvenile Threadfin Butterflyfishes do not have the long filament from the rear of the dorsal. The eye-spot on the dorsal fin does not fade with adulthood in Indo-Pacific specimens, but adults of the subspecies* C.a.auriga *from the Red Sea may lose it.*

Below: **Chaetodon capistratus** *Colourful Butterflyfishes also inhabit areas other than the usual Indo-Pacific regions. This species comes from the Caribbean.*

Chaetodon capistratus
Four-eyed Butterflyfish
● **Distribution:** Western Atlantic and Caribbean.
● **Length:** 150mm/6in (wild), 100mm/4in (aquarium).
● **Diet and feeding:** Crustaceans, coral polyps, algae. Grazer.
● **Aquarium behaviour:** Once settled in the aquarium it should thrive, but it may be difficult to acclimatize at first.

The white body has a series of dark 'V' stripes and a false eye-spot on each side of the caudal peduncle. This extra pair of 'eyes' on the rear of the body is an excellent target for any predator; imagine its annoyance when the target swims rapidly away in the opposite direction to that indicated by the false decorations. (These, together with the real pair of eyes, give the fish its common name.) It may be very difficult to accustom this species to aquarium foods and it may starve to death. Although attractive, therefore, this is not really a beginner's fish.

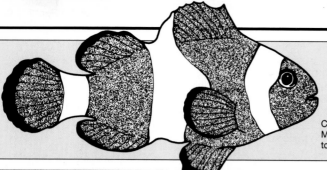

Common Clown (*Amphiprion ocellaris*)
Mature at 80mm (3.2in) and shown as a guide
to the maximum wild size of each species.

Chaetodon chrysurus
Pearlscale Butterflyfish
● **Distribution:** Indo-Pacific, Red Sea.
● **Length:** 150mm/6in (wild).
● **Diet and feeding:** Crustaceans, vegetable matter. Grazer.
● **Aquarium behaviour:** A shy species.

The scales on this species are partially dark-edged, giving the fish a lattice-covered, or checkered, pattern. The main feature is the bright orange arc connecting the rear of the dorsal and anal fins; a repeated orange band appears in the caudal fin. The fish's habitat is thought to be nearer to Africa, Mauritius and the Seychelles rather than spread widely over the Indo-Pacific area. It is rarely imported. The Red Sea variant *C.chrysurus paucifasciatus* has a faint spot in the dorsal fin and a slightly different shape to the orange area. *C.mertensii* and *C.xanthurus* are also very similar in appearance to *C.chrysurus*.

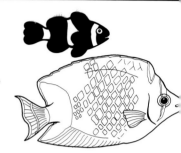

Left and below:
Chaetodon xanthurus
Despite having slightly different colorations, these two fishes are the same species. C.xanthurus is often confused with two other similarly marked species, but the almost identical C.chrysurus is imported less frequently; it can be distinguished by its smaller and less clearly defined scales.

Right: **Chaetodon ephippium**
The threadlike extension to the dorsal fin – typical of these fishes – can be clearly seen here, indicating a mature specimen.

A practical reminder
Be sure to remove chlorine and
chloramine from tapwater before using
it to make up synthetic sea water. There
are many proprietary additives widely
available for this purpose.

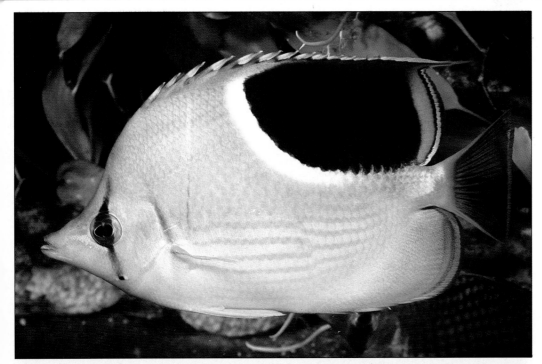

Chaetodon ephippium
Saddleback Butterflyfish
● **Distribution:** Indo-Pacific.
● **Length:** 230mm/9in (wild).
● **Diet and feeding:**Crustaceans.
Grazer.
● **Aquarium behaviour:** May be
intolerant of other members of its
own, or other, species.

Easily recognizable by the white-
edged dark 'saddle' that covers
the rear upper portion of the body
and dorsal fin. The females
become plumper at breeding time.
It may be difficult to accustom
these fish to a successful aquarium
feeding pattern.

Chaetodon collare
Pakistani Butterflyfish
● **Distribution:** Indian Ocean.
● **Length:** 150mm/6in (wild),
100mm/4in (aquarium).
● **Diet and feeding:** Meat foods
and greenstuff. Grazer.
● **Aquarium behaviour:** May be
intolerant of other members of its
own, or other, species.

The brown coloration of *C. collare*
is unusual for a Butterflyfish. It is
reputed to be difficult to keep,
although not all authorities agree
on this. Species from different
locations may have different
feeding requirements, the species
from rocky outcrops being easier
to satisfy in captivity than those
from coral reefs. Not a suitable fish
for the beginner.

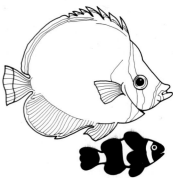

Left: **Chaetodon collare**
*From the coast of East Africa, right
across the Indian Ocean to
Melanesia, this fish is a common
sight around the coral reefs.*

107

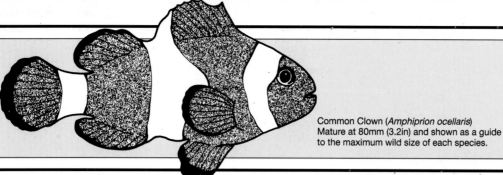

Common Clown (*Amphiprion ocellaris*)
Mature at 80mm (3.2in) and shown as a guide
to the maximum wild size of each species.

Chaetodon (Anisochaetodon) falcula

Double-saddled Butterflyfish; Pig-faced Butterflyfish

● **Distribution:** Indian Ocean.
● **Length:** 150mm/6in (wild), 100-125mm/4-5in (aquarium)
● **Diet and feeding:** Crustaceans, coral polyps, algae. Grazer.
● **Aquarium behaviour:** Aggressive towards similar species.

Two dark saddle markings cross the top of the body. The dorsal, anal and caudal fins are yellow, and there is a black spot or bar on the caudal peduncle. The body and head are white. A vertical black bar runs down the side of the head and there are many vertical thin lines on the body. This species is often confused with *C.ulietensis*, which is found across a wider area of the Pacific Ocean, and has slightly lower reaching 'saddles' and less yellow on top of the body and dorsal fin.

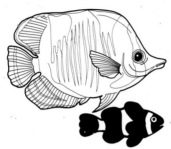

Right: **Chaetodon falcula**
The distribution of this Butterflyfish is confined to the Indian Ocean. C.ulietensis has similar markings, but is fairly easy to distinguish and is found in the wider-ranging Indo-Pacific waters.

A practical reminder
Find out the specific gravity of the water in your dealer's tanks before buying fishes so that you can adjust the initial conditions in your aquarium to suit your first introductions.

Left: Chaetodon frembli
The clearly visible dark spot just in front of the dorsal fin probably serves as an alternative 'eye-target' for any would-be predator. This species does not share the characteristic Butterflyfish pattern, in which the real eye is hidden in a vertical dark band.

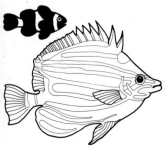

Chaetodon frembli
Blue-striped Butterflyfish
● **Distribution:** Indo-Pacific, Red Sea.
● **Length:** 200mm/8in (wild).
● **Diet and feeding:** Crustaceans, coral polyps, algae. Grazer.
● **Aquarium behaviour:** Calm community fish.

The yellow body is marked with upward slanting diagonal blue lines. A black mark appears immediately in front of the dorsal fin, and the black of the caudal peduncle extends into the rear of the dorsal and anal fins. The caudal fin has white, black and yellow vertical bars. This Butterflyfish lacks the usual black bar through the eye. Not an easy species to keep.

Chaetodon (Anisochaetodon) kleini
Klein's Butterflyfish; Sunburst Butterflyfish
● **Distribution:** Indo-Pacific.
● **Length:** 125mm/5in (wild), 100mm/4in (aquarium).
● **Diet and feeding:** Crustaceans, coral polyps, algae. Grazer.
● **Aquarium behaviour:** Peaceful.

This is a more subtly coloured fish; its black eye bar is followed by a grey bar and the white forebody changes to a golden yellow. The dorsal and anal fins, plus the front part of the caudal fin, are a matching gold-yellow. The mouth is black. *C.kleini* is considered to be the easiest of all Butterflyfishes to keep, being hardy once it has settled into the aquarium.

Above: **Chaetodon kleini**
The obvious wide bands on this juvenile fish will fade with adulthood. Only the black bar will remain as a contrast to the sunburst colour of the body.

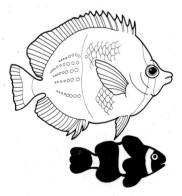

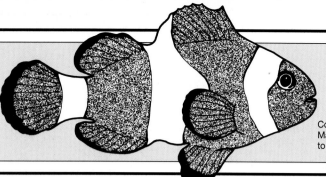
Common Clown (*Amphiprion ocellaris*)
Mature at 80mm (3.2in) and shown as a guide
to the maximum wild size of each species.

Chaetodon (Gonochaetodon) larvatus

Red-headed Butterflyfish
● **Distribution:** Red Sea.
● **Length:** 120mm/4.7in (wild).
● **Diet and feeding:** Crustaceans, coral polyps, algae. Grazer.
● **Aquarium behaviour:** Peaceful.

C.larvatus is reputed to be difficult to keep and a temperamental feeder. It has a dark brown-red head and the rear portion of body is black. The caudal fin is divided by a grey area crossed with white and yellow chevron markings.

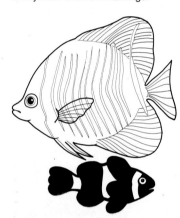

Chaetodon lunula

Racoon Butterflyfish
● **Distribution:** Indo-Pacific.
● **Length:** 200mm/8in (wild)
● **Diet and feeding:** Crustaceans, coral polyps, algae. Grazer. Feeds well.
● **Aquarium behaviour:** Peaceful.

A white-edged black bar runs down over the eye and immediately sweeps up again into the mid-dorsal area. A white bar crosses this bar immediately behind the eye. A black blotch appears on the caudal peduncle, a feature missing in the otherwise similar species, *C.fasciatus*. *C.lunula* is fairly long-lived in the aquarium and will readily accept most foods.

Above: **Chaetodon lunula**
Juvenile forms of the Racoon Butterflyfish have an 'eye-spot' in the rear part of the dorsal fin, but this fades with age. Another difference between young and adult fishes is that the adult fish has more yellow on the snout.

Below: **Chaetodon larvatus**
If you feel that the colour of the head is not quite the shade of red you expected from the fish's popular name, but more of an orange-brown colour, then perhaps the alternative name of Hooded Butterflyfish is more apt.

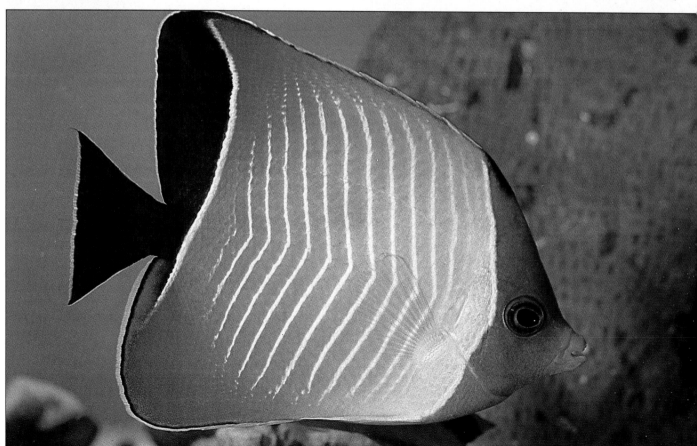

A practical reminder
Always use plastic clips to fix heater-thermostats and other equipment in place. Avoid introducing any form of metal into the marine aquarium as it is likely to poison the fishes.

Chaetodon melannotus
Black-backed Butterflyfish
● **Distribution:** Indo-Pacific.
● **Length:** 150mm/6in (wild).
● **Diet and feeding:** Crustaceans, coral polyps, algae. Grazer.
● **Aquarium behaviour:** Peaceful.

The white body is crossed by diagonal thin black stripes and bordered by yellow dorsal, anal and caudal fins. A black eye bar divides the yellow head.

Chaetodon meyeri
Meyer's Butterflyfish
● **Distribution:** Indo-Pacific.
● **Length:** 150mm/6in (wild).
● **Diet and feeding:** Coral polyps. Grazer.
● **Aquarium behaviour:** May be intolerant of other members of its own, or other, species.

The striking vertical and diagonal black stripes are enclosed by the yellow border to the dorsal, anal and caudal fins. This species is extremely difficult to keep in the aquarium as it feeds mainly on polyps.

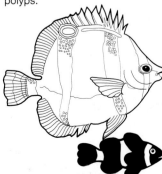

Above: **Chaetodon melannotus**
For hobbyists requiring absolute accuracy in fish descriptions, this species might be renamed the Black-sided Butterflyfish.

Below: **Chaetodon meyeri**
When young, diagonal stripes cover the whole body area behind the two vertical bars. The pattern becomes interrupted with age.

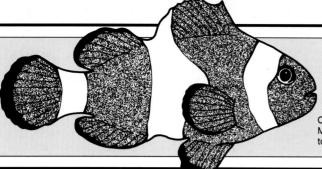

Common Clown (*Amphiprion ocellaris*)
Mature at 80mm (3.2in) and shown as a guide
to the maximum wild size of each species.

Chaetodon octofasciatus

Eight-banded Butterflyfish
● **Distribution:** Indo-Pacific.
● **Length:** 100mm/4in (wild).
● **Diet and feeding:** Coral polyps. Grazer.
● **Aquarium behaviour:** May be intolerant of other members of its own, or other, species.

The striking vertical black stripes are the main feature of this species. It is a difficult species to keep in the aquarium as its diet consists mainly of coral polyps. It may be worth trying brineshrimp.

Chaetodon ornatissimus

Ornate Coralfish
● **Distribution:** Pacific.
● **Length:** 180mm/7in (wild).
● **Diet and feeding:** Coral polyps. Grazer.
● **Aquarium behaviour:** May be intolerant of other members of its own, or other, species.

This fish is a swimming companion of *C.meyeri*. They share similar facial markings but in *C.ornatissimus* the diagonal lines are yellow. Like its companion, it can be difficult to keep because of feeding problems.

Below: **Chaetodon octofasciatus**
Try tempting this stunning, but difficult, fish with brineshrimp.

A practical reminder
Always increase the aeration rate in the treatment tank because many medications reduce the level of oxygen in the water. Vigorous aeration also helps to drive out carbon dioxide.

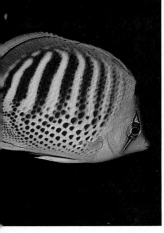

Above: **Chaetodon ornatissimus**
As in C. meyeri, *the diagonal stripes in the juvenile fish change to a more oval pattern as the fish reaches adulthood. This fish from the outer reefs ranges from the western Pacific to Hawaii, and needs plenty of swimming space.*

Left: **Chaetodon punctofasciatus**
This species' natural habitat ranges from the China Sea in the north, out to the Philippines and south as far as Australia's Great Barrier Reef. If you see it in your store, do buy it, since it is not difficult to keep, and may even obligingly take flaked foods.

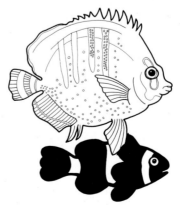

Chaetodon punctofasciatus
Spot-banded Butterflyfish
● **Distribution:** Pacific.
● **Length:** 100mm/4in (wild).
● **Diet and feeding:** Coral polyps. May accept flake foods in the aquarium. Grazer.
● **Aquarium behaviour:** May be intolerant of other members of its own, or other, species.

The vertical black stripes end halfway down the body, and turn into many spots. A black spot appears immediately in front of the dorsal fin. The eye bar is yellow with a black edge.

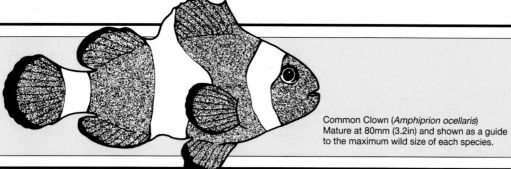

Common Clown (*Amphiprion ocellaris*)
Mature at 80mm (3.2in) and shown as a guide
to the maximum wild size of each species.

A practical reminder
Air pumps give better results with
wooden diffusers than with airstones.
Site the pump above the water level if
possible, or else fit an 'anti-siphon' loop
or a non-return valve in the air line.

Chaetodon semilarvatus
Addis Butterflyfish
Distribution: Indian Ocean,
Red Sea.
Length: 200mm/8in (wild).
Diet and feeding: Crustaceans,
coral polyps, algae. Grazer.
Aquarium behaviour: May be
intolerant of other members of its
own, or other, species.

The yellow body is crossed by thin
orange vertical lines. A blue-black
inverted teardrop patch covers the
eye. This species settles down
readily in captivity. Specimens
from the Red Sea are difficult to
obtain and therefore very
expensive.

Left: **Chaetodon semilarvatus**
*The bright colour and distinctive
markings of this species make it a
perfect photographic subject.*

Above: **Chaetodon striatus**
*Do the black and white stripes of
the Banded Butterflyfish remind
you of the freshwater Angelfish?*

Below: **Chaetodon trifascialis**
*This fish has a wide horizontal
black band with white blotches as
a fright, or night-time pattern.*

Chaetodon striatus
Banded Butterflyfish
● **Distribution:** Tropical Atlantic
Ocean.
● **Length:** 150mm/6in (wild).
● **Diet and feeding:** Crustaceans,
coral polyps, algae. Grazer.
● **Aquarium behaviour:** May be
intolerant of other members of its
own, or other, species.

An easily recognizable species
with four dark bands across its
body. A continuous dark band
passes through the outer edges of
the dorsal, caudal and anal fins to
connect with the ends of the third
vertical band. The juvenile form
has a white-ringed black spot on
the soft dorsal fin. A good
community fish.
 Take care not to shock or
otherwise stress this easily
frightened fish during
transportation and introduction
into the aquarium.

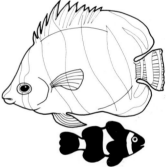

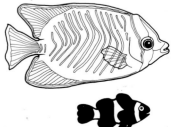

Chaetodon trifascialis
Chevron Butterflyfish
● **Distribution:** Indo-Pacific,
Red Sea.
● **Length:** 180mm/7in (wild).
● **Diet and feeding:** Coral polyps.
Grazer.
● **Aquarium behaviour:**
Aggressive.

In juveniles, the chevron-marked
area of the white body is bordered
by the black eye bar and a black
area at the rear of the body, dorsal
and anal fins. In adult fishes, the
black rear area extends to cover
the previously yellow caudal fin
completely. These fish are almost
impossible to keep due to the
problem of providing a suitable
diet; think twice before trying it.

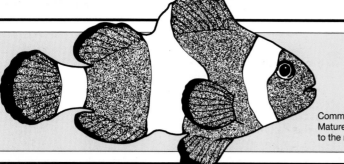

Common Clown (*Amphiprion ocellaris*)
Mature at 80mm (3.2in) and shown as a guide
to the maximum wild size of each species.

Chaetodon trifasciatus
Rainbow Butterflyfish, Redfin Butterflyfish
● **Distribution:** Indo-Pacific.
● **Length:** 150mm/6in (wild).
● **Diet and feeding:** Live coral polyps in nature. Grazer.
● **Aquarium behaviour:** Unknown.

In this species the blue-violet body is crossed with fine horizontal lines. Three crescent-shaped black bars cross the head. Variations in the colour of the front part of anal fin are said to indicate sexual differences: pink in the female, red in the male. Another difficult species to keep due to feeding problems, although juveniles seen feeding in dealers' tanks might be acclimatized with live brineshrimp, *Mysis* shrimp and/or *Tubifex*. *C.austriacus* from the Red Sea is similarly marked, but has less patterning in the anal fin.

Above: Chaetodon trifasciatus
Buying reasonably sized specimens of this stunningly beautiful fish is no guarantee that they will thrive in captivity; they may not adapt to aquarium foods.

Right: **Chaetodon austriacus**
The above species has a number of colour variants but this similar-looking fish is a different species altogether, being found in the Indian Ocean and the Red Sea.

A practical reminder
Avoid disturbing the substrate and tank decorations when filling the tank. To disperse the flow, direct the water carefully into a wide-mouthed jug or deep saucer standing on the substrate.

Chaetodon (Rhabdophorus) xanthocephalus

Yellowhead Butterflyfish; Goldrim Butterflyfish
- **Distribution:** Indian Ocean.
- **Length:** 200mm/8in (wild).
- **Diet and feeding:** Crustaceans, coral polyps, algae. Grazer.
- **Aquarium behaviour:** Hardy and peaceful; a good community fish. Once acclimatized, it will eat and thrive. Do not keep it with overly boisterous fishes.

This rare fish is much deeper-bodied than the other members of its Family, and it has a pronounced snout. The mouth and throat, and the dorsal and anal fins are yellow, and the thin eye bar is black. The lines on the body are bent and slightly chevron-shaped. Juveniles have more black in the dorsal and anal fins.

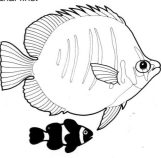

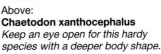

Below: **Chaetodon vagabundus**
The Vagabond Butterflyfish is a long-standing aquarium favourite, a good introduction to the Family.

Above:
Chaetodon xanthocephalus
Keep an eye open for this hardy species with a deeper body shape.

Chaetodon (Anisochaetodon) vagabundus

Vagabond Butterflyfish; Criss-cross Butterflyfish
- **Distribution:** Indo-Pacific.
- **Length:** 200mm/8in (wild).
- **Diet and feeding:** Crustaceans, coral polyps, algae. Grazer.
- **Aquarium behaviour:** Peaceful.

Diagonal lines cross the white body in two directions. Black bars cross the eye and fringe the rear part of the body. The rear part of the dorsal and anal fins are gold-yellow edged with black; the yellow caudal fin has two black vertical bars. A similar species is *C.pictus*, often classified as a subspecies or a colour variant. *C.vagabundus*, like all marines, appreciates good water conditions and regular partial water changes.

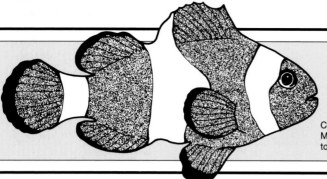

Common Clown (*Amphiprion ocellaris*)
Mature at 80mm (3.2in) and shown as a guide
to the maximum wild size of each species.

Chelmon rostratus

Copper-band Butterflyfish
● **Distribution:** Indo-Pacific,
Red Sea.
● **Length:** 170mm/6.7in (wild).
● **Diet and feeding:** Frozen foods,
small animal foods, algae. Picks in
between coral heads.
● **Aquarium behaviour:**
Aggressive towards members of
its own species.

The yellow-orange vertical bands
on the body have blue-black
edging. These distinctive colours,
coupled with the false 'eye-spot' at
the rear of the upper body, make
this fish difficult to confuse with
any other. It may take time to
acclimatize to aquarium foods but
should adapt if taught by other,
bolder tankmates. It is very
sensitive to deteriorating water
conditions in the aquarium.

Forcipiger flavissimus

Long-nosed Butterflyfish
● **Distribution:** Indo-Pacific,
Red Sea.
● **Length:** 200mm/8in (wild),
100-150mm/4-6in (aquarium).
● **Diet and feeding:** Small animal
foods, algae. Picks in between
coral heads.
● **Aquarium behaviour:** Not as
aggressive as the previous
species.

The body, dorsal, anal, and pelvic
fins are bright yellow, but a black
triangle disrupts the contours of
the head. The lower jaw is white,
and the caudal fin is clear. A false
'eye spot' on the anal fin confuses
predators. It is similar in its
aquarium requirements and
treatment to *C.rostratus*. The Big
Long-nosed Butterflyfish
(*F.longirostris*) is a similar species
with a proportionately longer
snout, although overall it is shorter
than *F.flavissimus*. It is less
frequently imported.

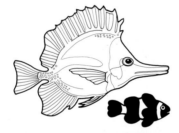

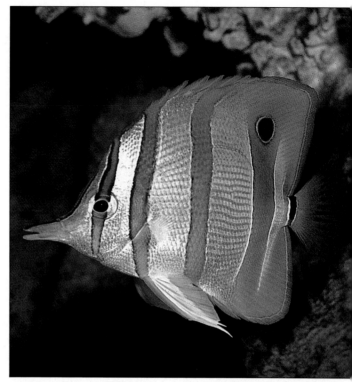

Above: **Chelmon rostratus**
*The outstanding colours and
attractive and slightly unusual
shape of the Copper-band
Butterflyfish should be all the
inducement you need to keep it in
the best aquarium conditions.*

Below: **Forcipiger flavissimus**
*If the Copper-band Butterflyfish
needed a rival in picking out food
from among the crevices in the
coral, then this fish would be a
good candidate. Note how the
black triangle camouflages the eye.*

A practical reminder
Reduce the pressure of water returning
from power filters by using a spray bar
to disperse the water across the surface
of the aquarium. Make sure that all hose
connections are securely fixed in place.

Above: **Heniochus acuminatus**
*The Wimplefish, with its long
trailing extension to the dorsal fin,
is often confused with the Moorish
Idol* (Zanclus *sp.). However, it
lacks the extraordinary facial
markings of that species. The plain
yellow dorsal and caudal fins are
other very useful features that help
to distinguish this fish.*

Left: **Forcipiger longirostris**
This species of Forcipiger *is at a
natural advantage over similar
long-snouted fishes when it comes
to searching for food; with its
much longer snout it is able to
probe into parts of the coral
inaccessible to other fishes.*

Heniochus acuminatus

*Wimplefish, Pennant Coralfish,
Poor Man's Moorish Idol*
● **Distribution:** Indo-Pacific,
Red Sea.
● **Length:** 180mm/7in (wild).
● **Diet and feeding:** Meat foods
and greenstuff. Grazer.
● **Aquarium behaviour:**
Companionable.

Two wide, forward-sloping black
bands cross the white body. The
rear parts of the dorsal, pectoral
and anal fins are yellow while the
pelvic fins are black. The front few
rays of the dorsal fin are much
extended. Young specimens act as
cleanerfishes and all these fish
appreciate plenty of swimming
room. Other species, such as the
Horned Coralfish (*H.chrysostomus*
or *H.permutatus*) are rarely
imported. While *H. acuminatus*
varies little in juvenile and adult
coloration, other species in the
genus do differ; some adults
develop protuberances on the
forehead.
    Heniochus is easier to keep than
the lookalike *Zanclus*. It is a
shoaling fish, but the natural leader
in a group in captivity may well
develop into a bully.

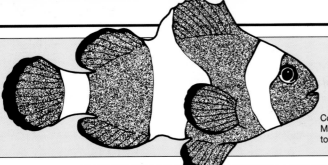

Common Clown (*Amphiprion ocellaris*)
Mature at 80mm (3.2in) and shown as a guide
to the maximum wild size of each species.

Family. CIRRHITIDAE
Hawkfishes

Family chacteristics
Despite their attractive appearance and friendliness, Hawkfishes are predators – albeit of small prey. They rest or 'perch' on a piece of coral and wait for food to pass by, at which point they dash out and seize it. Reproduction in these fishes is by demersal eggs, i.e. the eggs are laid and fertilized on a firm surface, where they subsequently hatch.

Diet and feeding
In the wild, these fishes will take small invertebrates – shrimps, etc. – and smaller fishes. In the aquarium, provide live foods and suitable meaty frozen foods.

Aquarium behaviour
Hawkfishes will appreciate plenty of 'perching places' in the aquarium. Despite their predatory nature, they appear not to harm sedentary invertebrates such as tubeworms, soft corals, etc.

Oxycirrhites typus
Longnosed Hawkfish
● **Distribution:** Indian Ocean mainly.
● **Length:** 100mm/4in (wild).
● **Diet and feeding:** Meat foods. Sits on a rock or coral, then dashes out to grab food.
● **Aquarium behaviour:** Peaceful. Does well in small groups.

The elongate body of this hardy fish is covered with a squared pattern of bright red lines. The snout is very long and suited to probing the coral crevices for food. There are small cirri, or crestlike growths, at the end of each dorsal fin ray and on the nostrils. The female is larger than the male and the male has darker red lower jaws. There are black edges to both the pelvic and caudal fins.

In nature, spawnings occur from dusk onwards. Reports of aquarium 'spawnings' suggest that the female lays patches of adhesive eggs after courtship activity.

Below: **Oxycirrhites typus**
The Longnosed Hawkfish cannot depend on its natural colouring for camouflage, as it perches on coral outcrops waiting to pounce on its next unsuspecting meal.

A practical reminder
Remove uneaten food once the fishes lose interest in it, otherwise it will begin to pollute the water. You should, in any case, feed most fishes only a little at a time, but at regular intervals.

Family: DIODONTIDAE
Porcupinefishes

Family characteristics
Porcupinefishes are very similar to the other 'inflatable' fishes, the Puffers. They can be distinguished from the Pufferfishes, however, by the spines on their scales and by their front teeth, which are fused together. Hard crustacean foods present little problem to them. The pelvic fins are absent. Normally the spines are held flat, but in times of danger they stand out from the body as the fish inflates itself. Their appearance and inflatability make them interesting subjects for the aquarium.

Diet and feeding
Earthworms, shrimps, crab meat and other meaty foods can be given, but cut food into pieces for smaller specimens. Young fish, such as livebearing fry, are also accepted.

Aquarium behaviour
Although they grow very large in the wild, Porcupinefishes rarely grow as big in captivity. Nevertheless, be sure to keep them alone in a large aquarium. You may find that specimens measuring 125-180mm/5-7in appear to recognize the fishkeeper.

Chilomycterus schoepfi
Spiny Boxfish; Striped Burrfish; Burrfish
● **Distribution:** Tropical Atlantic, Caribbean.
● **Length:** 300mm/12in (wild).
● **Diet and feeding:** Crustaceans, molluscs, meat foods. Bold.
● **Aquarium behaviour:** Aggressive among themselves. Do not keep them with small fishes.

The undulating dark lines on its yellow body provide *C.schoepfi* with excellent camouflage, and a first line of defence; then the short spines – fixed and usually held erect – may be called upon to play their part. Not as liable to inflate itself as other species. Importations of this fish are rare.

Diodon hystrix
Common Porcupinefish; Porcupine Puffer
● **Distribution:** All warm seas.
● **Length:** 900mm/36in (wild), considerably smaller in the aquarium.
● **Diet and feeding:** Crustaceans, molluscs, meat foods. Bold.
● **Aquarium behaviour:** Generally peaceful with other fishes.

This species has longer spines held more flatly against the body. They are not constantly active, remaining at rest for long periods until hunger or some other action-provoking event stirs them. Keep the tank efficiently filtered to cope with these fishes that can sometimes prove 'messy eaters'.

Top: **Chilomycterus schoepfi**
The short spines of this species are kept erect, a constant defence against predation or capture.

Above: **Diodon hystrix**
Despite its formidable adult size, the Common Porcupinefish poses little threat to smaller fishes.

Diodon holacanthus
Long-spined Porcupinefish
● **Distribution:** All warm seas.
● **Length:** 500mm/20in (wild), 150mm/6in (aquarium).
● **Diet and feeding:** Crustaceans, molluscs, meat foods. Bold.
● **Aquarium behaviour:** Do not keep with small fishes.

The colour patterning on this species is blotched rather than lined, but it serves the same excellent purpose – to disguise the fish as part of the surrounding underwater scenery.

Right: **Diodon holacanthus**
The Long-spined Porcupinefish is one of the most commonly found species, being native worldwide. It feeds on crustaceans, using its powerful front teeth, so do not include it in a tank containing invertebrates.

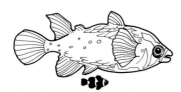

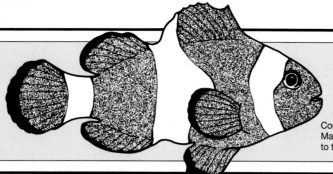

Common Clown (*Amphiprion ocellaris*)
Mature at 80mm (3.2in) and shown as a guide
to the maximum wild size of each species.

Family: GOBIIDAE
Gobies

Family characteristics
Comparatively little is known about this very large Family, which – paradoxically – contains one of the smallest vertebrates (*Pandaka* sp). In the wild, Gobies are found in several different locations: tidal shallow beaches; on the coral reef itself; and on the muddy seabed. Some species are found in fresh water. All rely on having a secure bolthole in which to hide when danger threatens. Such 'boltholes' may be located within sponges, caves, crevices or simply burrows in the seabed.

The Gobies are endearing little characters for the aquarium. Unlike the Blennies, the colours of the Gobies can be quite brilliant. Their bodies are elongate, the head blunt with high-set eyes. Gobies can be further distinguished from Blennies, with whom they share a similar habitat, by the presence of a 'suction-disc' formed by the fusion of the pelvic fins.

Sexing Gobies is difficult, although females may become distended with eggs at breeding time and there are the typical differences in the size and shape of the genital papillae – if you can see them! (The genital papillae are breeding tubes that extend from the vent of each fish; usually longer in females than in males.) In some species, the male may change colour or develop longer fins during the breeding period. Spawning occurs in burrows or in sheltered areas, with the eggs being guarded by the male. Several Gobies have been spawned in captivity. *Gobiosoma oceanops* and *Lythrypnus dalli*, for example, will breed willingly in the aquarium, but rearing the young fry is not easy. The young of *G.oceanops* have been reared with more success than the smaller fry of *L.dalli*.

Diet and feeding
Gobies are carnivorous bottom-dwelling fishes that will eat brineshrimp, finely chopped meat foods, dried foods and *Daphnia* in the aquarium.

Aquarium behaviour
Many reef-dwelling species provide cleaning services for larger fishes, the cleaning sequence following the pattern described for the Cleaner Wrasse (see page 130).

Gobiosoma oceanops
Neon Goby
● **Distribution:** Western Atlantic, especially Florida, and the Gulf of Mexico.
● **Length:** 60mm/2.4in (wild), 25mm/1in (aquarium)
● **Diet and feeding:** Parasites, small crustaceans and plankton. Bold nibbler; bottom feeder.
● **Aquarium behaviour:** Peaceful and uninhibited.

Two characteristics distinguish this most familiar Goby: the electric blue coloration of the longitudinal line on the body and the cleaning services it offers to other fishes. The species can be positively identified by the gap visible between the two blue lines on the snout when the fish is seen from above; other species have connected lines or other markings between the ends of the lines.

G.oceanops has been bred in the aquarium. Pairing occurs spontaneously, and if you intend breeding the fishes try to buy any 'pairs' of fishes seen to be keeping close company with each other. Before spawning, the male's colour darkens and he courts the female with exaggerated swimming motions, assuming a position on the aquarium floor until the female takes notice of him. Spawning activity occurs in a cave or other similar sheltered area – an upright plastic tube stuck in the aquarium floor is often more than acceptable. The fertilized eggs

hatch after 7-12 days. In the wild, the fry feed on planktonic foods for the first few weeks. In the aquarium, start the fry off with liquid fry foods, cultured rotifers and newly hatched brineshrimp. After three to four months, the young fish will pair off themselves, even though they will not spawn for another few months.

Unfortunately, these eminently suitable (and practicable) aquarium subjects are relatively shortlived – perhaps only a year, but their breeding possibilities should enable you to continue the species without too much trouble.

Lythrypnus dalli
Blue-banded Goby; Catalina Goby
● **Distribution:** Californian Pacific coast.
● **Length:** 60mm/2.4in (wild), 25mm/1in (aquarium).
● **Diet and feeding:** Small crustaceans and other small marine organisms. Bottom feeder.
● **Aquarium behaviour:** Peaceful with small fishes.

The red body is crossed by brilliant blue vertical lines and the first dorsal fin has an elongated ray. The male has longer dorsal fin spines than the female. Several fish will share even a reasonably small aquarium quite happily, but they are not naturally a longlived species. This species does not require the same high water temperatures as other marine fish; do not exceed a maximum of 22°C(72°F). This fish has been bred successfully in the aquarium; the fry are much smaller than those of the Neon Goby.

Left: **Gobiosoma oceanops**
The brilliantly coloured Neon Goby has much in its favour as a subject for the marine aquarium. Its tank need not be too large, and the fish will spawn quite readily.

A practical reminder
Remember that many marine fishes are herbivorous and welcome green matter in their diet. This is another reason for the bright lighting; it encourages lush growths of algae for fishes to feed on.

Above: **Lythrypnus dalli**
A number of Blue-banded Gobies could share a reasonably sized tank without too much quarrelling.

Left: **Nemateleotris splendida**
Also known as a 'hovering' Goby, the Firefish never ventures too far from the safety of its bolthole.

Nemateleotris splendida
Firefish
● **Distribution:** Indo-Pacific.
● **Length:** 60mm/2.4in (wild).
● **Diet and feeding:** Small crustaceans, plankton and other small live foods. Bottom feeder.
● **Aquarium behaviour:** Peaceful once established.

This beautifully coloured fish makes a burrow in the substrate and only when it has organized this bolthole will it settle down in the aquarium. The blue, green and yellow on the body gradually give way to a magnificent fiery red on the rear of the body and on the dorsal, anal and caudal fins. The first dorsal fin is much elongated.

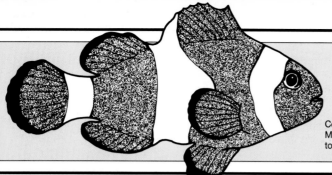

Common Clown (*Amphiprion ocellaris*)
Mature at 80mm (3.2in) and shown as a guide
to the maximum wild size of each species.

Family: HOLOCENTRIDAE
Squirrelfishes

Family characteristics
Squirrelfishes are large-eyed nocturnal fishes that hide by day
among crevices in the coral reefs of the Indo-Pacific and Atlantic
Oceans. They usually have red patterning on their elongate bodies,
spines on the gill covers and sharp rays on the fins. The dorsal fin
looks as if it has two separate parts: a long-based spiny part at the
front and a high triangular softer rayed section at the back.

Diet and feeding
In the aquarium, they rapidly adjust to a daytime eating routine and
a diet consisting of chopped worm foods and small fish.

Aquarium behaviour
Squirrelfishes are very active and need a sufficiently large
aquarium to accommodate their energetic way of life. Remember
that small fishes may not welcome such boisterous companions.

Holocentrus (Adioryx) diadema
Common Squirrelfish
- **Distribution:** Indo-Pacific.
- **Length:** 300m/12in (wild).
- **Diet and feeding:** All foods. Bold.
- **Aquarium behaviour:** Do not keep with small fishes.

Horizontal red lines and a red
dorsal fin make this common fish a
very colourful addition to any
sufficiently large aquarium. In
nature, it is a nocturnal species
and therefore needs some hiding
places in which to rest during the
day. It does adapt to aquarium life,
however, and will swim around in
daylight hours.

Below: **Holocentrus diadema**
*In the wild, these strikingly
attractive fishes swim in large
shoals among the coral reefs. Their
relatively large size and constant
activity render them less suited to
an aquarium of modest
proportions. However, if you can
provide adequate swimming space
and plenty of companions, the
Common Squirrelfish will prove a
worthwhile addition to the tank.*

A practical reminder
Always use non-metallic (non-toxic)
containers when making up synthetic
sea water. Similarly, you should use
plastic containers to store sea water for
future partial water changes.

Holocentrus rufus
White-tip Squirrelfish
● **Distribution:** Western Atlantic.
● **Length:** 200mm/8in (wild).
● **Diet and feeding:** Crustaceans
and meaty foods. Bold.
● **Aquarium behaviour:** Shoaling
fish for a large aquarium.

Holocentrus rufus is a similar
colour to other Squirrelfishes, but it
has a white triangular mark on
each dorsal fin ray.

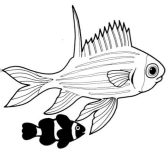

Right: **Holocentrus rufus**
*A feature of this species is the long
rear part of the dorsal fin; the
upper part of the caudal fin is
larger than the lower. Reasonably
fearless, predatory Squirrelfishes
can hold their own with Grunts and
even Moray Eels; they will meet
any attempts to threaten their
territorial safety with grunting
noises and quivering actions.*

Left: **Myripristis murdjan**
*The Big-eye Squirrelfish clearly
lives up to its popular name! The
organs in question are used to
good advantage at night, when the
fish is active. It lacks the spine on
the rear of the gill cover that is
carried by members of the genus
Holocentrus. Although peaceful,
do not be tempted to include
smaller fishes in their tank.*

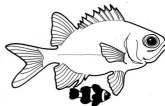

Myripristis murdjan
Big-eye Squirrelfish; Blotcheye
● **Distribution:** Indo-Pacific.
● **Length:** 300mm/12in (wild).
● **Diet and feeding:** Crustaceans
and meaty foods. Bold.
● **Aquarium behaviour:** Peaceful.

The red edge on each scale gives
this fish a reticulated appearance.
There is a dark red vertical area
immediately behind the gill cover.

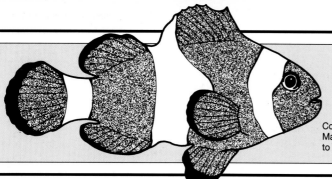

Common Clown (*Amphiprion ocellaris*)
Mature at 80mm (3.2in) and shown as a guide
to the maximum wild size of each species.

Family: LABRIDAE
Wrasses and Rainbowfishes

Family characteristics
The Labridae is a very large Family, encompassing about 400 species. It is not surprising, therefore, that the body shape varies; some Wrasses are cylindrical, while others are much deeper bodied. Like many other marine fishes, Wrasses swim without making much use of the caudal fin, which is mainly used for steering or held in reserve for emergencies. The main propulsion comes from the pectoral fins.

Sex reversal is quite common in Wrasses, the necessary change occurring in single-sexed groups as required. Reproductive activity can occur between pairs or collectively in groups. In both cases, the fishes spiral upwards towards the surface to spawn. Occasionally, this activity is based around a preselected territory. Coastal species take advantage of the outgoing tide to sweep the fertilized eggs away from the reef to safety. Species from temperate zones in Europe and the Mediterranean build spawning nests of algae or sand.

Diet and feeding
Feeding habits vary from species to species, but most relish molluscs and crustaceans. They will take brineshrimps, shrimps, earthworms and also green foods.

Aquarium behaviour
Juvenile forms are quite suitable for the aquarium. Wrasses and Rainbowfishes are interesting for several reasons: the juvenile coloration patterns are different from those of adult fishes; many bury themselves at night, or spin mucus cocoons in which to rest; and a number of fishes perform 'cleaning services' on other species, removing parasites in the process. Fishes in this group are usually quite active and therefore may disturb more sedate fishes in the aquarium.

Bodianus pulchellus
Cuban Hogfish
● **Distribution:** Western Atlantic.
● **Length:** 250mm/10in (wild), 150mm/6in (aquarium)
● **Diet and feeding:** Crustaceans, shellfish meat. Bold bottom feeder.
● **Aquarium behaviour:** Generally peaceful although small fishes in the aquarium may not be entirely safe.

The front of the body is red, divided by a white horizontal band; the upper part of the back is bright yellow. There is a black spot at the end of the pectoral fins. Juveniles are yellow with a dark spot on the front of the dorsal fin, a colour scheme similar to that of the juvenile form of *Thalassoma bifasciatum* (see page 132). It is likely that both these species have evolved similar markings to signal their cleaning services. Usually it is quite easy to acclimatize these fishes to aquarium foods.

Bodianus rufus
Spanish Hogfish
● **Distribution:** Western Atlantic.
● **Length:** 600mm/24in (wild), 200mm/8in (aquarium)
● **Diet and feeding:** Crustaceans, shellfish meat. Bold bottom feeder.
● **Aquarium behaviour:** Peaceful.

Juvenile specimens are yellow with an area of blue along the upper body. Adult fishes show the standard red and yellow coloration, although the proportions may vary according to the habitat and depth of water. Like other members of the genus, juveniles perform cleaning actions on other fishes.

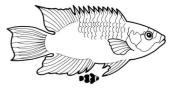

Coris angulata
Twin-spot Wrasse
● **Distribution:** Indo-Pacific, Red Sea.
● **Length:** 1200mm/48in (wild), 200-300mm/8-12in (aquarium).
● **Diet and feeding:** Small marine animals, live foods. Bottom feeder.
● **Aquarium behaviour:** Peaceful but grows very quickly.

A spectacularly coloured species, both as a juvenile and as an adult. When young, this fish is white with two prominent orange spots on the dorsal surface (hence the above common name). The front of the body, together with the fins, is covered with dark spots and there are two white-edged black blotches on the dorsal fin. The adult fish is green with yellow-edged purple fins.

Left: **Bodianus pulchellus**
This smart Cuban Hogfish from the western Atlantic is easy to acclimatize to aquarium life.

Above right: **Bodianus rufus**
A brightly coloured juvenile specimen of this wrasse from the Caribbean. A peaceful fish.

Right: **Coris angulata**
The adult Twin-spot Wrasse not only loses the two spots seen in this juvenile, but also outgrows the domestically sized aquarium.

A practical reminder
You can lessen the risk of disease in the
aquarium by using only the highest
quality foods from reliable sources.
Gamma-irradiated foods are safe, fish
from the local fishmongers may not be.

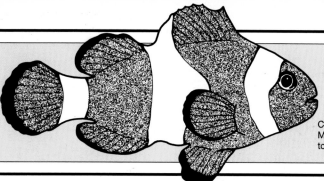

Common Clown (*Amphiprion ocellaris*)
Mature at 80mm (3.2in) and shown as a guide
to the maximum wild size of each species.

Coris formosa
African Clown Wrasse
● **Distribution:** Indian Ocean.
● **Length:** 300mm/12in (wild),
200mm/8in (aquarium).
● **Diet and feeding:** Small marine
animals, live foods. Bottom feeder.
● **Aquarium behaviour:** Peaceful
but grows large.

The juvenile fish is dark brown with
a thick vertical white band crossing
the body and dorsal fin just behind
the gill cover. Two shorter bands
cross the head and two more
appear on the rear of the dorsal fin
and caudal peduncle. The caudal
fin is white. In the adult, the head
and body are green-brown and
two green-blue stripes run in front
of and behind the gill cover. The
dorsal fin is red with an elongated
first ray, the anal fin is green and
purple, and the caudal fin is red,
bordered with white.

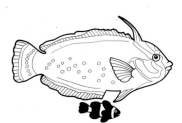

Above right: **Coris formosa**
*The African Clown Wrasse
eventually loses the juvenile white
markings shown here. The adult's
dorsal fin has an extended first ray.*

Below: **Coris gaimardi**
*The first colour stage of the Clown
Wrasse is orange, with similar, but
less extensive, white markings on
the body than the above species.*

Above opposite: *As the Clown
Wrasse matures, the orange body
of the juvenile fades, accompanied
by darkening of the fins, head, and
edges of the white markings.*

Below opposite: *Here, the final
adult colours are established. The
blue facial markings and spotted
body bear little resemblance to the
appearance of the young fish.*

A practical reminder
Marine fishes are very susceptible to shock. Equalize temperatures in the transportation bag and tank and release the fishes into the aquarium under dim lighting conditions, if possible.

Coris gaimardi
Clown Wrasse; Red Labrid
● **Distribution:** Indo-Pacific.
● **Length:** 300mm/12in (wild), 150mm/6in (aquarium).
● **Diet and feeding:** Crustaceans, shellfish meat. Bold bottom feeder.
● **Aquarium behaviour:** May quarrel among themselves.

Juveniles are similar to *C.formosa* but are orange rather than brown; the middle white band does not extend right down the body and the dorsal fin lacks a spot. Adults are brown-violet with many blue spots. The dorsal and anal fins are red, the caudal fin is yellow. There are blue markings on the face. These can be nervous fishes that dash about when first introduced into the aquarium, so try not to shock them.

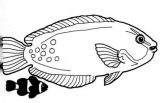

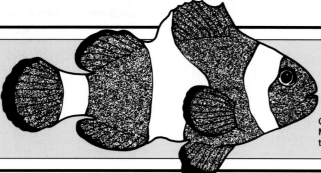

Common Clown (*Amphiprion ocellaris*)
Mature at 80mm (3.2in) and shown as a guide
to the maximum wild size of each species.

Gomphosus coeruleus

Birdmouth Wrasse
● **Distribution:** Indo-Pacific.
● **Length:** 250mm/10in (wild).
● **Diet and feeding:** Small animal life gathered from coral crevices. In the aquarium, they will take brineshrimp, *Mysis* shrimp, krill and chopped fish meats, plus some green foods. Grazer.
● **Aquarium behaviour:** Peaceful.

The body in adult males is blue-green; younger males, and females, are brown. The snout is elongated. A very active fish that is constantly on the move around the aquarium. This species looks and swims like a dolphin. Young fishes act as cleaners.

Labroides dimidiatus

Cleaner Wrasse
● **Distribution:** Indo-Pacific.
● **Length:** 100mm/4in (wild).
● **Diet and feeding:** Skin parasites of other fishes in the wild; in captivity, finely chopped meat foods make an excellent substitute. Bold.
● **Aquarium behaviour:** Peaceful.

This is the most familiar of the Wrasses because of its cleaning activities. This cleaning process, also practised by some Gobies and Cleaner Shrimps, is almost ritualistic. When approached by a Cleaner Wrasse, the subject fish – or host – often remains stationary with fins spread, in a head-up or head-down attitude. Sometimes the colours of the host fish fade, maybe so that the Cleaner Wrasse can see any parasites more clearly. The elongate blue body of the Cleaner Wrasse has a horizontal dark stripe from snout to caudal fin. The mouth is terminal, and it is this feature that distinguishes *L.dimidiatus* from the predatory lookalike *Aspidontus taeniatus*, the so-called False Cleanerfish.

Below: **Gomphosus coeruleus**
The Birdmouth Wrasse is a very active species, always on the move around the aquarium. Generally, it is very peaceful, and minds its own business, but its constant movement may annoy more leisurely or smaller species.

Right: **Labroides dimidiatus**
One of the true assets to the marine aquarium, the Cleanerfish provides a service much appreciated by the other inmates of the tank. Be sure that the fish you introduce is the true Cleanerfish; look for the mouth at the extreme tip of the snout: an underslung mouth indicates the False Cleanerfish, (Aspidontus taeniatus), which will bite instead of clean its host.

Below opposite: Here, a beautiful Butterflyfish (Chaetodon trifasciatus) is taking advantage of the Cleanerfish's services. Many fishes make a point of visiting the territory of the Cleanerfish, literally a 'cleaning station'. They wait their turn to have parasites removed from their skin, gills or even mouth, advertising their willingness to be cleaned by adopting a motionless head-up or head-down attitude.

A practical reminder
Reject any fishes which are too thin,
have obvious physical faults or will not
feed. Not all marine fishes swim with
erect fins and so clamped fins are not
necessarily a sign of ill health.

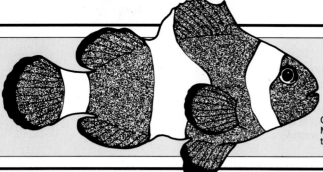

Common Clown (*Amphiprion ocellaris*)
Mature at 80mm (3.2in) and shown as a guide
to the maximum wild size of each species.

Novaculichthys taeniurus

Reindeer Wrasse
● **Distribution:** Indo-Pacific.
● **Length:** 30mm/1.2in (wild).
● **Diet and feeding:** Crustaceans, meaty foods. Bottom feeder.
● **Aquarium behaviour:** Peaceful.

The blotchy green coloration and elongated first rays of the dorsal fin are features of the juvenile; adult fishes are brown with marks radiating from the eye; these fade as the fish grows older. Because this fish is so small, be sure to keep it with similarly sized or non-predatory tankmates.

Right: **Novaculichthys taeniurus**
Keep this Wrasse in a species tank or with equal-sized tankmates.

Below: **Thalassoma bifasciatum**
Only dominant males of the species have the blue head.

Thalassoma bifasciatum

Bluehead (Juveniles are known as Banana Wrasse)
● **Distribution:** Caribbean.
● **Length:** 140mm/5.5in (wild).
● **Diet and feeding:** Crustaceans, meaty foods. Bottom feeder. Most specimens have a very healthy appetite but may need weaning off live brineshrimp on to other, more convenient, meaty foods.
● **Aquarium behaviour:** Peaceful.

This fish undergoes remarkable colour changes: juveniles are yellow (the shallow water types are white) with a dark spot on the front of the dorsal fin and/or a dark horizontal stripe along the body. Dominant males then develop the characteristic blue head and green body separated by contrasting black and white bands.

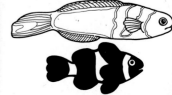

A practical reminder
Choose compatible fishes; big fishes
may eat smaller ones or boisterous
fishes intimidate shy ones. Even fishes
which shoal in the wild will not
always tolerate each other in captivity.

Thalassoma lunare
Moon Wrasse; Lyretail Wrasse;
Green Parrot Wrasse
● **Distribution:** Indo-Pacific,
Red Sea.
● **Length:** 330mm/13in (wild).
● **Diet and feeding:** All meaty
foods. Greedy bottom feeder.
● **Aquarium behaviour:** Active all
day, then sleeps deeply at night.
Its constant daytime movement
may disturb smaller fishes and it
may attack new additions to the
tank, regardless of their size.
Needs plenty of room.

Adult specimens lose the dark
blotches of the juvenile and are
bright green with red and blue
patterns on the head. The centre of
the caudal fin is bright yellow.

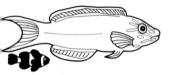

Right: **Thalassoma lunare**
The radiating facial patterns
around the eye of this adult Moon
Wrasse are a feature of its adult
coloration; many species share
this striking characteristic.

Below: **Thalassoma lunare**
A Moon Wrasse in adult colours. A
distinguishing feature of this
species is the bright yellow central
section to the caudal fin.

Common Clown (*Amphiprion ocellaris*)
Mature at 80mm (3.2in) and shown as a guide
to the maximum wild size of each species.

Family: MONOCANTHIDAE
Filefishes

Family characteristics
Filefishes, like the Triggerfishes to whom they are related (and with whom they are classified by some authorites), have two dorsal fins, the first being a rudimentary spine which can be locked into position. The ventral fins are reduced to a single spine. The skin is rough in texture, which has given rise to the fishes' alternative common name of Leatherjackets.

Diet and feeding
In the wild, these fishes use their tiny mouths to feed mainly on polyps and algae. This may cause initial problems in the aquarium until they can be persuaded to accept alternative foods.

Aquarium behaviour
Despite their scientific similarity to Triggerfishes, Filefishes are generally smaller, less active and – once acclimatized and feeding well – make good additions to the aquarium community.

Oxymonocanthus longirostris
Long-nosed Filefish; Orange-green Filefish; Beaked Leatherjacket
● **Distribution:** Indo-Pacific.
● **Length:**100mm/4in (wild).
● **Diet and feeding:** Polyps and algae in the wild; animal foods such as crustaceans and shellfish meat in captivity. Grazer.
● **Aquarium behaviour:** Shy; best kept in groups of two or more with non-boisterous fishes, or in a species aquarium.

The body is bright green with orange spots, and this pattern continues into the caudal fin. The dorsal and anal fins are yellow. The orange eyes have radial patterning and the snout is also orange. The green and orange first dorsal fin is held erect. The male has orange in the fins, and a black-edged red ventral flap of skin that joins the body to the rudimentary ventral fins. Females have colourless fins and a black-edged grey ventral flap.

Below:
Oxymonocanthus longirostris
The head-standing attitude of this fish is quite normal behaviour.

A practical reminder
Some fishes are difficult to acclimatize to aquarium diets. Be guided by your dealer and don't be tempted by very exotic species – they may be a bad investment if they simply won't feed.

Family: MONOCENTRIDAE
Pine-cone Fishes

Family characteristics
This small Family contains some interesting fishes known to have existed millions of years ago. Their bodies are enclosed in the rigid covering of a few large scales fused together. They are deepwater fishes and it is thought that they use their light-generating organs to attract prey. These fishes are only occasionally available through dealers and therefore command a high price.

Diet and feeding
Because of their deepwater origins, little is known of their natural diet. It probably consists mainly of small marine animals attracted to them by their light-generating organs. In the aquarium, offer live foods and then try to wean them on to other suitable foods.

Aquarium behaviour
You may find it advisable to keep these fishes in a species tank so that you can study them more closely.

Monocentrus japonicus
Pine-cone Fish
● **Distribution:** Indo-Pacific.
● **Length:** 160mm/6.3in (wild), 100-150mm/4-6in (aquarium).
● **Diet and feeding:** Provide chopped white fish meat or shellfish meat, such as boiled mussel. Also supply frozen meaty foods.
● **Aquarium behaviour:** Keep in a dimly lit species aquarium.

The head forms about one third of the body size. The large brass-coloured scales have dark edges and spiny centres. Spiny dorsal rays alternate from left to right. The pelvic fins are restricted to strong spines. Does not thrive if kept at temperatures above 23°C(74°F) for long periods.

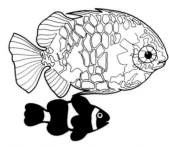

Below: **Monocentrus japonicus**
The Pine-cone Fish, one of the more unusual fishes for the aquarium, can boast an ancestry going back some millions of years. Although not commonly encountered in retail outlets, it is worth considering if you are looking for something different for the marine aquarium.

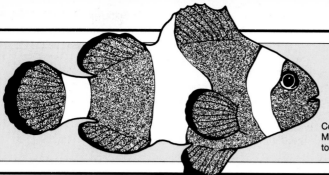

Common Clown (*Amphiprion ocellaris*)
Mature at 80mm (3.2in) and shown as a guide
to the maximum wild size of each species.

Family: MONODACTYLIDAE
Fingerfishes

Family characteristics
These silver rhomboidal fishes are reminiscent of the freshwater Angelfishes. They are found in coastal waters, particularly estuaries, often entering brackish or even fresh water. Although young specimens will thrive in slightly brackish water, they do even better in full strength salt water. Along with *Scatophagus* spp, they are scavengers, frequently found in dirty waters, where they appear to thrive in the conditions!

Diet and feeding
These fishes will eat any foods, including *Tubifex* worms.

Aquarium behaviour
Fast-moving shoaling fishes that may reach up to 150mm(6in) long in captivity.

Below: **Monodactylus argenteus**
Although young specimens may be kept successfully in freshwater or brackish water tanks, as it grows, the Fingerfish really thrives in full-strength sea water. In common *with its relative, the similar but less widely seen Striped Fingerfish (M.sebae), this is an active shoaling species that needs plenty of swimming space in the aquarium to really feel at home.*

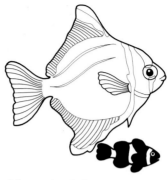

Monodactylus argenteus
Fingerfish; Malayan Angel; Silver Batfish
● **Distribution:** Indo-Pacific.
● **Length:** 230mm/9in (wild).
● **Diet and feeding:** Will eat anything. Bold scavenger.
● **Aquarium behaviour:** Peaceful but constantly active.

One or two black bars cross the front part of the silver body and the fins are yellow. The pelvic fins are rudimentary. These fishes are very fast swimmers when disturbed, and can be difficult to catch in the aquarium.

Monodactylus sebae
Striped Fingerfish
● **Distribution:** Eastern Atlantic, West African coast.
● **Length:** 200mm/8in (wild).
● **Diet and feeding:** Will eat anything. Bold scavenger
● **Aquarium behaviour:** Peaceful, but restless.

Monodactylus sebae is slightly darker than the previous species and the body is much taller. Two additional dark vertical stripes cross the body, one connecting the tips of the dorsal and anal fins, the other crossing the extreme end of the caudal peduncle. The pelvic fins are rudimentary. They appear to be less hardy than the more commonly kept species.

A practical reminder
Marine fishes will often accept aquatic
livefoods as used in the freshwater
aquarium, but remember that such food
may not live as long in sea water.
Livebearer fry may survive longer.

Family: MURAENIDAE
Moray Eels

The tropical eels are often splendidly marked and all grow very
long. Many are nocturnal and are hardly seen during the day, since
they hide among caves and crevices. They detect their food by
smell and are usually quite undemanding in captivity, providing
that they have sufficient room, refuges and food. Keeping them in
the company of small 'bite-sized' fishes is tempting providence a
little too much. Needless to say, the aquarium should be tightly
covered – and beware your fingers when feeding them.

Breeding Moray Eels in captivity is unlikely because sexual
maturity is reached only when the eels attain a large size. This
stage is not normally reached in the confines of a domestic
aquarium, and so successful breeding is doubtful even if a
sufficient number of specimens are kept together to allow natural
pairings to take place. A further complication is that many eels
need to undertake migratory journeys before spawning occurs.

Gymnothorax tesselatus
Reticulated Moray; Leopard Moray
● **Distribution:** Indo-Pacific.
● **Length:** 1500mm/60in (wild).
● **Diet and feeding:** Will eat
anything they can swallow.
Predatory ambushers.
● **Aquarium behaviour:** Do not
keep with anything small.

The dark body is covered with a
reticulated pattern of pale
markings, producing an effect very
similar to a giraffe's markings. The
nostrils are tubular. This species is
sometimes called *Lycodontis
tesselata.*

Below: **Gymnothorax tesselatus**
*Concentrating on the 'business
end' of this species is very wise.
The bite can be very painful, even
leading to infection (and that's only
for humans). Just imagine
encountering this predator if you
were a fish! Only for the 'big tank'
hobbyist or public aquariums.*

Above:
Rhinomuraenia amboinensis
*Asking anyone to estimate the
length of this fish in your tank
could lead to you winning a few
bets. Putting two in your tank
could really confuse people. It
does attract a lot of attention, with
its fine colours, length and coils.*

Rhinomuraenia amboinensis
Blue Ribbon Eel
● **Distribution:** Pacific.
● **Length:** 750mm/30in (wild).
● **Diet and feeding:** Meat eater
that needs live foods. Often
difficult to feed. Nocturnal.
● **Aquarium behaviour:** Usually
peaceful, but boisterous inquisitive
fishes, such as Damsels, may
annoy it.

The body is dark blue-black and
the dorsal fin is bright yellow. The
long nostrils, positioned at the very
tip of the pointed snout, are
constantly erect.

Evidence has shown that a
certain amount of hermaphroditism
exists within this species, and this
has led to some confusion with
species identification.
R.amboinensis is black, but
appears to transform with age, first
into the blue form known as
R.quaesita and then into a yellow
female form. (It may be that
R.quaesita is the only valid
species, merely passing through
several colour phases during its
development.)

These are favourite show fishes.
Be sure to fit a secure lid on their
tank; these snakelike fishes can
escape very easily.

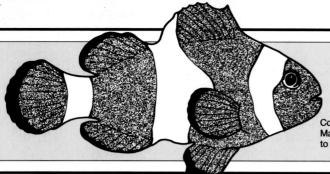

Common Clown (*Amphiprion ocellaris*)
Mature at 80mm (3.2in) and shown as a guide
to the maximum wild size of each species.

Family: OPISTHOGNATHIDAE
Jawfishes

Family characteristics
Behind the large mouth and eyes of these fish is a tapering
cylindrical body. The main appeal of Jawfishes is their habit of
constructing tunnels or burrows in the substrate into which they
retreat when threatened. At night they use a small pebble or shell
to cover the entrance.

While the commonly kept Yellow-headed Jawfish
(*Opisthognathus aurifrons*) shows no sexual dimorphism, males of
other less familiar species, such as the Atlantic Yellow Jawfish
(*O.gilberti*) and the Pacific Blue-Spotted Jawfish do undergo colour
changes at breeding times. Perhaps the best guide to the sexes
is the fact that males take on the incubation of the eggs.

Diet and feeding
Hovering close to their burrowed tunnels, Jawfishes wait for their
prey of crustaceans, small fishes and plankton. Some species are
not so adventurous, preferring to remain in their holes waiting for
small live foods to pass by.

Aquarium behaviour
Providing sufficient 'accommodation' is available, a number of
these fishes can be kept together. They are very hardy but easily
frightened, retreating into their holes like lightning. These tolerant
fishes bother nobody, but may be harassed by other cave-dwelling
species that may have designs on their living quarters. Jawfishes
are excellent jumpers, so ensure that the aquarium has a closely
fitting cover to prevent escapes.

Above: **Opisthognathus aurifrons**
*The normal pose, at peace with the
world. How the fish manages to
retreat into its hole tail-first at such
speed almost defies belief.*

Below: **Opisthognathus aurifrons**
*Once seen outside its usual safe
retreat, the Yellow-headed Jawfish
reveals that its slim body has the
most delicate coloration.*

Opisthognathus aurifrons

Yellow-headed Jawfish
● **Distribution:** Western Atlantic.
● **Length:** 125mm/5in (wild).
● **Diet and feeding:** Finely
chopped shellfish meat. Makes
rapid lunges from a vertical
hovering position near its burrow
to grab any passing food.
● **Aquarium behaviour:** Peaceful
and rarely disturbed by other
fishes, although the Royal Gramma
(*Gramma loreto*) may try to steal its
territory given the opportunity.

The delicately coloured yellow
head is normally all you see of this
fish, but the rest of the body is an
equally beautiful pale blue. The
eyes are large. It needs a
reasonably soft substrate in which
to excavate a burrow, entering the
hole tail first at any sign of trouble.
A good jumper.

A practical reminder
Reduce the risk of introducing disease by screening all new fishes for signs of ailments. You can use the time that some fishes may need in quarantine to acclimatize them to aquarium foods.

Family: OSTRACIONTIDAE
Boxfishes and Trunkfishes

Family characteristics
These fishes have a rigid body made up of bony plates covered with a sensitive skin that may be damaged by Cleanerfishes. The only flexible part is the caudal peduncle, where the most obvious growth occurs rearwards. The pelvic fins are missing, although bony stumps may appear at the corners of the body box in some species. They are slow moving – some have been designated 'hovercraft fishes' by imaginative authors – and they do indeed have a similar form of locomotion, making rapid movements of the dorsal, anal and pectoral fins to good effect. When buying these fishes, avoid any with concave looking sides, as these never recover from this probable semi-starved state.

Most are poisonous, releasing a poison into the water when threatened. In the confines of the aquarium, or in the transportation container, this often proves fatal both to the Boxfish and to other fishes. Some authorities advocate introducing these fish into the aquarium in advance of other fishes to reduce the chances of fatal consequences should the Boxfishes become frightened.

Diet and feeding
These fishes will try anything, but appear to relish worm foods, especially *Tubifex* (obtained from a disease-free source).

Aquarium behaviour
Some reports suggest that these fish resent the attentions of Cleaner Gobies or any other inquisitive fishes perhaps attracted by their slow swimming action.

Lactoria cornuta
Long-horned Cowfish
● **Distribution:** Indo-Pacific.
● **Length:** 500mm/20in (wild), 400mm/16in (aquarium).
● **Diet and feeding:** Crustaceans and greenstuff. Shy bottom feeders.
● **Aquarium behaviour:** Intolerant of each other.

The two 'horns' on the head and two more projections at the bottom rear of the body make for easy identification. The body is brilliant yellow with bright blue spots in the centre of each segment of body 'armour plating'. Specimens in domestic aquariums do not reach very large sizes.

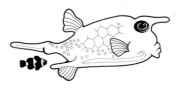

Above: **Lactoria cornuta**
The large horny projections serve a more specific purpose than merely providing the fish with its popular name of Long-horned Cowfish: they make the fish hard to swallow by predators, although its poisonous flesh would inflict justifiable retribution in any event.

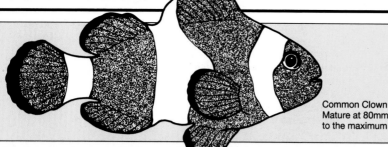

Common Clown (*Amphiprion ocellaris*)
Mature at 80mm (3.2in) and shown as a guide
to the maximum wild size of each species.

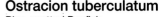

A practical reminder
Calculate copper-based medication doses accurately by using a copper test kit. Do not use activated carbon in filters used in treatment tanks as it will remove the medication from the water.

Left: **Ostracion lentiginosum**
Although named lentiginosum, *there are strong grounds for believing that this fish is the male form of O.meleagris. The confusion arises because of the obvious differences in colour patterning on the body, which make it hard to believe that the two are related.*

Below left: **Ostracion meleagris**
Although often confused with young specimens of Pufferfish, especially Arothron meleagris, *Boxfishes rely on poisonous secretions to ward off predators rather than inflating their bodies. According to recent information, the fish shown here is probably a female or juvenile form of the vividly coloured fish above.*

Below right:
Ostracion tuberculatum
This species really lives up to its popular name of Boxfish, especially when viewed from the angle captured here. However, a side view would soon reveal yellow fins, a pointed snout and longish caudal peduncle.

Ostracion lentiginosum
Blue-spotted Boxfish
● **Distribution:** Indo-Pacific.
● **Length:** 200mm/8in (wild), 100mm/4in (aquarium).
● **Diet and feeding:** Crustaceans. Bottom feeder.
● **Aquarium behaviour:** Peaceful, but do not keep in the same aquarium as inquisitive fishes.

This is a most colourful species. The top of the body is black with white spots and the lower flanks are violet with yellow spots. The two sections are separated by a yellow line. The eye is yellow-gold and the face is a similar colour. The body patterning dwindles away two-thirds of the way through the caudal fin. The male is much darker than the female.

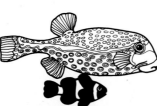

Ostracion meleagris
White-spotted Boxfish; Pacific Boxfish
● **Distribution:** Indo-Pacific.
● **Length:** 160mm/6.3in (wild).
● **Diet and feeding:** Crustaceans and greenstuff. Bottom feeder.
● **Aquarium behaviour:** Peaceful.

There is much confusion between this and the previous species since *O.meleagris* is also black with a covering of white spots. Some authorities believe that both are the same species, one being the male, the other the female. The problem is that they cannot agree which one is which! Start feeding with brineshrimp, *Daphnia* etc.

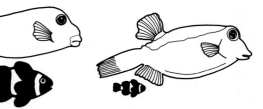

Ostracion tuberculatum
Blue-spotted Boxfish
● **Distribution:** Indo-Pacific.
● **Length:** 450mm/18in (wild).
● **Diet and feeding:** Crustaceans and greenstuff. Bottom feeder.
● **Aquarium behaviour:** Peaceful; best left undisturbed.

The almost cube-shaped body of juveniles is light cream or yellow with dark blue spots; it is easy to imagine that they are animated dice, slowly swimming around looking for food. Adult fishes develop a more elongate body and the colour changes to a yellowy green, while the armoured plates on the body become more clearly defined. The fins are tinted yellow.

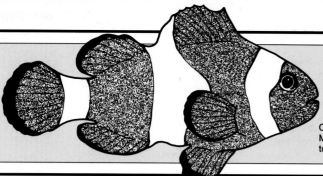

Common Clown (*Amphiprion ocellaris*)
Mature at 80mm (3.2in) and shown as a guide
to the maximum wild size of each species.

Family: PLATACIDAE
Batfishes

Family characteristics
The oval-bodied, high-finned Batfish is unmistakable. It is found in coastal and brackish waters and in mangrove swamps. It often lies on its side 'playing dead', floating like a leaf to avoid capture or detection. There is still unresolved speculation as to whether there is only one true species, with the variously coloured forms being regarded as subspecies. According to commercial sources, there may be three species of Batfishes available, with possibly a rarer fourth: *Platax orbicularis*, *P.tiera* (Longfinned Batfish), *P.pinnatus*, and a marbled type as yet un-named. In the light of such varied speculations, it is not surprising that positive species identification is difficult, but it is known that adult fishes have less coloration than juveniles.

Diet and feeding
These greedy fishes will usually accept all manner of foods.

Aquarium behaviour
The Batfish usually adapts to captivity well, not quarrelling with similarly sized tankmates. It does need a spacious tank, however, as it grows very quickly.

Platax orbicularis
Batfish; Orbiculate Batfish;
Round Batfish
● **Distribution:** Indo-Pacific.
● **Length:** 500mm/20in (wild), 380mm/15in (aquarium).
● **Diet and feeding:** Will eat anything. Scavenger.
● **Aquarium behaviour:** Peaceful, but grows fast. Keep away from boisterous fin-nipping species.

The body is round, with large rounded fins. There are one or two dark stripes on the head and front part of the body, but these fade with age. Young specimens have more elongated fins and also more red coloration.

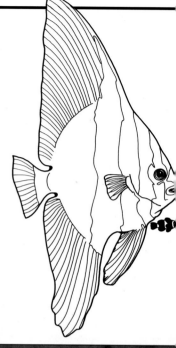

Below: **Platax orbicularis**
A young specimen, showing the typical dark red-brown stripes. Allow a generous depth of water for these tall-finned fishes.

A practical reminder
Do not leap to conclusions in
diagnosing fish diseases or treat fishes
with more than one remedy at a time.
Avoid treating a tank containing
invertebrates with copper-based cures.

Platax pinnatus
Red-faced Batfish
● **Distribution:** Indo-Pacific.
● **Length:** 500mm/20in (wild),
450mm/18in (aquarium).
● **Diet and feeding:** Will eat
anything. Scavenger.
● **Aquarium behaviour:** Peaceful,
but grows fast. Keep away from
boisterous fin-nipping species.

Platax pinnatus may be a separate
species of Batfish; the body shape
is much shorter and higher than in
P.orbicularis and the fins are very
elongate. The colour is much
darker, with a red outline to the
body and fins. It is a pity that it
should lose such magnificent
colours and gracefulness with
advancing age.

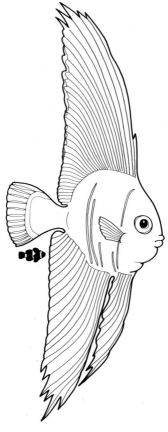

Left: **Platax pinnatus**
*This splendid fish makes a
majestic picture, the red edges of
the fins outlining the fish to
perfection. It is quite easy to see
how tempting the tall fins might be
to other fishes with a fin-nipping
disposition. Luckily (for the fish
although not for the hobbyist)
these attractive colours fade with
increasing age. Similar in body
shape to the freshwater Angelfish,
the fish's slender body enables it
to move with ease through dense
mangrove roots in coastal areas.*

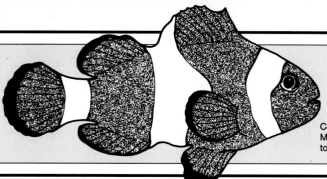

Common Clown (*Amphiprion ocellaris*)
Mature at 80mm (3.2in) and shown as a guide
to the maximum wild size of each species.

Family: PLECTORHYNCHIDAE
Sweetlips

Family characteristics
Fishes in this Family are often classified in the Pomadasydae. They resemble Snappers, but differ from them in dentition details. The coloration of juveniles and adults differs quite dramatically. The Sweetlips are confined to the Indo-Pacific Ocean areas.

Diet and feeding
Crustaceans, live animal and meaty foods. Shy slow eaters.

Aquarium behaviour
Juveniles are excellent subjects for a large quiet aquarium.

Plectorhynchus albovittatus

Yellow Sweetlips; Yellow-lined Sweetlips
- **Distribution:** Indo-Pacific, Red Sea.
- **Length:** 200mm/8in (wild).
- **Diet and feeding:** Crustaceans, animal and meaty foods. Bottom feeder.
- **Aquarium behaviour:** Hardy, but keep with non-boisterous fishes.

In juveniles the body is yellow, with two white-bordered dark bands

running the length of the body. The lower band is level with the terminal mouth and centre line of the fish. The patterning of the body extends into the rear of the yellow dorsal fin and into the caudal fin. Adult fishes lose this interesting coloration and become brown.

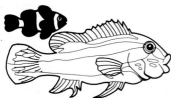

Below:
Plectorhynchus albovittatus
When seen in dealer's tanks, the juveniles look very appealing, but they lose these colours with age.

Above and right:
Plectorhynchus chaetodonoides
Another striking difference in body colours, this time between young and adult Harlequin Sweetlips.

144

A practical reminder
Collect seashore specimens carefully. If you have to remove them from stones, replace these with substitutes to retain natural refuges. Don't transport fishes and invertebrates in the same container.

Plectorhynchus chaetodonoides

Harlequin Sweetlips; Clown Sweetlips; Polka-dot Grunt
● **Distribution:** Pacific.
● **Length:** 450mm/18in (wild).
● **Diet and feeding:** Crustaceans, animal and meaty foods. (Small live or frozen shrimps will often get them feeding in the aquarium.) Bottom feeder.
● **Aquarium behaviour:** Shy; keep with non-boisterous fishes.

Juveniles have a dark brown body covered with well-defined white blotches and this pattern is repeated on the fins. Adult fishes are a drab brown with dark dots. Feeding requires special attention; be sure to offer only small portions.

Plectorhynchus orientalis

Oriental Sweetlips
● **Distribution:** Indo-Pacific.
● **Length:** 400mm/16in (wild).
● **Diet and feeding:** Crustaceans, animal and meaty foods. Bottom feeder.
● **Aquarium behaviour:** Shy; keep with non-boisterous fishes.

Juvenile fishes have large cream-yellow patches on a dark background. Adults may sometimes be confused with young *P.albovittatus*, although there are more stripes on *P.orientalis* and the coloration is not quite so yellow.

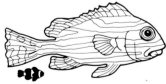

Left: **Plectorhynchus orientalis**
Members of the Sweetlips group are surprisingly shy; another even more unexpected feature is their habit of taking small morsels of food. Adult Oriental Sweetlips, similar in coloration to the juvenile Yellow Sweetlips shown opposite, reverse the usual colour sequence, ending up with stripes in contrast to the juvenile's creamy patches.

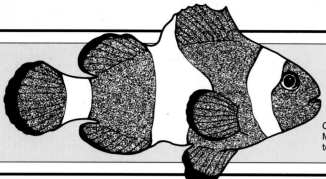

Common Clown (*Amphiprion ocellaris*)
Mature at 80mm (3.2in) and shown as a guide
to the maximum wild size of each species.

Family: PLOTOSIDAE
Catfishes

Family characteristics
Two features make it easy to identify the marine Catfishes: the second dorsal and anal fins merge with the caudal fin, and there are barbels around the mouth. The spines preceding the dorsal and pectoral fins are poisonous.

These fishes are very gregarious when young – species grouping together in a tight ball for safety – but this habit is lost (along with any colour pattern) when adult. In the wild, adult fishes may enter river systems.

Diet and feeding
Chopped shellfish meats form an ideal food in the aquarium.

Aquarium behaviour
Only juvenile specimens are suitable for the aquarium, as the adult fishes not only outgrow their juvenile coloration but also can become dangerous to inexperienced handlers.

Plotosus lineatus
Saltwater Catfish
- ● **Distribution:** Indo-Pacific.
- ● **Length:** 300mm/12in (wild).
- ● **Diet and feeding:** Chopped shellfish meats. Bottom feeder.
- ● **Aquarium behaviour:** Peaceful.

Two parallel white lines run along the length of the dark body. The second dorsal and anal fins are very long-based and merge with the caudal fin. In the wild, young specimens shoal together, forming a tight, ball-like clump when threatened. In the aquarium, they are best kept in small shoals, since solitary specimens seem to pine away. The spines are poisonous, so handle these fishes with care. (For action if stung, see page 168 – introduction to Scorpaenidae.)

This species presumably spawns in the same way as the freshwater Plotosid *Tandanus*, which constructs a nest of debris, sand or gravel. The male (usually identified simply because it does not lay the eggs) is said to guard the eggs after spawning has taken place. This fish is also known as *Plotosus anguillaris*.

Top right and right:
Plotosus lineatus
The horizontal stripes of the young Catfish make for a smart-looking fish, and the habit of young specimens congregating together suggests that it may be a good community subject. However, this fast-growing species soon loses its stripes and sociable nature as it matures in the aquarium.

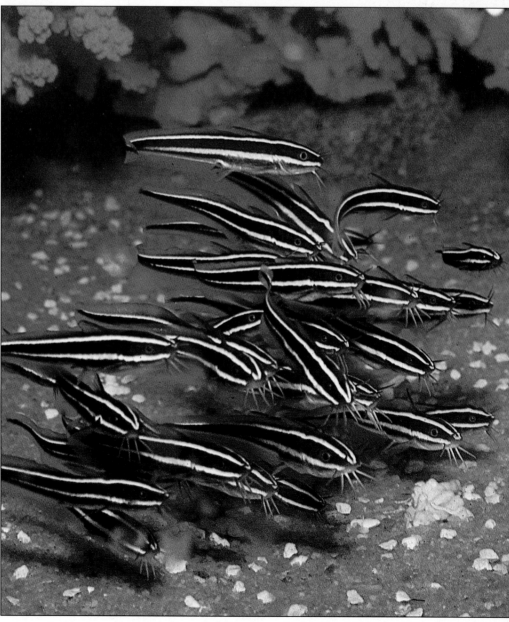

A practical reminder
Never collect more native animals than
you can accommodate in the tank. If the
specimens outgrow their quarters, you
can return them to the wild and capture
smaller replacements at the same time.

Family: POMACENTRIDAE

Anemonefishes (Clownfishes) and Damselfishes

Family characteristics

Fishes within this Family are usually divided into two distinct
groups: the Anemonefishes and the Damselfishes. They are very
important to the marine aquarist, because they are brilliantly
coloured, of modest size, and are also very hardy. These attributes
make them ideal starter fishes, Damselfishes being especially
suitable because they are nitrite tolerant. Here, we discuss the
Anemonefishes. Damselfishes are described from page 154.

The curious 'waddling' swimming action of the Anemonefishes,
together with their clearly defined markings, has given them their
other collective common name of Clownfishes. As their principal
common name suggests, the Anemonefishes live in close
association with sea anemones, especially *Discosoma*, *Radianthus*
and *Stoichactus* species. The Anemonefish was thought to be
immune to the stinging cells of the sea anemone, but it now
appears that the mucus on the fish prevents the stinging cells from
being activated. This relationship is usually referred to as being
symbiotic, but 'commensalism' might be a more accurate
description. In this context, commensalism means that the fishes
and sea anemones live in close proximity to one another, often to
their mutual benefit. There may be some doubt about the benefit
derived by the sea anemone in return for not stinging the fish. One
belief is that the fish drops morsels of food for the sea anemone to
eat, or entices would-be predators near enough to the sea
anemone to be stung by its tentacles. Another theory is that the
Anemonefishes, being territorial by nature, chase away fishes that
might eat the sea anemone.

It could be that the Clownfish/sea anemone relationship is more
like that of a patient and doctor. Some observers have noticed that
the sea anemone appears to remove *Oodinium* parasites, not only
from the Clownfish but also from any other similarly infected fish
that cares to enter the sea anemone's tentacles. However, it is only
the Clownfish that carries on with further visits to the sea anemone

once the parasitic infection has cleared up. (It would appear that
non-infected fishes cannot avoid the effects of the stings.)

Not all Anemonefishes are dependent upon sea anemones to the
same degree. It seems that poor swimmers are the most reliant,
whereas the more able swimmers venture further away with more
confidence in their ability to survive without the immediate
protection offered by the embracing tentacles.

Despite their close relationship in the wild, Anemonefishes will
live quite happily in the aquarium without a sea anemone (and
vice-versa), but then you will not see the fish behave as it does in
nature. Large sea anemones can 'accommodate' several
Anemonefishes. A single fish occupying a small sea anemone, on
the other hand, will become territorial, defending its 'own'
anemone from intruders. In the absence of a sea anemone, the
fishes do not develop this territorial behaviour.

There may be some variation in the colour patterns of juvenile
and adult forms and also between the same species from different
localities. However, in most cases there are very few external
physical differences between the sexes, although *Amphiprion
perideraion* is reported to offer more positive clues in this respect
(see page 150). Also, studies of some species in the wild have
shown that, generally, mature females are longer than males. Like
the Damselfishes, Anemonefishes exhibit hermaphrodite
capabilities (i.e. fishes will change sex to 'even up' the numbers) to
ensure the continuity of the species. Spawning has occurred in the
aquarium and the eggs are laid on a selected site and guarded.

Diet and feeding

In the wild, small crustaceans, plankton and algae are the main
diet. In the aquarium, these fishes will take live foods, algae, fish
meat-based foods and flakes, etc.

Aquarium behaviour

Because of their territorial tendencies, Anemonefishes are
eminently suitable for keeping in the aquarium, where they will
naturally associate with suitable anemones. In this way, you can
keep a few Anemonefishes in a relatively small tank.

ANEMONEFISHES

Amphiprion akallopisos
Yellow Skunk Clown
● **Distribution:** Indo-Pacific.
● **Length:** 75mm/3in (wild),
40-50mm/1.6-2in (aquarium).
● **Diet and feeding:** Small
crustaceans, small live foods,
algae, vegetable-based foods.
Bold feeder.
● **Aquarium behaviour:** Peaceful.

A white line runs along the very top
of the brown-topped golden body,
from a point level with the eye to
the caudal peduncle. Some
Anemonefishes do not live up to
the Family's reputation as sea
anemone dwellers, but this species
seems to need the association
more than others.

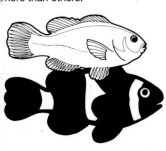

Above: **Amphiprion akallopisos**
Here, the Yellow Skunk Clown is
doing what comes naturally,
resting among the tentacles of its
home sea anemone which,
providing it is large enough, can
play host to several fishes.
*Radianthus ritteri is a sea anemone
often associated with this fish.*

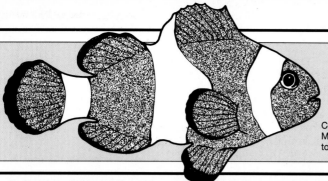

Common Clown (*Amphiprion ocellaris*)
Mature at 80mm (3.2in) and shown as a guide
to the maximum wild size of each species.

Amphiprion bicinctus

*Two-banded Anemonefish;
Banded Clown*
● **Distribution:** Red Sea, Indo-Pacific.
● **Length:** 120mm/4.7in (wild), 75mm/3in (aquarium).
● **Diet and feeding:** Small crustaceans, small live foods, algae, vegetable-based foods. Bold feeder.
● **Aquarium behaviour:** Peaceful.

The body is predominantly dark brown but for the ventral regions, which are yellow. All the fins, with the exception of the paler caudal fins, are bright yellow. Two tapering white vertical bars divide the body into thirds; in juvenile forms, there is a third white bar across the rear of the body.

Amphiprion ephippium

Tomato Clown; Fire Clown; Red Saddleback Clown
● **Distribution:** Indo-Pacific.
● **Length:** 120mm/4.7in (wild), 75mm/3in (aquarium).
● **Diet and feeding:** Small crustaceans, small live foods, algae, vegetable-based foods. Bold feeder.
● **Aquarium behaviour:** Can be aggressive.

This fish is often confused with *A.frenatus*, since both are a rich tomato-red with a black blurred blotch on the body rearwards of the gill cover. Occasionally, juveniles have a white vertical bar just behind the head, but some authorities maintain that this is never the case. According to some sources, imported species of *E.ephippium* are really *E.rubrocinctus*.

Amphiprion frenatus

Tomato Clown; Fire Clown; Bridled Clownfish
● **Distribution:** Pacific.
● **Length:** 75mm/3in (wild).
● **Diet and feeding:** Small crustaceans, small live foods, algae, vegetable-based foods. Bold feeder.
● **Aquarium behaviour:** May be quarrelsome in confined spaces.

A.frenatus is very similar to *A.ephippium*, but it has the white stripe behind the head (sometimes two in juveniles) and the body blotch is often larger. The confusion between the two species is not helped by the fact that some authorities call this fish *A.ephippium* or *A.melanopus*. Another name for it is *A.polylepis*.

Above: **Amphiprion bicinctus**
An adult specimen. Juvenile forms are darker in body colour; there may also be dark patches in the caudal fin and rear of the dorsal fin, both disappearing with age. Two other species are similarly marked: the Indian Ocean A. allardi, the juveniles having saddle-like markings on the caudal peduncle, and A. chrysopterus, in which the adult is less orange.

Opposite top:
Amphiprion ephippium
This juvenile Tomato Clown is but one species of Amphiprion so named, many others having the similar rich red body coloration with a dark patch. The distinctions centre upon the presence or absence of the white vertical stripe; true adult A. ephippium do not have one, although it may persist from the juvenile for a time.

Right: **Amphiprion frenatus**
Unlike the previous species, adult specimens of this Tomato Clown retain the vertical white stripe into adulthood. As with all fishes with similar features that are gathered over very wide areas by collectors not aware of other's efforts or descriptions, there is bound to be confusion with classifications.

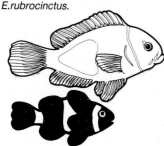

A practical reminder
A coldwater marine tank may overheat in the summer months. To compensate, increase aeration, add ice cubes in a plastic bag, or pass the filter's output tube through a bucket of cold water.

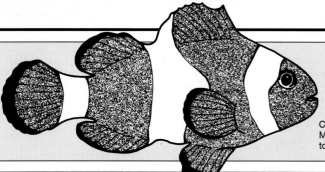

Common Clown (*Amphiprion ocellaris*)
Mature at 80mm (3.2in) and shown as a guide
to the maximum wild size of each species.

Amphiprion nigripes

Black-footed Clownfish
- **Distribution:** Indian Ocean.
- **Length:** 80mm/3.2in (wild), 50mm/2in (aquarium).
- **Diet and feeding:** Eats plankton and crustaceans in the wild, but finely chopped foods are ideal in captivity. Bold feeder.
- **Aquarium behaviour:** Best kept with other Anemonefishes.

Although it is similar to the two previous species, *A.nigripes* is much more subtly coloured. It is a soft golden brown with a white stripe just behind the head. The ventral fins are black, but the anal fin is not always so, hence the common name.

Amphiprion ocellaris

Common Clown; Percula Clown
- **Distribution:** Indo-Pacific.
- **Length:** 80mm/3.2in (wild), 50mm/2in (aquarium).
- **Diet and feeding:** Finely chopped foods. Bold feeder.
- **Aquarium behaviour:** Will sometimes exclude other Anemonefishes from its territory.

This is the Clownfish that everyone recognises, for the simple reason that it is the species most often imported. It is frequently confused with *A.percula*, which has slightly more black, especially in the dorsal fin, between the first two white bands, and on the pectoral and caudal fins.

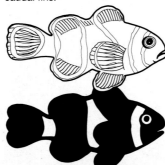

Amphiprion perideraion

Salmon Clownfish; Pink Skunk Clownfish
- **Distribution:** Pacific Ocean.
- **Length:** 80mm/3.2in (wild), 38mm/1.5in (aquarium).
- **Diet and feeding:** Finely chopped foods. Not quite as bold as other species.
- **Aquarium behaviour:** Shy.

This species is very similar in colour to *A.akallopisos*, but can be easily distinguished from it by the vertical bar just behind the head. The body colour is perhaps a little more subdued and a white stripe reaches the snout. *A.perideraion* is rather more sensitive than other species and is best kept in a species tank with adequate space for sea anemones. Males have orange edging to the soft-rayed part of the dorsal fin and at the top and bottom of the caudal fin.

Below: Amphiprion nigripes
The Black-footed Clownfish is found off the Maldive Islands in the Indian Ocean. Its colours are not as rich as those of some other Clownfishes, and in this respect it is very similar to A.perideraion.

Right: **Amphiprion ocellaris**
The Common Clown can be found with some variations in its body colour. Based on scientific experimentation in similar species, this has been attributed to the relatively darker colours of their chosen sea anemones; it would seem that pale Anemonefishes become darker to blend in with their host anemone.

Below right:
Amphiprion perideraion
The Skunk Clownfish has a vertical bar, and a pink hue to the body, which helps distinguish it from similar white-backed species. It is also one of the few Clownfishes that show signs of sex differences.

A practical reminder
Keep a close-fitting lid on the tank,
especially if it contains invertebrates, as
many are great escape artists. Provide
hermit crabs with variously sized shells
to use as continuing 'homes'.

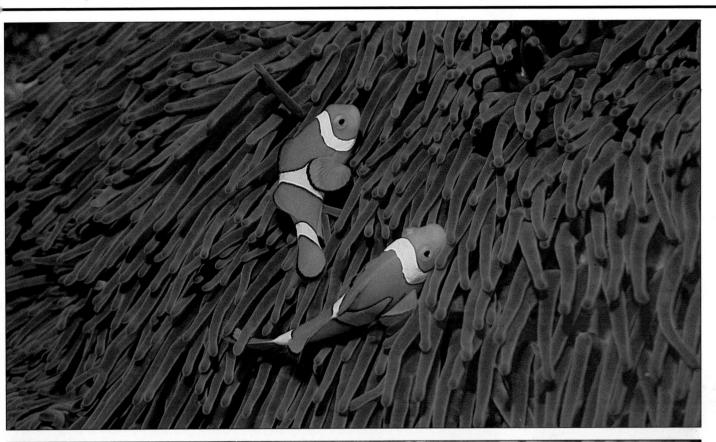

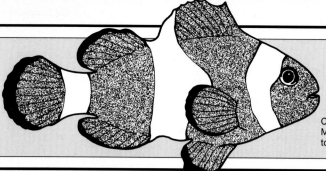

Common Clown (*Amphiprion ocellaris*)
Mature at 80mm (3.2in) and shown as a guide
to the maximum wild size of each species.

Above: **Amphiprion polymnus**
The white markings on the dorsal area make recognition quite positive. An alternate scientific name offered for the White-saddled Clownfish is A.laticlavius.

Amphiprion polymnus
White-saddled Clownfish
● **Distribution:** Pacific.
● **Length:** 120mm/4.7in (wild), 100mm/4in (aquarium).
● **Diet and feeding:** Small crustaceans, small live foods, algae, vegetable-based foods. Bold feeder.
● **Aquarium behaviour:** Can be territorial.

The dark red-brown body is marked by two white bands; one broad band lies just behind the head, the other begins in the middle of the body and curves upwards into the rear part of the dorsal fin. There is also a dash of white along the top of the caudal fin. Not an easy fish to maintain.

Premnas biaculeatus
Maroon Clownfish
● **Distribution:** Pacific Ocean.
● **Length:** 150mm/6in (wild), 100mm/4in (aquarium).
● **Diet and feeding:** Finely chopped foods. Bold.
● **Aquarium behaviour:** Aggressive towards other Anemonefishes.

This larger species differs from other Clownfishes by having two spines beneath the eye, as well as the usual small spines on the back edge of the gill cover. The body is a deep rich red colour with three narrow white bands crossing it, one behind the head, one midway along the body and one just behind the dorsal and anal fins.

Right: **Premnas biaculeatus**
Recent scientific work has put forward the suggestion that the genus Premnas should be treated as a subgenus of Amphiprion, but aquarium hobbyists are sometimes slow to readjust to such moves, just in case the names change again in a short space of time!

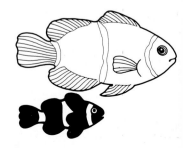

A practical reminder
You should take extra care when handling fishes that have venomous, or even merely sharp, spines. Even if fishes become hand-tame it may be prudent to offer food impaled on a stick.

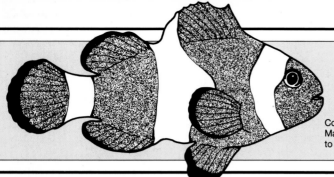

Common Clown (*Amphiprion ocellaris*)
Mature at 80mm (3.2in) and shown as a guide
to the maximum wild size of each species.

Family: POMACENTRIDAE
Damselfishes

Family characteristics
Damselfishes are small, busy fishes that bob constantly around the coral heads, using them as their territory and retreating into them when threatened. Consequently, they are among the most agile of fishes – particularly when you are trying to catch them!

There are a number of similar looking 'Electric-blue' or 'Blue Devil' fishes and also several blue-and-yellow coloured species. Because of these similarities, there is much confusion about the correct taxonomic classification. Sometimes Damsels lose their brilliant colours in captivity. Fading the colours may be a response that helps the fishes to blend in more effectively with the surroundings.

Normally, there are no clear distinctions between the sexes. An internal examination – usually beyond the scope or immediate interest of the hobbyist – will reveal differences more clearly. However, during courtship and breeding periods, colour changes do occur: *Abudefduf* males usually turn pale; the Atlantic *Eupomacentrus* species develop a mask over the eyes, head or other dorsal part of the body; and Pacific *Eupomacentrus* develop a contrasting colour around the pupil of the eye. There is one method of determining sex by external observation – a technique similar to that used for determining sex in freshwater Cichlids – and that is by looking at the genital papillae (often called the ovipositor). The male genital papilla is narrower and more pointed than the female's. Unfortunately, it takes a keen eye to make the necessary observations and these are best delayed until breeding activity is noticed, when the papillae are easier to see.

Spawning in Damselfishes entails the selection of a site and the laying and subsequent guarding of eggs.

Diet and feeding
Finely chopped meats, algae and greenstuff, but all species of Damselfishes will take dried foods readily.

Aquarium behaviour
When confident of a nearby safe refuge, they are delightful fishes, but they may transfer their nervous energy into quarrels among themselves. They can be aggressive. Provide a spacious aquarium if you wish to keep several fishes together.

Abudefduf cyaneus
(A. assimilis)
Blue Damsel
● **Distribution:** Indo-Pacific.
● **Length:** 60mm/2.4in (wild).
● **Diet and feeding:** Finely chopped meats, algae and greenstuff. Will take dried food. Bold feeder.
● **Aquarium behaviour:** May squabble with members of its own species. Keep singly or in shoals.

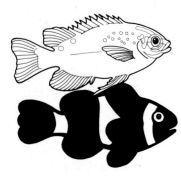

Although some specimens may have yellow markings on the caudal fin and ventral area, the predominant colour of this fish is a stunning royal blue. There is some confusion about the positive classification of this species, since some authorities refer to it as *Glyphidodontops*.

Above right: **Abudefduf cyaneus**
One of the many blue Damselfishes, this species probably has more synonyms than most. Doubts will always arise due to colour variations between fishes of different age, sex and location.

Right:
Glyphidodontops hemicyaneus
This is another name often applied to several bright blue species, all with varying amounts of yellow on fins and body. Such a coloration may be merely intermittent or a locality feature, rather than a positive identification factor.

A practical reminder
Make sure you can differentiate
between species and their lookalikes,
which may be predatory. The true
Cleanerfish removes parasites from
fishes; the False Cleaner takes skin!

Above: **Abudefduf oxyodon**
*As with all marine fishes, it is vital
that imported specimens are in the
very best of health if they are to*
*thrive in captivity. This handsome
fish from the Pacific Ocean may
not always adapt well if in less
than tip-top condition.*

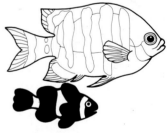

Abudefduf oxyodon
*Blue-velvet Damselfish; Black
Neon Damselfish*
● **Distribution:** Pacific.
● **Length:** 110mm/4.3in (wild),
75mm/3in (aquarium).
● **Diet and feeding:** Finely
chopped meats, algae and
greenstuff. Bold.
● **Aquarium behaviour:**
Aggressive.

A vertical yellow stripe crosses the
deep blue-black body just behind
the head. The electric blue wavy
lines on the head and upper part of
the body may fade with age.

Left: **Abudefduf saxatilis**
*The Sergeant Major is widely
distributed throughout the tropics.
The male changes colour and an
ovipositor appears from the vent
during spawning, which occurs
between territorial males and
visiting females. Eggs are laid on
rocks, shells or coral branches.*

Abudefduf saxatilis
Sergeant Major
● **Distribution:** Indo-Pacific,
tropical Atlantic.
● **Length:** 150mm/6in (wild),
50mm/2in (aquarium).
● **Diet and feeding:** Finely
chopped meats, algae and
greenstuff. Bold grazer.
● **Aquarium behaviour:** Juveniles
are very active; adults can become
aggressive.

Five vertical dark bars cross the
yellow/silvery body. Depending on
the geographic location of the
individuals, the caudal fin may be a
dusky colour. Juvenile forms in the
Atlantic have bright yellow upper
parts on an otherwise silver body.
However, it may lose its colours
when disturbed. This is a hardy
fish, and a good choice for the
beginner. A shoal in a large tank is
impressive. A.saxatilis is a good
teacher fish for 'educating' new
fish to accept food and to help
mature a newly set up aquarium.

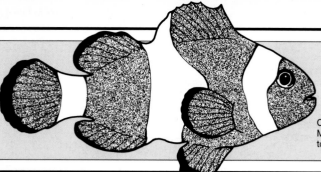

Common Clown (*Amphiprion ocellaris*)
Mature at 80mm (3.2in) and shown as a guide
to the maximum wild size of each species.

Chromis caerulea
Green Chromis
● **Distribution:** Indo-Pacific, Red Sea.
● **Length:** 100mm/4in (wild), 50mm/2in (aquarium).
● **Diet and feeding:** Chopped meats. Shy.
● **Aquarium behaviour:** Generally peaceful.

This hardy colourful shoaling species has a brilliant green-blue sheen to the scales. The caudal fin is more deeply forked than in some Damselfishes. Keep these fishes in shoals; individuals may go into decline in the aquarium.

Chromis cyanea
Blue Chromis
● **Distribution:** Tropical Atlantic.
● **Length:** 50mm/2in (wild).
● **Diet and feeding:** Chopped meats. Dried foods. Average.
● **Aquarium behaviour:** A peaceable shoaling fish that prefers to be with some of its own kind to feel at home.

This species thrives in vigorously aerated water. The body colour is brilliant blue with some black specks, topped with a black dorsal surface. There are black edges to the dorsal and caudal fins. The eye is also dark. In shape and size (but not colour) *C.cyanea* closely resembles *C.multilineata*, the Grey Chromis. The Blue Hamlet (*Hypoplectrus gemma*) is a colour mimic of *Chromis cyanea*, using its 'disguise' to prey upon unsuspecting fishes and crustaceans – which assume the 'Blue Chromis' to be harmless.
　At breeding time, a brown ovipositor extends from just in front of the anal fin in a similar manner to that of freshwater Cichlids (see also page 154).

Right: Chromis cyanea
The normally narrow black area on the top of the male Blue Chromis spreads during spawning time and a brown ovipositor appears. The male usually guards the eggs.

Below right: Chromis xanthurus
Compare this species to the picture on p.154. There appears to be more yellow in the pelvic fins, a spot on the gill cover and at the bottom of the rear dorsal fin.

Below: Chromis caerulea
Like many Damselfishes, the peaceful Green Chromis has a gregarious nature and appreciates being kept in a small shoal. A lively and attractive species.

A practical reminder
Replenish water losses through
evaporation by adding *fresh* water, as
none of the sea salt is lost during
evaporation. Adding sea water would
alter the specific gravity of the water.

Chromis xanthurus
Yellow-tailed Damselfish
● **Distribution:** Indo-Pacific.
● **Length:** 100mm/4in (wild),
50mm/2in (aquarium).
● **Diet and feeding:** Chopped
meats. Dried foods. Bold.
● **Aquarium behaviour:** A
peaceable shoaling fish that
prefers to be with some of its
own kind to thrive.

The deep royal blue body
contrasts sharply with the bright
yellow caudal fin and caudal
peduncle. Again, there is some
confusion over the correct name of
this species, both *Pomacentrus
caeruleus* and *Abudefduf
parasema* are given by other
sources.

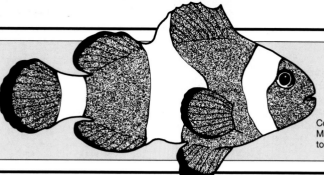

Common Clown (*Amphiprion ocellaris*)
Mature at 80mm (3.2in) and shown as a guide
to the maximum wild size of each species.

Dascyllus aruanus
Humbug
● **Distribution:** Indo-Pacific.
● **Length:** 80mm/3.2in (wild), 75mm/3in (aquarium).
● **Diet and feeding:** Chopped meats. Bold feeder.
● **Aquarium behaviour:** Aggressive towards its own kind and very territorial.

This white fish has three black bars across the body. The front bar covers the eye and follows the slope of the head up into the first rays of the dorsal fin. The rear two bars extend into the pelvic and anal fins and also into the dorsal fin, where they are linked by a horizontal bar along the top part of the fin. The caudal fin is unmarked. This is the hardiest of the Damsels.

Below: **Dascyllus aruanus**
Was the Humbug named by someone with a sweet tooth? It shares its popular name with a similarly coloured confection.

Dascyllus carneus
Cloudy Damsel
● **Distribution:** Indo-Pacific.
● **Length:** 80mm/3.2in (wild).
● **Diet and feeding:** Chopped foods. Dried foods. Bold.
● **Aquarium behaviour:** Aggressive towards its own kind.

All the fins, except the white caudal, are black and the body is greyish brown with a pattern of blue dots. There is a white patch on the top of the body, towards the front part of the dorsal fin and immediately behind a black bar, which covers the pectoral fin. A similar fish, *D.reticulatus*, is more an overall grey in colour, lacks the white patch and has a vertical black bar running from the rear dorsal to the rear of the anal fin.

Right: **Dascyllus carneus**
Of a similar size, but less starkly coloured than the previous species, the Cloudy Damsel has more grey-brown in its body.

A practical reminder
Keep a careful watch on algae growing in the tank. Although it should be thriving for the benefit of the fishes, thin it out if it becomes too lush; if it dies, it could cause pollution problems.

Left: **Dascyllus marginatus**
No doubt the dark margin to the dorsal fin inspired this fish's popular and scientific name.

Dascyllus marginatus

Marginate Damselfish; Marginate Puller

● **Distribution:** Red Sea.
● **Length:** 100mm/4in (wild).
● **Diet and feeding:** Chopped meats. Dried foods. Bold feeder.
● **Aquarium behaviour:** Aggressive and territorial.

A brown area slopes backwards from the front of the black-edged dorsal fin to the point of the anal fin. The rest of the body is cream in colour. Like all *Dascyllus* species, this fish occasionally makes quite audible purring or clicking sounds. This active fish will shelter among coral during the night.

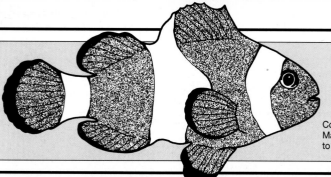

Common Clown (*Amphiprion ocellaris*)
Mature at 80mm (3.2in) and shown as a guide
to the maximum wild size of each species.

Dascyllus melanurus

Black-tailed Humbug
● **Distribution:** West Pacific.
● **Length:** 75mm/3in (wild).
● **Diet and feeding:** Chopped
foods. Dried foods. Bold feeder.
● **Aquarium behaviour:**
Aggressive and territorial.

This fish is very similar to
D.aruanus, except that the black
bars are more vertical and, as
indicated by the common name, a
black bar crosses the caudal fin.

Above: **Dascyllus melanurus**
*This black and white Damsel is,
like its almost lookalike relative the
Humbug, a shoaling fish. It is
found over a more limited area,
however, being limited to the
western Pacific Ocean around the
Philippines and Melanesia.*

Right: **Dascyllus trimaculatus**
*This very common Damselfish, the
Domino, is instantly recognizable
by the three white spots on the
body, and it would be very hard to
imagine any other popular name
for it. A similarly marked species
from Hawaii,* D.albisella, *also
carries three spots when young
but these are more likely to fade.*

A practical reminder
Even if you know how many fishes your tank can hold, always build up to this figure gradually so that the biological filter can cope with the increasing amounts of waste products.

Dascyllus trimaculatus
Domino Damsel; Three-spot Damselfish

● **Distribution:** Indo-Pacific, Red Sea.
● **Length:** 125mm/5in (wild), 75mm/3in (aquarium).
● **Diet and feeding:** Chopped meats and dried foods. Bold.
● **Aquarium behaviour:** Territorial.

This fish is velvety black overall, including the fins. The only markings are the three spots from which the comon name is derived. There is one white spot on each upper flank, midway along the length of the dorsal fin; the third spot is situated on the centre of the head, just behind the eye. The spots may fade with age.

Eupomacentrus leucostictus
Beau Gregory

● **Distribution:** Caribbean.
● **Length:** 150mm/6in (wild), 50mm/2in (aquarium).
● **Diet and feeding:** Animal and vegetable matter. Dried foods. Bold feeder.
● **Aquarium behaviour:** Aggressive.

The yellow body is topped by a golden brown area covered in bright blue dots. There is a dark blotch at the rear of the dorsal fin. All the other fins are yellow. This common Damsel is hardy enough for the beginner, but may bully fishes with similar feeding habits; kept alongside species with different feeding habits it is not so aggressive.

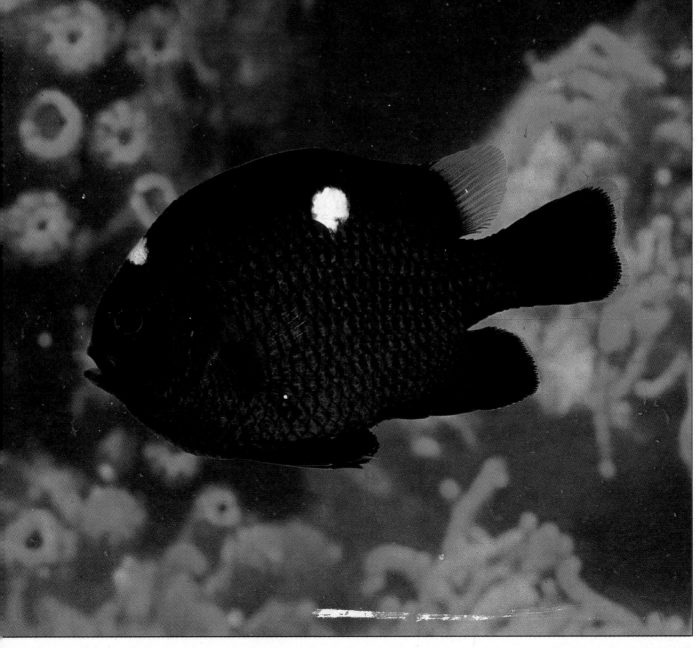

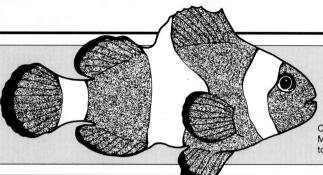

Common Clown (*Amphiprion ocellaris*)
Mature at 80mm (3.2in) and shown as a guide
to the maximum wild size of each species.

Paraglyphidodon (Abudefduf) melanopus

Yellow-backed Damselfish
- **Distribution:** Indo-Pacific.
- **Length:** 75mm/3in (wild).
- **Diet and feeding:** Chopped meats. Bold feeder.
- **Aquarium behaviour:** May be aggressive towards its own, and smaller, species.

An oblique bright yellow band runs from the snout to the tip of the dorsal fin above a pale violet body. The anal and pelvic fins are light blue, edged with black. The caudal fin is edged with yellow. A spacious tank with plenty of hiding places suits this brilliantly coloured fish very well.

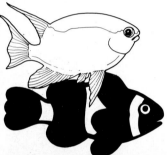

Pomacentrus coeruleus

Blue Devil; Electric-blue Damsel
- **Distribution:** Indo-Pacific.
- **Length:** 100mm/4in (wild), 50mm/2in (aquarium).
- **Diet and feeding:** Chopped meats. Dried food. Bold feeder.
- **Aquarium behaviour:** Pugnacious.

The bright blue coloration of this fish really makes it stand out in the aquarium. There may be some black facial markings. It is a hardy species and, being smaller than most *Dascyllus* sp., poses less of a threat to other tank inmates. It lives peacefully in small groups when young but may turn aggressive when adult.

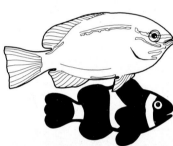

Pomacentrus melanochir

Blue-finned Damsel
- **Distribution:** Pacific.
- **Length:** 80mm/3.2in (wild).
- **Diet and feeding:** Chopped meats. Dried foods.
- **Aquarium behaviour:** Pugnacious. Less of a threat than *Dascyllus* sp.

At first sight, this looks like yet another yellow-tailed blue fish. However, closer inspection will reveal that each scale is dark-edged and that the blue patterning on the head is more obvious. The pelvic fins are yellowish.

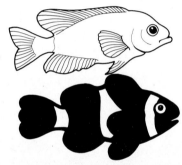

Below:
Paraglyphidodon melanopus
The combination of black-edged pelvic fins and brilliant colours of this Damselfish has inspired several alternative common names: Bow-tie Damsel, Bluefin Damsel and Royal Damsel being just a few more to conjure with. This superbly attractive fish is found over a wide area of the Indo Pacific Oceans.

Right: **Pomacentrus coeruleus**
The brilliant electric blue colour of the Blue Devil makes it an instant eye-catcher in the dealer's tanks, and it will certainly add an extra splash of colour to the home aquarium. Although generally peaceful, it may well alter its ways.

Below right:
Pomacentrus melanochir
Apparently, it takes one of two factors to make a positive identification of the many bright blue fishes with yellow markings: a reliable source of information or a large slice of luck. Such is the confusion over the many similar-looking species that the hobbyist often depends on the second.

A practical reminder
When setting up a new aquarium, plan
everything in advance and make sure
you have all you need close at hand.
Draw a plan of the tank decoration and
always seek advice on electrics if unsure.

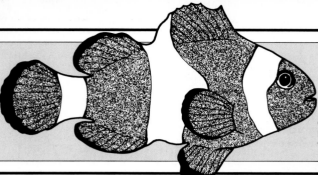

Common Clown (*Amphiprion ocellaris*)
Mature at 80mm (3.2in) and shown as a guide
to the maximum wild size of each species.

Pomacentrus violascens
Yellow-tailed Demoiselle
● **Distribution:** Pacific.
● **Length:** 80mm/3.2in (wild),
50mm/2in (aquarium).
● **Diet and feeding:** Chopped
meats. Dried food. Bold feeder.
● **Aquarium behaviour:**
Pugnacious.

The markings on *Pomacentrus
violascens* resemble those of
P.melanochir, but the tips of the
dorsal and anal fins are yellow and
the yellow of the caudal fin does
not spread so far on to the body.

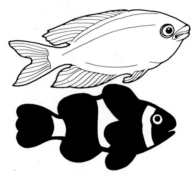

Right: **Pomacentrus sp**
*Contradictory classifications aside,
Damsels remain beautiful.*

Below: **Pomacentrus violascens**
*An intensely coloured specimen.
Also known as* Neopomacentrus.

164

A practical reminder
Use light fittings with waterproofed connectors for the aquarium. Cover glasses reduce the risk of spray or condensation damage to lamps, and also prevent dust entering the tank.

Family: POMADASYIDAE
Grunts

Family characteristics
Grunts can be distinguished from the similar-looking Snappers by differences in their dentition. Many grind their pharyngeal teeth, the resulting sound being amplified by the swimbladder. Juveniles often perform cleaning services for other fishes.

Diet and feeding
Members of this Family of fishes eat well, enjoying a diet of small fishes, shrimps and dried foods.

Aquarium behaviour
Grunts may grow too quickly for the average aquarium.

Below: **Anisotremus virginicus**
This fine adult specimen displays the typical bright blue streaks and dark vertical bars. A similarly marked 'twin' species, A.taeniatus occurs in the Pacific Ocean.

Anisotremus virginicus
Porkfish
● **Distribution:** Caribbean.
● **Length:** 300mm/12in (wild), 150mm/6in (aquarium).
● **Diet and feeding:** In the wild, brittle starfish, crustaceans, etc. In the aquarium, worms, chopped meat foods, etc. Nocturnal feeder.
● **Aquarium behaviour:** Keep juvenile specimens only. A large tank will suit them well.

The body is triangular, the highest part being just behind the head. The steep forehead is fairly long and the eyes are large. The yellow body is streaked with bright blue lines and two black bars cross the head region, one through the eye and one just behind the gill cover.

The juvenile coloration is different: the cream body has black horizontal stripes and a black blotch on the caudal peduncle. The head is yellow and the larger fins have red marks on their edges.

The common collective name of Grunts comes from the noise these fishes make when they are taken from the water. They are very similar to the Majestic Snapper, *Symphorichthys spilurus*.

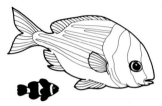

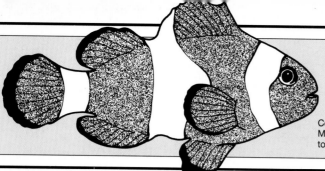

Common Clown (*Amphiprion ocellaris*)
Mature at 80mm (3.2in) and shown as a guide
to the maximum wild size of each species.

Family: SCATOPHAGIDAE
Butterfishes

Family characteristics
Like the Monodactylidae, the fishes in this Family are also estuarine and can be kept with some success in brackish water or even freshwater aquariums.

Diet and feeding
These fishes will eat anything, including greenfood, such as lettuce, spinach and green peas.

Aquarium behaviour
It is usual to keep Scats in the company of *Monodactylus* species.

Below: **Scatophagus argus**
The Scat is a familiar fish to hobbyists, as it can be kept with varying degrees of success in both brackish and fresh water. Adult specimens require full-strength sea water to develop fully. An active fish that will eat anything.

Scatophagus argus
Scat; Argus Fish
● **Distribution:** Indo-Pacific.
● **Length:** 300mm/12in (wild).
● **Diet and feeding:** Will eat anything, including greenstuff. Scavenger.
● **Aquarium behaviour:** Peaceful.

Like *Monodactylus* sp., the Scat is almost equally at home in salt, brackish or even fresh water, but it thrives best in sea water. It frequents coastal and estuarine waters, where it is assured of a good supply of animal waste and other unsavoury material. (Its scientific name means 'excrement eater'). The oblong body is laterally compressed and reminiscent of Butterflyfishes and Angelfishes. It is green-brown with a number of large dark spots, which become less prominent on adult fishes. A deep notch divides the spiny first part and the soft-rayed rear section of the dorsal fin. Juveniles have more red coloration, especially on the fins.

A practical reminder
Remember that the number of tropical marine fishes you can keep is much smaller than the number of coldwater or tropical freshwater species that you could accommodate in a similar tank.

Family: SCIAENIDAE
Croakers and Drums

Family characteristics
Most of the species likely to be suitable for the aquarium come from the western Atlantic, although a species from the opposite side of the American continent, in the eastern Pacific, is another possible contender.

The fishes in this Family are also capable of making sounds by resonating the swimbladder. Their strikingly marked bodies are usually elongated, often with a high first dorsal fin.

Diet and feeding
Most species may pose problems in their day to day care, being somewhat fussy eaters; success in the aquarium relies upon a constant supply of small live foods.

Aquarium behaviour
Fine with peacable tankmates. Will spawn in ideal conditions.

Equetus acuminatus
Cubbyu; High Hat
● **Distribution:** Caribbean.
● **Length:** 250mm/10in (wild), 150mm/6in (aquarium).
● **Diet and feeding:** Crustaceans, molluscs, soft-bodied invertebrates; live foods preferred in captivity. Slow bottom feeder.
● **Aquarium behaviour:** The long fins may be tempting to other fish, so be sure to keep them with non-agressive tankmates.

The main feature of this fish is the very tall first dorsal fin, which is carried erect. The pale body is covered with many horizontal black bands and the black fins have white leading rays. The chin barbels are used to detect food swimming below the fish, which then snaps downward to catch its prey. This species is probably the hardiest of the genus.

Equetus lanceolatus
Jack-knife Fish; Ribbonfish
● **Distribution:** Caribbean.
● **Length:** 250mm/10in (wild).
● **Diet and feeding:** Crustaceans, molluscs, soft-bodied invertebrates. Slow bottom feeder.
● **Aquarium behaviour:** Its fins may be attacked by other fish. Can be aggressive towards its own kind when adult.

The high first dorsal fin of this very beautiful fish has a white-edged black line through it, that continues like a crescent through the body to the tip of the caudal fin. This gives the fish a forward sloping appearance. Further vertical black bars cross the eye and the body just behind the head. A delicate fish in captivity, which may be susceptible to skin infections for no apparent reason.

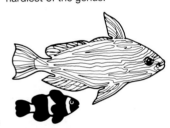

Left: **Equetus acuminatus**
The small barbels underneath the mouth are a good indication that the Cubbyu, or High Hat, is a bottom-feeding species.

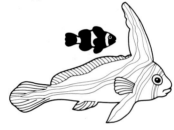

Below: **Equetus lanceolatus**
The strikingly attractive Jack-knife Fish is unfortunately rather delicate, and succumbs easily to shock and stress.

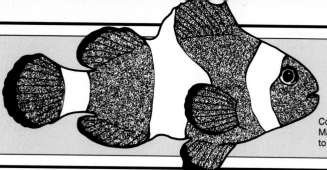

Common Clown (*Amphiprion ocellaris*)
Mature at 80mm (3.2in) and shown as a guide
to the maximum wild size of each species.

Family: SCORPAENIDAE
Dragonfishes, Lionfishes, Scorpionfishes and Turkeyfishes

Here are the exotic 'villains' of the aquarium. They are predatory carnivores that glide up to their prey and engulf it with their large mouths. The highly ornamental fins are not just there for decoration, since they have poisonous stinging cells and will inflict a very painful wound. HANDLE THESE FISHES WITH CARE. If you are stung, bathing the affected area in very hot water will alleviate the pain and help to 'coagulate' the poison.

During spawning, the pair of fishes rises to the upper levels of the water and a gelatinous ball of eggs is released. When they are 10-12mm (about 0.5in) long, the fry sink to the bottom.

Diet and feeding
As you might expect, these fishes require some form of live food – usually goldfishes – if they are to thrive in captivity. Feeding periods can be spaced apart, providing enough food has been taken; in practical terms this can be several goldfish at one 'sitting'. However, they can quite easily be weaned on to a diet of fish meats, suitable frozen foods and dead Lancefish.

Aquarium behaviour
Members of the Scorpaenidae are usually peaceful in captivity, but do not put temptation their way by keeping them with small fishes.

Dendrochirus (Brachirus) brachypterus
Turkeyfish
● **Distribution:** Indo-Pacific, Red Sea.
● **Length:** 170mm/6.7in (wild), 100mm/4in (aquarium).
● **Diet and feeding:** Small fishes, meat foods. Sedentary, engulfs passing prey.
● **Aquarium behaviour:** Keep in a species aquarium or together with larger fish.

A very ornate fish. The red-brown body has many white-edged vertical bars. The dorsal fin is multirayed and tissue spans the elongated rays. When spread, the fins have more obvious transverse patterning. The male has a longer pectoral fin and larger head than the female. At breeding time, the male darkens in colour; females become paler. This species does not grow as large as *Pterois* spp. It has attracted the alternative popular name of Dwarf Lionfish.

Below:
Dendrochirus brachypterus
It is well worth spending some time examining the very fine details of finnage, coloration and the overall appearance of this fish. Camouflage and species-recognition colour patterns, very poisonous defence mechanisms, together with a very healthy appetite, are all combined in this magnificent fish. A talking point for any visitor who sees one of these fishes in your aquarium.

A practical reminder
Fishes caught by means of drugs and explosives are often cheaper, but they are a lot less hardy and likely to have a shorter lifespan than fishes caught by more traditional, respectable methods.

Pterois antennata

Scorpionfish

● **Distribution:** Indo-Pacific, Red Sea.

Length: 250mm/10in (wild), 100-150mm/4-6in (aquarium).

Diet and feeding: Generally live foods such as small fishes, but all lionfishes can be acclimatized to take frozen shrimps and similar items in the aquarium.

Aquarium behaviour: Predatory.

The red bands on the body are wider and less numerous than on *P.volitans*. The white rays of the dorsal and pectoral fins are very elongated. It is possible to distinguish the sexes of all *Pterois* sp. at breeding time since the males darken and the females become paler and have noticeably larger abdomens. A slow-swimming fish that takes sudden gulps of food.

Above: **Pterois antennata**
Considering the bewildering array of fins slowly undulating in the water currents, it is not surprising that the stationary lurking Scorpionfish is often dismissed by its unsuspecting victims as a harmless piece of floating seaweed - until it is too late to escape that great gulping mouth. Perhaps this is its true fascination for some hobbyists who keep these fishes.

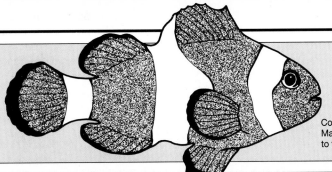

Common Clown (*Amphiprion ocellaris*)
Mature at 80mm (3.2in) and shown as a guide
to the maximum wild size of each species.

Above: **Pterois radiata**
*The dark bars across the head
(from the hornlike growths to the
bottom rear edge of the gill cover)
and body are accentuated by thin
white borders on each side.
Lionfishes often remain motionless
under ledges or in cave mouths
waiting for a potential meal to pass.*

Pterois radiata

White-fin Lionfish
● **Distribution:** Indo-Pacific,
Red Sea.
● **Length:** 250mm/10in (wild),
150mm/6in (aquarium).
● **Diet and feeding:** Smaller fishes
and meaty foods as described for
P. antennata. Slow-swimming
sudden gulper.
● **Aquarium behaviour:** Predatory.

Again, the red bands on the body
are wider and less numerous than
on *P.volitans*. The white rays of the
dorsal and pectoral fins are very
elongated and give this fish a very
graceful appearance. This species
is also known by the alternative
name of *Pteropterus radiatus*.

Pterois volitans

Lionfish; Scorpionfish
● **Distribution:** Indo-Pacific.
● **Length:** 350mm/14in (wild).
● **Diet and feeding:** Smaller fishes
and suitable meaty foods. Slow-
swimming sudden gulper.
● **Aquarium behaviour:**
Unsociable.

Pterois volitans is the most well-
known fish in this group. The
dorsal fin rays are quite separate
and the pectoral fins are only
partially filled with tissue. The
pelvic fins are red, and the anal
and caudal fins are comparatively
clear. Thick and thin red bands
alternate across the body and
there are tentacle-like growths
above the eyes.

Right: **Pterois volitans**
*This 'victim's eye view' of the
Lionfish illustrates another method
of capture; prey is manoeuvred
into a corner or area of no retreat,
the outspread fins preventing any
possibility of escape. Then the
usual quick gulp, and it's all over.*

A practical reminder
It is vitally important that you keep a
constant check on the water conditions
in your marine aquarium; the fishes are
less tolerant of changing conditions
than their freshwater counterparts.

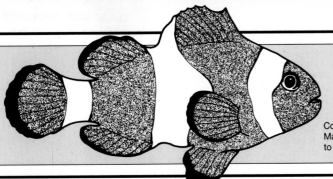

Common Clown (*Amphiprion ocellaris*)
Mature at 80mm (3.2in) and shown as a guide
to the maximum wild size of each species.

Family: SERRANIDAE
Sea Basses and Groupers

Family characteristics
Many juvenile forms of this large Family of predatory fishes have become aquarium favourites. Equally popular are the Basslets, whose brilliant colours ensure them a permanent place in the marine aquarium.

Most of the species within this group are hermaphrodite and therefore lack any clear sexual dimorphism. Even so, many species undergo colour changes during breeding, turning darker, paler, or taking on a bicolour pattern. Not surprisingly, 'females' become distended with eggs – another clue to their likely functional sex.

Diet and feeding
Include crustaceans and meaty foods in the diet of these fishes.

Aquarium behaviour
The majority of species need a large aquarium.

Anthias squamipinnis
Wreckfish; Orange Sea Perch;
Lyre-tail Coralfish
● **Distribution:** Indo-Pacific.
● **Length:** 125mm/5in (wild).
● **Diet and feeding:** Preferably live foods, or meat foods. Bold and prefers moving foods.
● **Aquarium behaviour:** Peaceful.

This very beautiful orange-red fish has elongated rays in the dorsal fin, a deeply forked caudal fin and long pelvic fins. It is a shoaling species that needs companions of the same species. Males have an elongated third dorsal spine are usually larger and more conspicuously coloured than females. Dominant males are quite happy for a harem to follow them.

Below: **Anthias squamipinnis**
The gorgeous colour and extended fins of the male Wreckfish are bound to attract the attention of a passing female, only too happy to join a growing band of admirers.

A practical reminder
Maintain the pH value of the water in the aquarium in the range 7.9-8.3. A falling pH value means that the water is losing its ability to remain in a stable condition; carry out a water change.

Calloplesiops altivelis
Marine Betta
● **Distribution:** Indo-Pacific.
● **Length:** 150mm/6in (wild).
● **Diet and feeding:** Small fishes, meaty foods. Predatory.
● **Aquarium behaviour:** Err on the side of caution, and do not keep with small fishes.

A very beautiful and deceptive fish: the trick is to decide which way it is facing, since the dorsal fin has a 'false-eye' marking near its rear edge. The dark brown body is covered with light blue spots and all the fins are very elongated. This species swims near the top of the aquarium.

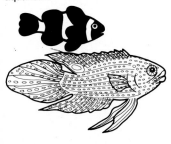

Right: **Calloplesiops altivelis**
The fins of this fish are very similar to those of the freshwater Siamese Fighting Fish, Betta splendens, *hence the popular name.*

Left: **Cephalopholis miniatus**
Ranging from the Red Sea to the mid-Pacific, the Coral Trout inhabits the coral reefs, looking for a meal of smaller fishes. It often hides away in caves or under ledges, denying the fishkeeper a view of its spectacular colouring. An alternative, and very apt, name for this species is Jewel Bass.

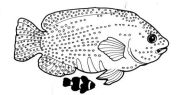

Cephalopholis miniatus
Coral Trout; Red Grouper
● **Distribution:** Indo-Pacific.
● **Length:** 450mm/18in (wild).
● **Diet and feeding:** Smaller fishes and meaty foods. Predatory.
● **Aquarium behaviour:** Do not keep with small fishes.

The body and the dorsal, anal and caudal fins of C. miniatus are bright red and covered with bright blue spots. However, the pectoral and pelvic fins are plain red. Other fishes bear a resemblance to this species, but they do not have the distinguishing rounded caudal fin.

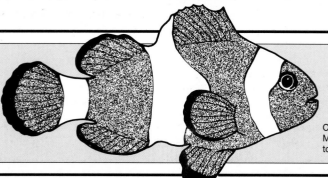

Common Clown (*Amphiprion ocellaris*)
Mature at 80mm (3.2in) and shown as a guide
to the maximum wild size of each species.

Chromileptis altivelis

Pantherfish; Polka-Dot Grouper
- **Distribution:** Indo-Pacific.
- **Length:** 500mm/20in (wild), 300mm/12in (aquarium).
- **Diet and feeding:** Live foods. Bold feeder.
- **Aquarium behaviour:** It is better not to keep this species with smaller fishes. However, its smallish mouth makes it the least harmful of all the Grouper fishes.

Juveniles have black blotches on a white body – effective disruptive camouflage. As the fish matures, these blotches increase in number but decrease in size. The result is a very graceful fish, and one that is constantly on the move in the tank.

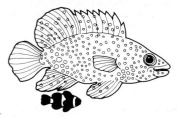

Above: **Chromileptis altivelis**
A splendid juvenile in fine colour, living up to its common name of Polka-Dot Grouper. As is often the case, the most beautiful of fishes are quite likely to be the most predatory. For this reason, do not be tempted to keep this fish with smaller species in the aquarium.

A practical reminder
Cutting corners to reduce expenses is a false economy, especially in the delicately balanced world of the marine tank. Neglecting regular maintenance practices is another recipe for failure.

Gramma loreto
Royal Gramma
● **Distribution:** Western Atlantic.
● **Length:** 130mm/5in (wild), 75mm/3in (aquarium).
● **Diet and feeding:** Eats a wide variety of foods, including chopped shrimp, greenstuff and dried foods.
● **Aquarium behaviour:** This cave-dwelling fish should be acclimatized gradually to bright light. It may resent other cave-dwelling species, particularly the Yellow-headed Jawfish, *Opisthognathus aurifrons.* Aggressive towards its own kind.

The main feature of this species is its remarkable colouring. The front half of the body is magenta, the rear half bright golden-yellow. A thin black line slants backwards through the eye. These somewhat secretive cave dwellers should not be kept with boisterous species. An almost identical species, *Pseudochromis paccagnellae*, has a narrow white line dividing the two main body colours.

Spawning activity has been observed – paradoxically, not in nature but in captivity. Four fish grouped themselves into two 'pairs', each comprising one small and one large fish. The larger fish lined a cave with algal threads and then appeared to incubate a mouthful of eggs. The eggs were later rejected and proved to be infertile, but this does shed light on the possible reproductive methods practised by this species. The dissimilar sizes of the fishes making up the 'pairs' seems to bear out other reports that the male fish is usually larger than the female.

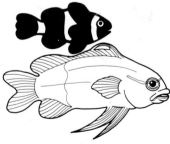

Left: **Gramma loreto**
As far as coloration goes, if big is beautiful then small can be simply stunning – as this Royal Gramma clearly demonstrates. A cave-dwelling fish, it is often very possessive, positively resenting any intrusion by other fishes into its chosen home. An aquarium stocked with many soft corals and hideaways suits this fish perfectly.

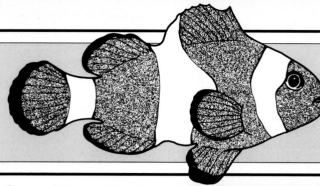

Common Clown (*Amphiprion ocellaris*)
Mature at 80mm (3.2in) and shown as a guide
to the maximum wild size of each species.

Grammistes sexlineatus

*Golden-striped Grouper; White/
Black-Striped Sea Bass*
● **Distribution:** Indo-Pacific.
● **Length:** 250mm/10in (wild).
● **Diet and feeding:** Animal and
meaty foods. Bold.
● **Aquarium behaviour:** Do not
keep with smaller fishes.

Alternate black and white
horizontal stripes cover the body.
Although a good aquarium subject,
it can give off toxic secretions
when frightened, annoyed or even
in the process of dying. It is
unlikely to reach its full size when
kept in captivity.

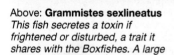

Above: **Grammistes sexlineatus**
*This fish secretes a toxin if
frightened or disturbed, a trait it
shares with the Boxfishes. A large*
aquarium containing this grouper
(introduced ahead of suitably sized
tankmates), may prove successful;
the grouper may become tame.

Lutjanus sebae

Emperor Snapper
● **Distribution:** Indo-Pacific.
● **Length:** 900mm/36in (wild).
● **Diet and feeding:** Animal and
meaty foods. Bold.
● **Aquarium behaviour:** Although
peaceful, do not keep this species
with smaller fishes. Despite its
attractive coloration, it will soon
outgrow the tank, and is therefore
not really suitable for anything but
the largest public aquarium.

The white body has three red-
brown transverse bands: the first
runs from the snout up the
forehead and the second is
'L-shaped' running vertically down
from the dorsal fin to the pelvic fins
and along the ventral surface into
the front half of the anal fin. The
third band is crescent shaped,
beginning in the rear of the dorsal
fin and crossing the caudal
peduncle into the lower half of the
caudal fin, which has a similarly
coloured bar on the top edge.

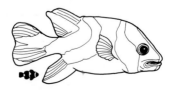

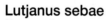

Right: **Lutjanus sebae**
*This Emperor Snapper is not only a
favourite with marine aquarists, it
also makes good eating! Sadly, the
bold coloration fades with age.*

Mirolabrichthys tuka

Purple Queen; Butterfly Perch
● **Distribution:** Pacific.
● **Length:** 125mm/5in (wild).
● **Diet and feeding:** Chopped
meaty foods. Bold.
● **Aquarium behaviour:** Generally
peaceful.

The sides of the body are purple,
topped with yellow. The head is
also yellow, while the fins are light
blue. Its gorgeous colours and
pointed snout make this fish easy
to recognize. Unfortunately, this
species does not survive long in
captivity. In the similarly coloured
species, *M.evansi*, the yellow at
the top of the body extends into
the caudal fin.

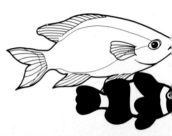

A practical reminder
Cultivate a good relationship with your dealer. This will enable him to get to know your system and your fishes and thus be in a better position to offer advice in the event of any problems.

Left: **Mirolabrichthys tuka**
The delicate colours and 'snouty' appearance make this species both easy to identify and tempting to own, but it is a delicate species.

Above: **Mirolabrichthys evansi**
Another very attractive and related species, the yellow extending into the caudal fin; like M.tuka, it is difficult to keep in captivity.

Pseudochromis paccagnella

False Gramma; Dottyback; Royal Dottyback; Paccagnella's Dottyback
● **Distribution:** Pacific.
● **Length:** 50mm/2in (wild).
● **Diet and feeding:** Finely chopped meat foods, brineshrimp.
● **Aquarium behaviour:** Do not keep with lively fishes. May tend to nip at other fishes.

This species is almost identical to *Gramma loreto*, but a thin white line – often incomplete or hard to see – divides the two main body colours.

Left:
Pseudochromis paccagnella
The False Gramma – or Dottyback – requires similar aquarium conditions to its lookalike relative, the Royal Gramma. Provide a tank well stocked with soft corals and convenient retreats to ensure a sense of security.

Common Clown (*Amphiprion ocellaris*)
Mature at 80mm (3.2in) and shown as a guide
to the maximum wild size of each species.

Symphorichthys spilurus
Majestic Snapper
- **Distribution:** Pacific.
- **Length:** 320mm/12.6in (wild).
- **Diet and feeding:** Meaty foods. Bold feeder.
- **Aquarium behaviour:** Do not keep with smaller fishes.

This fish is almost identical in colour to *Anisotremus virginicus*, the Atlantic Porkfish. The yellow body has horizontal blue lines and the fins are yellow. Two vertical black bars cross the head and there is a distinguishing white-ringed black blotch on the caudal peduncle. The dorsal fin develops extremely long filamentous extensions.

Above: **Symphorichthys spilurus**
Only the narrow band of land between the Pacific and Atlantic cuts off this species from the almost identical Atlantic Porkfish, Anisotremus virginicus *(described on page 165), which lacks the long extensions and caudal spot.*

Family: SIGANIDAE
Rabbitfishes

Family characteristics
The Rabbitfishes have deep oblong bodies and are fairly laterally compressed. The mouth is small and equipped for browsing on algae and other vegetation. The spines on the dorsal and anal fins are poisonous and so be sure to handle these fishes extremely carefully. Their alternative common name is 'Spinefoot', a reference to the fact that unsuspecting waders who disturb grazing fish risk a wound on the foot caused by the fishes' spines. Juveniles are often more brightly coloured than adults.

Only a dozen or so species belong to this Family, but they have an economic significance in the tropics, where they are caught for food. The one species that is especially familiar to hobbyists, *Lo (Siganus) vulpinus*, has a tubular mouth, which contrasts with the normal rabbit-shaped mouth of the Family.

Some reports of spawning in captivity – albeit of species not featured here – indicate that changing some of the water, or even decreasing its depth, may trigger off spawning activities.

Diet and feeding
Rabbitfishes must have vegetable matter in their diet, although they will adapt to established dried foods and live foods in the aquarium.

Aquarium behaviour
Active, fast-growing fishes that need plenty of swimming space.

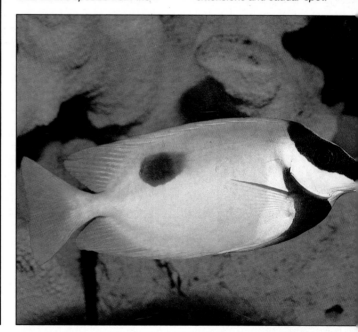

Lo (Siganus) vulpinus

Foxface; Fox-fish; Badgerfish
- **Distribution:** Pacific.
- **Length:** 250mm/10in (wild).
- **Diet and feeding:** Most foods, but must have vegetable matter. Bold grazer that adopts a typical 'head-down' feeding attitude.
- **Aquarium behaviour:** Lively but peaceable, although it may be aggressive towards members of its own species.

The white head has two broad black bands: one runs obliquely back from the snout, through the eye and up the forehead; the second band is triangular, beginning below the throat and ending behind the gill cover. This coloration obviously gave rise to the common name of Badgerfish among European hobbyists, more familiar with the Badger than other hobbyists who, for some reason, feel the fish's face looks more like that of a fox. Although physically similar to the Surgeonfishes, it has no spine on the caudal peduncle, and the pelvic fins are not very well developed, having only a few rays.

Females are generally larger than males; at breeding time, the females are plumper, with larger genital openings.

Above: **Lo vulpinus**
The Foxface, or Badgerfish, has a tubular mouth, which is rather at variance with the more rabbitlike shape characteristic of other members of this Family.

Above right: **Siganus virgatus**
The Silver Badgerfish has a more typically shaped mouth, which is ideally suited to grazing and rasping algae from firm surfaces. Remember that the dorsal and anal spines are dangerous.

A practical reminder
If you can consistently patronize one dealer you will be able to locate the source of any problems. This will be frustrated if you have bought fishes or equipment from many different sources.

Family: SYNANCEIIDAE
Stonefishes

Family characteristics
Like sharks, these fishes hold a morbid fascination for many fishkeepers. The lifestyle of these fishes is quite simple; they lie almost completely concealed among rocks and seaweed, or semi-buried in the sand, waiting for food to come along. Their body colour and irregular shape provide the perfect disguise. These very dangerous fishes have erectile spines that can inject an extremely poisonous toxin. Although a wound may not be fatal, an affected limb may have to be amputated. Handle these species with extreme caution. If you should ever visit the natural habitat of these fish, always wear protective shoes and investigate rocks and corals with a stick, never with your hands.

Diet and feeding
Predators, but almost by default in that they wait for unsuspecting prey to venture too close to them.

Aquarium behaviour
Apart from their 'horror' value, these fishes are not likely to display a great deal of activity. They are usually kept as 'status symbols' in species tanks.

Above: **Synanceja horrida**
If you were a fish, this is about the only part of the Stonefish that you would recognize as it lies in wait for passing prey, the rest being perfectly camouflaged against the substrate. As a fishkeeper, be sure to handle this fish with extreme care, principally because of the very poisonous spines.

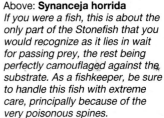

Synanceja horrida
Stonefish
● **Distribution:** Indo-Pacific.
● **Length:** 300mm/12in (wild).
● **Diet and feeding:** Will eat anything that it can swallow. Sedentary.
● **Aquarium behaviour:** Keep only with larger fish; in a species aquarium it will not require quite as much space as the more free-swimming species.

So effective is the natural camouflage of this species that it is almost impossible to describe! Generally, it is a mottled brown, with spots of more brown or red. The interior of the mouth is a paler colour. Beware of moving rocks or other similar decorations in the tank, just in case they aren't entirely what they seem!

Siganus virgatus
Silver Badgerfish
● **Distribution:** Pacific.
● **Length:** 260mm/10.2in (wild).
● **Diet and feeding:** Live foods, meat foods and plenty of greenstuff. Bold grazer.
● **Aquarium behaviour:** Lively but peaceable, although it may be aggressive towards fellow members of its own species.

The silvery yellow body is more oval and the head more rounded than in the previous species. Again, the head has two badger-like black bars, the second of which begins narrowly just below the pectoral fins and broadens as it runs up to the top of the body. The head and forepart of the body are covered with blue lines, producing an intricate pattern.

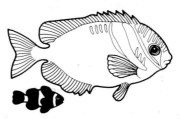

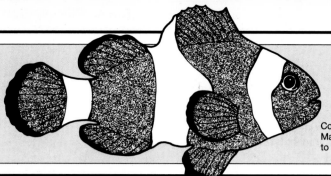

Common Clown (*Amphiprion ocellaris*)
Mature at 80mm (3.2in) and shown as a guide
to the maximum wild size of each species.

Family: SYNGNATHIDAE
Pipefishes and Seahorses

Family characteristics
Every fishkeeper loves the Seahorse, and the equally appealing Pipefish, which could be described as a 'straightened out' version of the Seahorse. Pipefishes are found among crevices on coral reefs, whereas Seahorses, being poor swimmers, anchor themselves to coral branches with their prehensile tails. Many Pipefishes are estuarine species, and are therefore able to tolerate varying salinities, even entering fresh water.

When Seahorses reproduce, the female uses her ovopositor tube to deposit the eggs into the male's abdominal pouch, where they are fertilized and subsequently incubated. Incubation periods range from two weeks to two months, depending on the species.

Diet and feeding
Seahorses and Pipefishes have small mouths and require quantities of small live foods to thrive; brineshrimp and rotifers are suitable, but some fishkeepers use Guppy fry.

Aquarium behaviour
Pipefishes and Seahorses do best in a quiet aquarium.

Dunkerocampus dactyliophorus
Banded Pipefish

● **Distribution:** Pacific.
● **Length:** 180mm/7in (wild).
● **Diet and feeding:** Very small live foods. Browser.
● **Aquarium behaviour:** Needs a quiet aquarium.

The entire length of the body is covered with alternate light and dark rings. The most distinctive feature of the fish is the disproportionately large caudal fin, which is white with a red central blotch. The other fins are small and hard to see, and there are no pelvic fins. The snout is very long. The eggs are carried by the male on the ventral surface of the body.

Right: **Hippocampus hudsonius**
A pinkish individual of this elegant species. Seahorses adopt a vertical position when at rest. When swimming, they lean forward, propulsion being provided by the fan-like dorsal fin.

Below:
Dunkerocampus dactyliophorus
The Banded (or Harlequin) Pipefish is a brightly coloured and fascinating addition to a quiet aquarium. Note the tiny pectoral fins and dorsal fin halfway along.

A practical reminder
As interest in marine fishkeeping grows around the world, the hobby magazines have increased their marine-orientated articles. These offer a good source of information on up-to-date practices.

Hippocampus hudsonius

Florida Seahorse
- **Distribution:** Western Atlantic.
- **Length:** 150mm/6in (wild).
- **Diet and feeding:** Small animal foods. Browser.
- **Aquarium behaviour:** Needs a quiet, non-boisterous aquarium.

The pelvic and caudal fins are absent, and the anal fin is very small. The tail is prehensile. The coloration of this species is variable; individuals may be grey, brown, yellow or red. The male incubates the young in the abdominal pouch.

Hippocampus kuda

Yellow Seahorse
- **Distribution:** Indo-Pacific.
- **Length:** 250mm/10in (wild) – measured vertically.
- **Diet and feeding:** Plenty of live foods, young freshwater livebearer fry, very small crustaceans, brineshrimp. *Daphnia* etc. Browser.
- **Aquarium behaviour:** Best kept in a species tank.

Newly imported specimens may be grey, but once they have settled into the aquarium, the body takes on the a yellow hue. An irresistible fish with a fascinating method of reproduction. The male incubates the fertilized eggs in his pouch for four to five weeks before they hatch. This species needs anchorage points in the aquarium, such as marine algae and other suitably branched decorations.

Above: **Hippocampus kuda**
Apart from the fascination of its unusual body shape, with its equine appearance, and amusing activity among the coral branches, the Seahorse also displays a very different method of reproduction – the male incubating the fertilized eggs in his abdominal pouch.

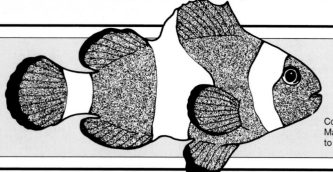

Common Clown (*Amphiprion ocellaris*)
Mature at 80mm (3.2in) and shown as a guide
to the maximum wild size of each species.

Family: TETRAODONTIDAE
Puffers

Family characteristics
Puffers are generally smaller than Porcupinefishes and smooth scaled. Their jaws are fused, but a divided bone serves as front teeth. 'Tetraodon' means four toothed (two teeth at the top and two at the bottom), whereas 'Diodon' means two teeth (one at the top and one at the bottom). These fishes use their pectoral fins to achieve highly manoeuvrable propulsion, but the pelvic fins are absent. Their inflating capabilities vary from species to species; *Tetraodon* sp. – among which are some freshwater members – are 'fully-inflatable', but members of the genus *Canthigaster* can only manage partial inflation. The flesh is poisonous.

Diet and feeding
Puffers will eat readily in the aquarium, taking finely chopped meat foods. They have a bold feeding manner.

Aquarium behaviour
Generally peaceful but occasionally may be aggressive towards other fishes. Do not keep with invertebrates.

Arothron hispidus
White-spotted Blow fish
● **Distribution :** Indo-Pacfic, Red Sea.
● **Length:** 500mm/20in (wild).
● **Diet and feeding:** Finely chopped meat foods. Cruncher.
● **Aquarium behaviour:** Peaceful. Do not keep with invertebrates.

The distinctive features of this species are the number of bluish white spots over the patchy grey body. These spots are not so pronounced in adult fishes. Just behind the gill cover, and at the base of the pectoral fins, there is a dark patch surrounded by a circular yellow pattern. Like most Puffers, the flesh is poisonous.

Arothron meleagris
Spotted Puffer; Guinea Fowl Puffer; Golden Puffer
● **Distribution:** Indo Pacific, Red Sea.
● **Length:** 300mm/12in (wild).
● **Diet and feeding:** Finely chopped meat foods. Cruncher.
● **Aquarium behaviour:** Peaceful, but do not keep with invertebrates.

Although a plain yellow colour phase occurs, normally the brown-grey body is densely covered with white spots, very similar to the female *Ostracion meleagris* (see page 140), although the mouth is clearly different in structure. When kept in a spacious aquarium, it will be less likely to release its poison under stress from other fishes.

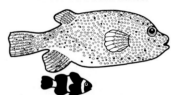

Below: **Arothron meleagris**
Like all Puffers, the Spotted Puffer will inflate its body when disturbed or frightened, but do not provoke it.

Left: **Arothron hispidus**
As members of the Tetraodontidae, *Pufferfish have their teeth fused together to form four powerful teeth (Tetra= four, odon= toothed) at the front of the mouth, which they use to crunch up molluscs and crustaceans. Just in front of the white-rimmed eyes, two tentacle-like nostrils are visible.*

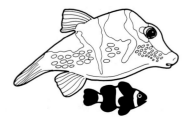

Canthigaster margaritatus (C. solandri)
Sharpnosed Puffer
● **Distribution:** Indo-Pacific, Red Sea.
● **Length:** 120mm/4.7in (wild), 50mm/2in (aquarium).
● **Diet and feeding:** Finely chopped meat foods. Bold cruncher.
● **Aquarium behaviour:** Peaceful, except towards members of its own kind.

This spectacularly patterned fish has a gold-brown body and a caudal fin covered with pale spots. A blue wavy line replaces the spots on the upper part of the body and a large white-edged black spot appears at the base of the dorsal fin. The fish swims with its caudal fin folded. The pelvic fins are absent. Some authorities place this genus in a separate group, the Canthigasteridae.

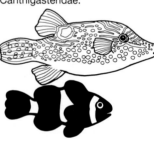

Canthigaster valentini
Black-saddled Puffer
● **Distribution:** Indo-Pacific.
● **Length:** 200mm/8in (wild), 75mm/3in (aquarium).
● **Diet and feeding:** Finely chopped meaty foods. Bold cruncher.
● **Aquarium behaviour:** Peaceful, although it has a reputation for nipping the fins of species with long fins, and may not tolerate its own kind.

The lower half of the body is cream in colour and covered with small brown dots. The upper part has four saddle-shaped dark areas; the one covering the forehead also has blue lines. These blue lines also occur on the two narrow vertical bars that reach three-quarters of the way down the sides of the fish between the head and dorsal fin. There is a final plain patch on the top of the caudal peduncle. A black spot at the base of the dorsal fin may merge with the other dark markings. The fins are red, but for the caudal fin, which is yellow. The pelvic fins are absent. This species is considered by some to be synonymous with *Canthigaster cinctus*.

A practical reminder
Breeding marine fishes is news! If you attempt to breed your fishes (or they oblige anyway), do keep records of successes, failures, methods used, to benefit the less experienced among us.

Above:
Canthigaster margaritatus
This Sharpnosed Puffer is decorated with a most attractive spotted pattern, with bright radiating stripes around the eyes and top of the body. The clamped caudal fin is a characteristic of this fish's swimming action. They make good scavengers around the aquarium, usually adopting a head-down attitude, always on the lookout for meaty foods, particularly relishing snails. This wide-ranging species has, not surprisingly, also earned alternative names of C.solandri *and* C.papua, *presumably from different discoverers.*

Left: **Canthigaster valentini**
The Black-saddled Puffer has strong jaws with which it can crunch coral in its search for food. A nip from its teeth can be very painful. Although its slow swimming actions presumably make it an excellent target, its poisonous skin secretions give it a good defence against predators.

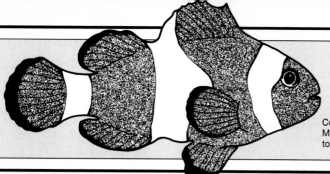

Common Clown (*Amphiprion ocellaris*)
Mature at 80mm (3.2in) and shown as a guide
to the maximum wild size of each species.

Family: THERAPONIDAE
Tigerfishes

Family characteristics
The most familiar species in this Serranid-related Family, the Target Fish, is not confined to the marine aquarium, as it can be kept in brackish and even freshwater tanks. It is a common inshore fish, entering bays and estuaries. The dorsal fin appears to be divided, the front spiny part being separated by a notch from the softer rayed rear half.

The adhesive eggs are deposited in hollows or under stones and guarded by the male until they hatch.

Diet and feeding
These are carnivorous fishes that need meaty animal foods.

Aquarium behaviour
Can be quarrelsome with their own species if kept in overcrowded conditions, so allow plenty of space in the aquarium.

Therapon jarbua
Target Fish; Crescent Bass; Tiger Bass
● **Distribution:** Indo-Pacific.
● **Length:** 250mm/10in (wild), 150mm/6in (aquarium).
● **Diet and feeding:** Animal foods. Predatory.
● **Aquarium behaviour:** A constantly moving fish, possibly too lively (and too fast-growing) for other species in the same aquarium. It does well in brackish water aquariums with species such as *Monodactylus* (page 136) and *Scatophagus* (page 166).

This species is easily recognizable by the dark horizontal markings on the body, which appear concentric around the dorsal fin – and thus target-shaped when viewed from above. The two dorsal fins and each lobe of the striped caudal fin have dark tips.

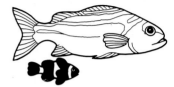

Below: **Therapon jarbua**
Fishkeepers fortunate enough to take their vacation in the tropics and taking their morning constitutional walk along the beach, can often see the Target Fish as it cruises into the shallows almost around their feet.

A practical reminder
If you have reached this page, then you
are well on your way to becoming a
successful marine aquarist and your
aquarium should soon be the envy of all
who see it. Good fishkeeping!

Family: ZANCLIDAE
Tobies

Family characteristics
The single species of this Family, *Zanclus canescens*, is a shoaling
fish found throughout the Indo-Pacific Ocean. Scientifically, it is
more closely related to the Acanthuridae (through the Suborder
Acanthuroidea), particularly because of the physical form of the
young fish, although it is difficult to see any resemblance at first
glance in the adult. Other authorities feel that it is superficially
nearer to the Chaetodontidae Family, especially to the similar
genus *Heniochus*. The common name of Moorish Idol is derived
from the high esteem in which the fish is held by some Moslem
populations. When caught by them it is returned to the water with
some ceremony.

Diet and feeding
Small crustaceans, chopped meat foods and plenty of greenstuff.

Aquarium behaviour
Since it may quarrel with others of the same species, it is best to
keep only a single Moorish Idol in the aquarium.

Below: **Zanclus canescens**
*Although the Moorish Idol is more
closely related to Surgeonfishes
than to Butterflyfishes, it lacks
scalpels on the caudal peduncle,
but does have hornlike projections
in front of the eyes. There is often
some debate about the validity of
the scientific name or the often
quoted Z. cornutus.*

Zanclus canescens
Moorish Idol
● **Distribution:** Indo-Pacific.
● **Length:** 250mm/10in (wild),
125mm/5in (aquarium).
● **Diet and feeding:** Small
crustaceans, chopped meat foods
and plenty of greenstuff. Bold
grazer in nature but shy in the
company of other fishes.
● **Aquarium behaviour:** A
sensitive shoaling fish in the wild
that is difficult to acclimatize to
aquarium life, especially feeding,
and also may be intolerant of
disease remedies. In the close
confines of the aquarium, these
fishes may quarrel among
themselves. The ploy of keeping a
number of youngsters together
does not always turn out for the
best either, as the dominant fish
often bullies the rest into
submission and eventual decline.
On balance, therefore, it is best to
keep only one of these fishes in the
aquarium.

Three black vertical bands cross
the body: one from the pelvic fins
to the beginning of dorsal fin,
another midway along the anal and
dorsal fins, the third across the
caudal fin. Behind the first black
band, the body is yellow.
Immediately in front of the eyes,
across the beaklike snout, is a
yellow saddle marking. The dorsal
fin is extremely elongated, often
trailing well past the caudal fin.
Adult fishes have hornlike
protruberances in front of the eyes.

This is not really a fish for
beginners. However, if you obtain
a healthy specimen and the water
conditions are good, with low
nitrate levels, a Moorish Idol will
eat virtually anything and thrive in
the aquarium.

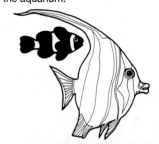

TROPICAL INVERTEBRATES

Right: *The Banded Coral Shrimp,*
Stenopus hispidus *makes a very
colourful addition to the aquarium.
When other shrimps become
rivals, it lives up to its alternative
common name of Boxing Shrimp.
It also performs cleaning actions,
removing parasites from fishes.*

*The attraction of the marine aquarium is not limited to the
fishes. The decorative corals, for example, add almost as
much beauty to the underwater scene. Anyone who has
travelled extensively under the sea – even if only as a
television viewer – will vouch for this. However, these
corals are usually dead skeletons and can only be brought
to some simulation of real life by adding other living
creatures that live on or around them in nature.*

*These animals include the sea anemones – which play
host to the anemonefishes – the very colourful crabs,
shrimps and prawns, tubeworms and featherdusters,
starfishes, sea cucumbers, sea slugs and sea urchins.
Providing sufficient care is taken to choose compatible
tankmates, many of these animals can be kept alongside the
fishes to present a truly complete underwater scene.
Alternatively, you may want to set up a completely
independent invertebrate collection, in which case you can
progress to the stunningly colourful and fascinating soft
corals, which open and close during the day like
underwater flowers in the moving water currents.*

*To keep invertebrates you will need to learn different
skills: many are normally sedentary, hardly moving from
their coral or rockbound sites. Feeding can be a collective
affair for filter feeding species – use a liquidizer to blend
normal aquarium foods into a more acceptable form – but
you will need to feed sea anemones by hand, placing
morsels of food into their tentacles with tweezers. Any food
that is missed will be taken by the scavenging crabs,
shrimps or starfishes, but do not include these animals in
the collection simply for this scavenging purpose.*

*Invertebrates will reproduce in the aquarium; sea
anemones, for example, will simply divide, or expel young
forms to increase their numbers. Hermit crabs make
fascinating subjects for observation, especially when they
are 'house hunting' for larger premises as they outgrow
their former dwellings. Even at night there is activity in the
aquarium; many of the soft corals and similar animals
emit small points of light in the darkness.*

Left: *The multitudinous tentacles of*
Radianthus ritteri *make it an ideal
safe 'home' for Clownfishes of the*
Amphiprion *genus. Several fishes
may take up tenancy in a large sea
anemone such as this.*

The invertebrates kept in the marine aquarium range from the sedentary tubeworms and fanworms to the more mobile sea anemones, shrimps, hermit crabs, starfish and sea slugs. (The care of live corals and 'living rock' is a specialist subject and beyond the scope of this encyclopedia.) In this section, we look at the general care of invertebrates and the range of specimens available for the marine aquarium.

General care

As a rule, only if you are an experienced fishkeeper with sufficient information about the compatibility (or otherwise) of fishes and invertebrates should you try to keep both in the same aquarium. Some combinations are easier than others. It is clear, for example, that the 'inoffensive' seahorses could be safely kept together with invertebrates to create a compatible underwater marine community.

Obviously, if you decide to keep invertebrates you will have to make special provision for feeding them. Many invertebrates are not mobile enough to chase, catch or even reach their food before it is snapped up by fast-moving fishes. Others require much finer foods than fish and, again, the food usually has to be brought to them and not the other way round.

Feeding methods vary too, and many invertebrates need to be fed individually. Sometimes the presentation of the food is important. For instance, it is normal practice to put finely liquidized fish meat in the aquarium for filter feeders. This emulsion of food will be taken in by filter feeders and, in addition, may help to spur the proliferation of microorganisms in the water, which will also be taken as food later on. Obviously, it will be very hard to judge how much has been taken, so after about an hour use an efficient power filter to clear the water of uneaten food.

It is not necessary to feed invertebrates as frequently as fish; every two days is usually quite sufficient for sea anemones, for example. However, you may well enjoy hand feeding creatures such as shrimps and crabs at more regular intervals – always taking care not to overfeed them of course! Useful clearing up operations are also performed by bottom-scavenging shrimps and crabs, as well as sea cucumbers.

Invertebrates appreciate water movement much more than fishes, because they rely on the water currents to bring food circulating near to them. A reverse-flow biological filtration system fulfils this purpose very adequately. It keeps the floor of the aquarium clear of packed-down debris and brings water currents up around the more sedentary life forms. It is also a good idea to vary the water direction around the aquarium from time to time; strategically placed airstones operated at intervals are ideal for this.

Like fishes, many invertebrates appreciate algae growths. These help to absorb nitrogenous wastes and also provide browsing material and hiding places. Accordingly, a well-lit aquarium should be the order of the day, a fact that is often borne out by the way in which some invertebrates bask in areas lit by strong spotlights.

A top layer of soft coral sand will benefit species that burrow into it at night and those that constantly sift the substrate for food, such as sea cucumbers.

Invertebrates are very susceptible to changes in water conditions; they cannot tolerate any metal pollution – particularly by copper. This can be a problem if you have to treat the mixed aquarium with proprietary copper-based medicines, and this is another good reason for keeping invertebrates in a separate tank.

Some invertebrates are more nitrite tolerant than others, which makes them ideal for introducing into an almost mature aquarium. Generally you should play safe and not introduce invertebrates into a brand new set up.

Selecting healthy specimens

As relatively little is known about invertebrates, it is not easy to be sure that you are buying a healthy specimen. Always try to carry out a thorough visual inspection before making a final choice.

Even if they are not moving around, most invertebrates show signs of life, constantly twitching their tentacles, for example. Make sure that creatures are complete, although it is true that a missing limb sometimes regenerates. Starfish and sea anemones should be firm to the touch and not hanging limp and 'empty'. Examine tubeworms to see if their tentacles retract when touched. When disturbed, most molluscs and other life forms shut or retract their tentacles. Avoid any specimens where the tentacles are hanging half in or half out of the tube and any where the tube is obviously empty or damaged.

Introducing invertebrates

The same general guide lines that apply to fishes should be observed when introducing invertebrates to the aquarium (see pages 44-45). Quarantine new additions in an *unmedicated* isolation tank before introducing them into the main collection. This isolation tank should closely resemble a permanently set-up tank and be complete with a good growth of algae. Here, the new additions can be screened for disease, although they cannot be treated with proprietary remedies, due to their intolerance of copper.

Below: *The fascination of watching life in an invertebrate aquarium is never ending. Many of the animals are so small that you may be unaware of their activities. They are only seen occasionally and then not always in the same place twice. More mobile invertebrates, such as shrimps or nudibranchs, constantly disappear and reappear amid the luxuriant growths of coral*

A SELECTION OF SPECIES

Clams

The genus *Tridacna* includes the Giant Clams (*T.gigas*) that are featured in all good underwater thriller movies. As well as obtaining food by filter feeding, the clam also digests the algae within its mantle. *T.elegans* is a smaller species. One problem with clams is that their normal activity is at such a low level that the fishkeeper does not always notice when they die. On the other hand, empty clam shells make excellent refuges and aquarium decorations.

Corals

Not all corals are hard, skeletal remains to be used simply as marine aquarium decorations. Living soft corals range in shape and form from delightfully delicate lace-like growths to the huge 'dining-table' configurations, topped with horizontal slabs. All are covered with millions of tiny tentacles that constantly wave in the water, both to breathe and to seize any passing planktonic foods. When tentacles retract, the surface of the coral becomes almost skin-like in its smoothness. At night, or under ultraviolet light, it is not unusual for the corals to emit tiny points of light. Obviously, such diverse forms of coral are not all suited for inclusion in the general bustle of the community aquarium, but a separate tank housing a self perpetuating number of soft corals and a few of the more mobile invertebrate life-forms will prove to be every bit as attractive as a marine aquarium stocked with fishes. A selection of corals suitable for inclusion in the marine aquarium are shown on this page.

Above: **Tridacna elegans**
The fringes of the shell are mirror images of one other, and form a tight fit when the Clam shuts.

Above:
Gorgonarie acanthomuricea
Gorgonarians take their name from their similarity to Medusa.

Above: **Tubipora musica**
The white tips on this piece of red Organ Pipe Coral – a favourite decoration – are the live polyps.

Below: **Dendronephthya sp.**
This soft coral makes its home either on rock surfaces or buried partially in the sand.

Left: **Euphyllia picteti**
This coral's skeleton has radiating ridges, but these are hidden by the mass of waving tentacles.

Above: **Xenia sp.**
The tentacles of this species of soft coral regularly open and close several times each minute.

Crabs

Many tropical crabs are ideal for the aquarium as they are smaller and usually more colourful than their relatives from cooler waters. However, the Anemone Crab, *Neopetrolisthes oshimai*, from the Indo-Pacific, is more closely related to the squat lobsters, since it has a tail, longer antennae and smaller back legs. As its common name suggests, it lives in close association with sea anemones, such as *Stoichactis*. It is tiny, barely reaching a length of more than 10mm (0.4in), even when mature. However, *Dardanus megistos*, the Hairy Red Hermit Crab (also from the Indo-Pacific) grows up to 200mm (8in). Hermit crabs are predatory scavengers and, while their lifestyles have a certain fascinating appeal, it is important to exercise care when choosing suitable tankmates for them – larger fishes and no small invertebrates.

Hermit crabs are particularly interesting because they carry their homes around with them in the shape of empty seashells; they have a soft abdomen which they can twist around in a spiral, thus enabling them to fit exactly into any chosen vacant shell of suitable size. As they grow, they are forced to come out of their shells and change their accommodation for larger premises; at this 'moving' stage, they are very vulnerable to predators, since their soft bodies no longer have the protection of the hard shell in which they previously lived. In an aquarium for hermit crabs, it is good policy to have a selection of various sized shells so that the crab can progress to more comfortable dwellings as it grows.

Lobsters

The highly coloured and intriguing *Enoplometopus occidentalis* is one species suitable for the aquarium. It is native to the Indo-Pacific and can reach a length of 200mm (8in). The large claws are covered with spines and the lobster does most of its feeding at night.

Nudibranchs

Sometimes it seems that these sea slugs achieve the impossible; at one and the same time they are incredibly ugly in shape and exceptionally beautiful in colour. They creep around the aquarium much like terrestrial slugs, but can also swim through the water with amazing convulsive actions. If handled, they can irritate the skin and may give off a poison to other animals as a defence mechanism. *Glossodoris* and *Casella* are just two striking examples of nudibranchs available to the marine fishkeeper.

Right: **Glossodoris sp.**
These slow-moving, brilliantly coloured sea slugs may take some time to find their way around the entire aquarium, but they are bound to brighten up the area wherever they eventually turn up.

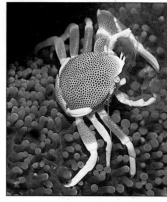

Above: **Neopetrolisthes oshimai**
This Anemone Crab is far shorter than its scientific name!

Left: **Dardanus megistos**
The rest of the Hairy Red Hermit is hidden deep inside its host shell.

Below:
Enoplometopus occidentalis
A colourful nocturnal lobster.

Above: The multi-jointed legs of this invertebrate make for agile movement across the aquarium floor in search of food. The high-set eyes are ideal for locating food and the claws are used to collect it, and as a first line of defence.

Sea anemones

Many fishkeepers will wish to keep a sea anemone in the aquarium, if only for the benefit of the Anemonefishes. The different species of sea anemone are not necessarily compatible, and one group often succumbs to the poisonous discharges of another. Many sea anemones have a low nitrite tolerance and you should seek advice on this point before buying any specimens for the aquarium. *Radianthus* species are a good choice, as they are more nitrite-tolerant than others, and are usually readily accepted by Anemonefishes. Other species also adopted by Anemonefishes include *Stoichactis* and *Discosoma*. A familiar sight in most aquatic stores is *Condylactis passiflora*, the Florida Sea Anemone, which has variously coloured tentacles that are more often than not tipped with violet.

Depending on their size, sea anemones have different feeding requirements. The smaller species need small particles of food – proprietary planktonic foods, cultured rotifers, brineshrimp, small freshwater *Daphnia*, *Cyclops* and maybe *Tubifex* can all be used. The larger species will be able to cope with morsels of suitable food placed within their tentacles. Crab, shrimp, mussel meat and frozen sea foods are readily taken, with the addition of pieces of liver, beef heart, and also proprietary aquarium granular and tablet foods.

Feeding twice a week is usually sufficient for large species, but smaller species can be fed with, say, brineshrimp a little more often. Needless to say, sea anemones should be offered food only when their tentacles are fully expanded. Be sure to remove any partially digested foods, ejected after a few hours or the next day, to prevent tank pollution.

Several sea anemones, although somewhat less brightly coloured, are also suitable for the coldwater marine aquarium, and are described on page 199.

Above: **Antheopsis koseiren**
The marine aquarium can be furnished just as artistically as a well-planted freshwater aquarium using contrasting colours of sea anemones and clumps of Caulerpa.

Left: **Stoichactis giganteum**
As its scientific name suggests, this short-tentacled sea anemone grows to a large size and can accommodate several clownfishes.

Sea apples

Sea apples belong to the Cucumariidae family, which includes the sea cucumbers. These strange animals are often quite brilliantly coloured. A favourite aquarium species is *Paracucumaria*, whose blue body has longitudinal yellow bars topped with bright red tentacles. Sea apples move across the aquarium floor, sifting the sand. There is generally enough food in an established aquarium for these animals, although they will take the extra foods provided for the benefit of other filter feeders.

Sea urchins

Sea urchins have a downward-facing mouth and vary in shape from roughly spherical to a flattened disc. Five rows of feet provide motive power; sometimes, the defensive spines that cover the body also assist movement. Despite being spine-covered, sea urchins are often preyed upon by large fishes such as Triggerfishes, although Cardinalfishes often use a sea urchin's spines as a convenient sanctuary from danger.

Do not take sea urchins out of water and always handle them extremely carefully; the spines are often venomous. Plant-eating sea urchins appreciate an aquarium where algae is plentiful but they may also eat morsels of meat or tablet food. The Long-spined Urchin, *Diadema antillarum*, from the tropical western Atlantic has particularly long black spines.

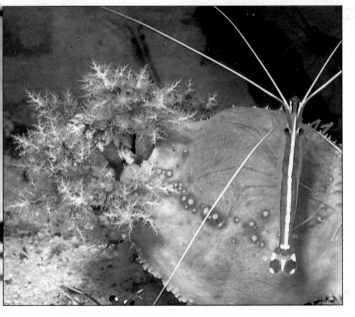

Above: *Spiny sea urchins make good subjects for the invertebrate aquarium, but be sure to handle them with the utmost care!*

Left: *Shrimps and sea apples help keep the aquarium clean by active scavenging; one picks up pieces, the other sifts the substrate.*

Shrimps

Many of the tropical shrimps are highly coloured and provide cleaner services to fishes. Shrimps and crabs shed their shells as they grow, so do not be alarmed if you find two identical bodies in the aquarium from time to time!

Stenopus hispidus, the Banded Coral Shrimp, is found in all warm seas and is easily recognized by the alternate red and white bands on its body and limbs. It grows to about 75mm (3in) and sets up a 'cleaning station', to which other fishes will come for its services. Because of its territorial behaviour, it is regarded as aggressive towards its own kind and has earned the alternative common name of Boxing Shrimp. Keep only single specimens or matched pairs. Sexing the shrimps is reasonably easy as the underside of the female is blue.

Hippolysmata grabhami, a Cleaner Shrimp from the western Atlantic, is easily identified by its red-topped yellow body and the white line that runs through the centre of the back. A feature of this genus is its ability to change sex over a period of time, from male to fully functioning female. Sperm can be stored in the female for long periods, enabling fertilized eggs to be produced in the absence of the male. You can keep these shrimps singly or in groups of any size.

Lysmata wurdemanni, another Cleaner Shrimp from the western Atlantic, has red and white longitudinal markings reminiscent of those on the Squirrelfish. (A Mediterranean species, *L.seticaudata*, is similarly marked.) *L.debelius* is a rich dark red with one or two white spots. *Rhynchochinetes uritae*, the Dancing Shrimp from Sri Lanka also has red and white stripes.

Hymenocera picta, the Indo-Pacific Harlequin Prawn, or Clown Shrimp, has a white body with blue ringed markings. It lives in association with sea anemones but

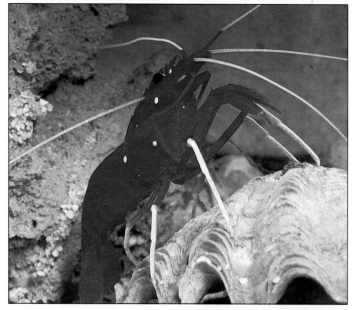

it feeds exclusively on starfishes, so do not keep it with these echinoderms. Indeed, you should buy it only if you have a ready supply of native starfish on which it can feed.

The Anemone Shrimps *Periclimenes* species (*P.brevicarpalis* and *P.pedersoni*) have transparent bodies with brightly coloured 'patch' markings that help to camouflage them should they clamber among the growths of *Caulerpa* in the aquarium. However, they rarely leave their chosen anemone.

Odontodactylus scyllarus, the Mantis Shrimp, is a highly aggressive creature that should only be kept with large fishes in spacious aquariums. It lives in caves or burrows waiting to pounce on anything edible that happens to be passing. Small specimens inadvertently introduced into the aquarium soon grow up to terrorize other inmates of the tank, and their repeated clubbing actions have even been known to shatter the glass.

Above left:
Hippolysmata grabhami
The central white line along the red back makes this Cleaner Shrimp easy to identify. As you can see, it gets along well with its own kind.

Above: **Saron marmoratus**
This bristly-backed Indo-Pacific species has a banded, or ringed, pattern to its legs. Males can be distinguished from females by their greatly enlarged front legs.

Left: **Lysmata debelius**
The white-spotted, port-wine red coloration of this defiant-looking shrimp shows up well against any background in the aquarium.

Below: **Stenopus hispidus**
You will need a large tank to accommodate these shrimps; they are always willing to pick a quarrel with intruding neighbours.

Starfishes

Starfishes are quite suitable for inclusion in the invertebrate aquarium, where they fare much better than when they are forced to compete with fishes for food. They are excellent scavengers, but do not leave them to forage for themselves in the belief that they will always find as much food as they require. They need green foods in their diet and, if the algae growth in the aquarium is insufficient, you should provide them with supplementary rations of lettuce or spinach.

Remarkably, starfishes are able to regenerate their entire body even when only the smallest part of it remains.

Not all starfishes conform to the standard shape; *Culcita*

schmideliana (the Pin-cushion Star), for example, becomes less obviously 'star-shaped' when adult. If overturned, it can right itself by inflating its body until the feet grip again. It grows up to 100mm (4in) across.

From the Indo-Pacific Oceans come the following species of starfish: *Fromia elegans*, which grows up to 80mm (3.2in) across (young specimens have black tips to the arms); *Linckia laevigata*, a bright blue starfish that may reach up to 400mm (16in); and the *Protoreaster* species, brilliantly coloured starfish that may be green, purple or bright red.

Oreaster nodosus is from the Caribbean, where it roams the sea-grass beds (rather than coral reefs) feeding on sponges.

Above: **Protoreaster lincki**
The stunning colours of this starfish are almost too vivid.

Below: **Fromia elegans**
Juvenile forms eventually lose the black tips to their legs with age.

Top: **Spirobranchus giganteus**
The long body of this tubeworm allows it to grow from deep within the corals yet still present its tentacles into clear water.

Above: **Sabella sp.**
The feathery tentacles of fanworms are very delicately constructed and well worth a closer look using a powerful magnifying glass.

Above right:
Spirographis spallanzani
The retractable tentacles of this fanworm are arranged spirally and may be white, red and brown. The length of the body may reach 200mm(8in), ideal for its habitat of soft mud in the Mediterranean and adjacent Atlantic Ocean. Keep this fanworm in the warmer waters of the tropical marine aquarium.

Tubeworms

The most commonly imported genera are *Sabellastarte* (Fanworms), and *Spirobranchus* and *Spirographis* (Tubeworms). All have tentacles – or, more accurately, gills – that perform the dual functions of respiration and the collection of food. The outer tube of *Sabellastarte* is mud-covered, while those of

Spirobranchus and *Spirographis* are calcium based. These tubeworms will accept suspension foods and newly hatched brineshrimp. Fanworms and tubeworms are very sensitive to abrupt changes of light, and may damage their tentacles by retracting them suddenly when the lights are switched off or on. (See page 19 for stress avoidance.)

COLDWATER FISHES AND INVERTEBRATES

Since sea water extends outside the tropical zones to all regions of the world, you should not overlook the possibility of keeping fishes from cooler waters.

It may seem paradoxical, but it is safe to assume that the greatest numbers of tropical fishes are kept by hobbyists in temperate regions far removed from the fishes' wild origins. If this is so, then shouldn't we try to redress the balance a little by turning our attention to the varied aquatic life around our own shores?

Because the sun shines less brightly at higher latitudes, less light penetrates the water in temperate regions. And the water is often less clear, due to pollution and the heavy concentration of silt and mud constantly stirred up by coastal traffic. Understandably, fishes from these waters are not as brilliantly coloured as their tropical relatives, but they do offer one very real advantage for the hobbyist – they are far less expensive to obtain. In fact, if you live relatively near to the seashore you can collect your own specimens absolutely free! A further bonus is that collecting the fishes will bring you enjoyment in terms of personal involvement and you will soon appreciate the conservationist's point of view, perhaps more fully than you did before.

Just as in a tropical collection, the coldwater aquarium can be further expanded by collecting invertebrate life as well as fishes, but again the same precautions apply about keeping only compatible species together. Many of the sea anemones are very colourful, bearing in mind their murky origins, and there is also the advantage that should any species outgrow the tank, or outstay its welcome by more antisocial adult behaviour, you can just as easily return it to the wild to continue its natural lifespan.

Despite the apparent convenience of keeping local species, you may find problems arising during the summer months; as you enjoy the warm sun, the water temperature in the aquarium may rise uncomfortably high for its occupants and you may need to take steps to cool it down.

Left: *The commonly found Tompot Blenny,* Blennius gattorugine, *often adopts this typical pose; perched on the top of a rock, or peering out from an underwater cave, it watches for a passing smaller fish as a potential meal. It is a belligerent-looking creature, with the almost threatening crests (cirri) above the eyes.*

Species of marine fish from cooler locations are not generally available from the usual aquatic stores, and hobbyists wishing to stock a coldwater marine aquarium will need to collect specimens from the wild. Blennies, Butterfishes, Gobies and the marine species of Stickleback are all small enough to be suitable for the aquarium in the long term. Juvenile forms of larger species, such as Bass, Grey Mullet and Wrasses, outgrow their aquarium before long and must be returned to the wild.

Family: BLENNIIDAE
Blennies

These are most common in rockpools, where they are found hiding under overhanging rocks. They are often confused with Gobies, but they lack the 'suction cup' formed by the fusion of the pelvic fins. Most Blennies have tentacles or a crest, described as 'cirri', positioned over the eye, giving them a distinctive appearance.

General care
Coldwater species require the same aquarium conditions as those described for tropical species (see page 16-31), with the obvious omission of heating equipment. Although substrate biological filtration is adequate, you should provide some extra water movement to create surface turbulence and to ensure well-oxygenated water.

As most of the species collected from the wild are likely to be rockpool inhabitants, you should furnish the aquarium with numerous retreats to recreate their natural habitat.

The biggest problem will be temperature regulation; in summer the average water temperature in the aquarium will be higher than you might expect to find in nature. Provide extra aeration at these times and improvise some kind of cooling system. Bags of ice cubes floated in the tank may help, and the serious hobbyist may even consider fitting a cooling plant, or using a second refrigerator to cool water in an outside filter system.

Feeding is not usually difficult as most fishes are more than willing to accept fish and shellfish meats. Only the fishes with the smallest mouths, such as Pipefishes and Sea Sticklebacks, will require copious amounts of tiny live food.

Regular monthly water changes will stabilize the water conditions. If you check the specific gravity, remember that it will give a higher reading at the lower water temperatures, probably about 1.025 at 15°C (59°F).

Collecting specimens
If you prepare the aquarium before you collect your fish, try to make sure that the water is the same specific gravity as the natural sea water in the rockpools. Otherwise, bring back as much natural water as you need to fill the tank or to reduce any differences in the specific gravity of the two bodies of water.

You must be well prepared to transport the livestock that you capture. Large plastic buckets with clip-on lids are ideal, although a double thickness of plastic film may be an adequate substitute for a lid. You will find that a battery-operated air pump, supplying air to an airstone in the water, will give the fish a better chance of surviving a long journey home. This is especially important during the summer months, when the journey may take longer. It is a good idea to take some extra sealable containers in which to collect some sea water, but make sure that it comes from an unpolluted or offshore site.

Collect specimens with care; rocks surrounding the rockpools are usually covered in very slippery seaweeds, so wear suitable footwear. Consult the tide timetables in advance to ensure that you get the maximum collecting time. DO NOT FORGET THE INCOMING TIDE. Remember also to leave the rockpool in a fit state for the animals left behind: if you collect invertebrates, such as sea anemones or starfishes, collect site and animal together, replacing any rocks that you remove with others to restore the number of hiding places in the pool. Transport anemones and other invertebrates separately from the fish; anemones will sting the fish in the close confines of a bucket, and fish may eat small invertebrates, such as shrimps, during transit.

NEVER OVER COLLECT. Not only is this bad practice from the conservation point of view, but it is also false insurance; it is better for the majority of specimens in a small collection to survive than to arrive home with none at all.

Above: **Blennius gattorugine**
The Tompot Blenny has some six attractive dark bars crossing its body vertically, easily seen once the fish comes out of its retreat.

Below: **Liophrys pholis**
The male Shanny's colours change from blotchy to very dark during the spawning period, but the mouth remains pale in contrast.

Aidablennius sphinx
Sphinx Blenny
● **Habitat:** Adriatic and Mediterranean.
● **Length:** 80mm (3.2in).
● **Diet:** All meaty worm foods.
● **Feeding manner:** Bottom feeder.
● **Aquarium compatibility:** May be territorial.

Once this fish leaves the security of its favourite bolt-hole, you can see that it is a most attractively coloured fish with dark bands crossing the body. It usually swims with the dorsal fin lowered, but raises it when alarmed. It spawns in caves, males physically covering any passing female inside.

Blennius gattorugine
Tompot Blenny
● **Habitat:** Mediterranean, Eastern Atlantic from West Africa to Scotland.
● **Length:** 200mm (8in).
● **Diet:** Live foods, meat and worm foods.
● **Feeding manner:** Bottom feeder.
● **Aquarium compatibility:** Can be territorial and may worry smaller fishes – and be themselves worried by larger ones.

These fishes prefer a tank decorated with medium-sized stones, under which they can hide. They can become tame, quite happy to make friends with you.

Using natural seawater

● Collect water some distance offshore to avoid pollution from sewage and industry and also to ensure the correct salinity. Inshore waters may have been diluted by recent heavy rainfall washing down from the land or from rivers.

● Avoid the risk of metal pollution by using only plastic containers for collecting and transporting specimens.

● Store collected water for several weeks or even months in sealed dark containers. During this time the sediment will settle, natural marine life (including disease-carrying organisms) will perish and the resulting bacterial activity will cease. The water can then be prepared for use.

● Aerate the siphoned off clean water for 12 hours or so before use. Test the water for pH value, ammonia and nitrite levels.

Blennius nigriceps

Black-headed Blenny
- **Habitat:** Mediterranean.
- **Length:** 40mm (1.6in).
- **Diet:** All meaty, worm foods.
- **Feeding manner:** Bottom feeder.
- **Aquarium compatibility:** May be territorial.

Whoever gave this fish its common name seems to have disregarded the predominant red of the body, concentrating instead on the darker reticulated patterning of the head region. *B.nigriceps* shares its habitat with the almost identical *Trypterygion minor*, from which it may be distinguished by the absence of a small extra dorsal fin in front of the main dorsal fins.

Lipophrys (Blennius) pholis

Shanny
- **Habitat:** Mediterranean, Eastern Atlantic from West Africa to Scotland.
- **Length:** 160mm (6.3in).
- **Diet:** Live foods, meat and worm foods.
- **Feeding manner:** Bottom feeder.
- **Aquarium compatibility:** Gregarious, but can be hard to please when it comes to a choice of hiding places; whelk shells are often acceptable.

Like all Blennies, these fish prefer a tank with plenty of hideaways. However, they also like to bask in the light, sometimes emerging from the water to do so. There are no cirri on the head.

Parablennius rouxi

Striped Blenny
- **Habitat:** Mediterranean.
- **Length:** 70mm (2.75in).
- **Diet:** All meaty, worm foods.
- **Feeding manner:** Bottom feeder.
- **Aquarium compatibility:** May be territorial.

A distinctive fish with a horizontal dark stripe from head to tail. The fins are colourless.

Salaria (Blennius) pavo

Peacock Blenny
- **Habitat:** Mediterranean.
- **Length:** 100mm (4in).
- **Diet:** Worm foods.
- **Feeding manner:** Bottom feeder.
- **Aquarium compatibility:** Territorial; needs plenty of retreats in which to hide.

Two obvious characteristics identify this species: the helmet-shaped hump above the eye in mature males and the blue-edged black spot just behind the eye. Blue-edged dark bands cross the green-yellow body.

Below: **Salaria pavo**
The Peacock Blenny tolerates wide extremes of temperature and salinities, and sometimes it will even enter fresh water.

Bottom: **Gobius jozo**
The somewhat misleadingly named Black Goby also tolerates brackish water. Mediterranean species spawn in the springtime.

Family: GASTEROSTEIDAE
Sticklebacks

Although freshwater Sticklebacks (*Gasterosteus* spp.) are able to tolerate some degree of salinity, there is one species within the family – *Spinachia spinachia* – that spends its entire life in marine conditions. Like its freshwater relatives, it also builds a nest in which to spawn, fabricating the structure from plant fragments stuck together with a secreted fluid.

Spinachia spinachia

Fifteen-spined Stickleback
- **Habitat:** Northeastern Atlantic.
- **Length:** 200mm (8in).
- **Diet:** Very small animal life.
- **Feeding manner:** Midwater feeder.
- **Aquarium compatibility:** Fin nipper; keep separately.

This species must have frequent meals of tiny live foods; brineshrimp are probably the most useful food for this purpose. The Stickleback lives for only about two years in the wild, and its life expectancy in the aquarium will be even shorter unless the feeding problem is solved.

Family: GOBIIDAE
Gobies

Gobies have no lateral line system along the flanks of the body; instead, sensory pores connected to the nervous system appear on the head and over the body. They can live quite a long time; records show they have survived for up to ten years. A very large Family, Gobies inhabit many types of water – tropical and temperate, freshwater, brackish and full salt water.

Gobius cruentatus

Red mouthed Goby
- **Habitat:** Eastern Atlantic, North Africa to southern Ireland.
- **Length:** 180mm (7in).
- **Diet:** Crustaceans, worms, shellfish meats, small fishes.
- **Feeding manner:** Bottom feeder.
- **Aquarium compatibility:** Territorial at times.

Gobies are found on both sandy and rocky shores. Sand-dwelling species are naturally camouflaged, whereas rock-dwellers can be much more colourful.

Gobius jozo

Black Goby
- **Habitat:** Mediterranean, Black Sea and eastern Atlantic.
- **Length:** 150mm (6in).
- **Diet:** Worm foods, small crustaceans.
- **Feeding manner:** Bottom feeder.
- **Aquarium compatibility:** Territorial at times.

A generally dark blotched fish, but how it 'colours up' in captivity depends a great deal on the colour of its surroundings. It is very rarely black! Another scientific name for this fish is *Gobius niger*.

Lepadogaster candollei

Connemara Clingfish
- **Habitat:** Eastern Atlantic, Mediterranean, Black Sea.
- **Length:** 75mm (3in).
- **Diet:** Worm foods.
- **Feeding manner:** Bottom feeder.
- **Aquarium compatibility:** Not known.

The common name refers to the ability of the fish to cling to rocks and other surfaces by means of a suction disc formed by the pelvic fins. Colours may vary but generally include reds, browns and greens; males have red dots on the head and on the lower part of the long-based dorsal fin.

Pomatoschistus minutus

Sand Goby
- **Habitat:** Eastern Atlantic, Mediterranean and Black Sea.
- **Length:** 95mm (3.7in).
- **Diet:** Worm foods.
- **Feeding manner:** Bottom feeder.
- **Aquarium compatibility:** Probably shy and likely to be predated upon by other fish. This species is best kept in a tank with its own kind.

Its natural camouflage colouring makes this fish difficult to see when you are collecting it. Being a sand colour, it will 'feel at home' with a similarly coloured covering on the aquarium floor.

Left: **Lepadogaster candollei**
The Connemara Clingfish has a variable coloration, mainly based on browns, reds and greens with some dotted markings. Male fish have red spots on the cheeks and at the base of the dorsal fin.

Family: LABRIDAE

Wrasses

Like their tropical relatives, Wrasses from temperate waters can also be brightly coloured. In fact, their colour can lead to identification and sexing problems; colour varies not only between the sexes (that of the male also changing at breeding time) but also depending on the mood of the fish and on the colour of the substrate! Sex reversals are also not uncommon. Young fishes act as cleanerfishes to other fishes, and many species hide away in crevices or bury themselves in the sand at night.

Coris julis
Rainbow Wrasse
● **Habitat:** Mediterranean, eastern Atlantic.
● **Length:** 250mm (10in).
● **Diet:** Small marine animals, live foods.
● **Feeding manner:** Bottom feeder, although it will take surface plankton.
● **Aquarium compatibility:** Peaceful.

The long, slender, green-brown body has a horizontal white-red stripe. The eyes are red. These fishes are hermaphrodites, the females turning into fully functional males. Aquarium specimens are active during the day, but bury themselves in the substrate at night. This behaviour has not been observed in this species in the wild. Like their tropical relatives, juveniles act as cleaner fishes.

Left: **Coris julis**
The Rainbow Wrasse has colour variants depending on location and sex. Those from deeper water are red-brown; females have a pale spot on the gill cover base.

Below left: **Anthias anthias**
For a fish that has such appealing coloration, it is quite surprising that collectors have not yet endowed it with a popular name.

Bottom left: **Serranus hepatus**
The Brown Comber frequents fairly shallow waters, where it feeds on small fish and crustaceans.

Family: PHOLIDIDAE

Gunnells

Often seen in the same areas as Blennies, members of the Pholididae are slender cylindrical fishes with a dorsal fin running the entire length of the back. The anal fin is also long based, occupying almost the rear half of the body. Both the dorsal and anal fins join with the caudal fin. The pectoral fins are small and the pelvic fins are limited to just one ray. Species are found on both sides of the North Atlantic Ocean and also on the northern Pacific coast of America.

Pholis gunnellus
Butterfish; Gunnell
● **Habitat:** Eastern and Western Atlantic.
● **Length:** 250mm (10in).
● **Diet:** Crustaceans, worms, molluscs, shellfish meats.
● **Feeding manner:** Bottom feeder.
● **Aquarium compatibility:** Do not keep with small invertebrates.

The eel-like body has a long-based dorsal fin that is twice as long as the anal fin. It may have transverse dark bands on the body and white-edged markings along the base of the dorsal fin. This species is found under stones.

Anthias anthias
● **Habitat:** Mediterranean, eastern Atlantic as far north as Biscay.
● **Length:** 240mm (9.5in).
● **Diet:** A varied selection of animal and meaty foods.
● **Feeding manner:** Bold.
● **Aquarium compatibility:** Peaceful.

The body is golden brown with blue speckling and the facial markings are blue. The long pelvic fins are yellow and blue. In the wild, the coloration may appear different because part of the colour spectrum of light is lost in deep waters due to absorption.

Serranus hepatus
Brown Comber
● **Habitat:** Mediterranean, eastern Atlantic (Senegal to Portugal).
● **Length:** 130mm (5in).
● **Diet:** Animal and meaty foods.
● **Feeding manner:** Bold.
● **Aquarium compatibility:** No reliable information is available, but do not keep with smaller fishes.

The reddish brown body has four or five vertical dark bars across it. The undersides of the body are pale. There is a black blotch on the dorsal fin at the junction of the hard and soft rays.

Family: SCORPAENIDAE

Scorpionfishes

Although they lack the ornate finnage of the tropical Scorpionfishes, species from temperate waters are just as dangerous. The spines on the head, which serve as positive species identifiers, are very venomous. When disturbed during the day, these sedentary nocturnal fishes swim only a short distance before settling down again to await any passing prey.

Scorpaena porcus
Scorpionfish
● **Habitat:** Mediterranean and eastern Atlantic (Biscay and further south).
● **Length:** 250mm (10in).
● **Diet:** Small fishes.
● **Feeding manner:** Lies in wait for prey.
● **Aquarium compatibility:** Distinctly unsociable; nocturnal. Keep in a separate tank.

The reddish brown mottled coloration makes this fish hard to see as it lies on the seabed. Not only is it a danger to other fishes, but also to swimmers who may inadvertently step on it. Use very hot water to bathe any wound, which may turn septic.

Above: **Scorpaena porcus**
Plume-like growths on the head, together with venomous spines on dorsal fin and gill covers make an attractive, but dangerous species.

Rockpools hold an extra fascination: they sustain a large number of life forms other than fish, and these, too, are well worth collecting. While it is true that temperate zone fishes and invertebrates do not match the brilliance of their tropical relatives, these animals will add colour and variety to the more subtle shades of the coldwater marine aquarium. The following is a representative selection.

Crabs
Although crabs seem to be endearing little creatures, the majority of 'free-swimming' species grow too large and become a disruptive influence in the aquarium. A better choice would be the smaller Hermit Crabs (*Pagurus* spp.), which interestingly shed their adopted shell for larger premises as they increase in size.

Nudibranchs
Relatively colourful species occur in the Mediterranean and northeastern Atlantic. *Chromodoris* and *Hypselodoris* are typical genera of these molluses.

Prawns and shrimps
It is easy to capture species of *Palaemon*, *Crangon* and *Hippolyte* - small shrimps and prawns – from rockpools in the northeastern and northwestern Atlantic and the Mediterranean. *Lysmata* is an interesting Mediterranean species, *L.seticaudata* being very similarly marked to the Indo-Pacific species *Rhynchonectes uritae*. Prawns and shrimps are excellent scavengers and often act as cleaners to other fishes. (See page 192 for tropical equivalents.) Egg-carrying females may provide extra numbers for the coldwater marine aquarium.

Above: **Palaemon serratus**
The Common Prawn is easily caught in rockpools – but be quick!

Above: **Actinia equina**
Strawberry Beadlet Anemones retract to form jelly-like blobs.

Sea anemones
Beadlet anemones (*Actinia equina*) can be found in a variety of colours. The columns can be red, green or brown and the tentacles are usually the same colour, but not always. They move around the aquarium, providing splashes of colour in an ever-changing pattern.

Actinia equina has two sub-species. *A.equina* var. *mesembryanthemum*, the Beadlet Anemone from the North and South Atlantic and the Mediterranean, is a very common sight in coldwater rockpools. The body and tentacles are bright red, but the body contracts to a dull red sphere just as you reach for it.

A.equina var. *fragacea*, the strawberry variant, is usually red with green spots – just like a strawberry. Its tentacles are usually red, but can be a paler pink. It is larger than the Beadlet and is found in the slightly deeper waters of the northeastern Atlantic and the Mediterranean.

The long tentacles of *Anemonia viridis (sulcata)*, the Snakelocks Anemone, are not fully retractable. Because it prefers strong light, it is found very close to the water surface in the northeastern Atlantic and Mediterranean. In the same waters you will find *Bunodactis verrucosa*, the Wartlet or Gem Anemone. It has tentacles with ringed markings and vertical rows of wartlike growths on its body, hence the common name.

Cerianthus membranaceus, the Cylinder Rose, is almost a cross between a sea anemone and a tubeworm, with a longer cylindrical body and less stocky in shape. The tube is often partially buried in the sand. It is a delicate animal that needs careful handling, although it may be able to regenerate a damaged tube fairly easily. Its tentacles vary in colour from species to species and are toxic to most fishes; for this reason, too, you should place other sea anemones beyond its reach. Unlike some sea anemones, *Cerianthus* does not move about the aquarium.

Although a fairly large anemone, *Condylactis aurantiaca* from the Mediterranean, has relatively short brown, white-tipped tentacles tipped with violet. Some *Epizoanthus* species are also native to the Mediterranean. They only grow to around 10mm (0.4in), but colonies can be found on rocks just below the waterline, where the constant water movement ensures a regular delivery of food.

Urticina (Tealia) felina var. *coriacea*, the Dahlia Anemone from the North Atlantic and northeastern

Pacific, has a body covered with warts, sand and fragments of shell. Tentacles surround the patterned mouth disc. A similar species, *U.crassicornis*, occurs on the east coast of North America. *U.lofotensis* has white and pink tentacles on a red body and, with the larger *U.columbiana*, occurs in the northeastern Pacific. There is also a deepwater species known as *U.eques*.

Sea squirts
Sea squirts are vase-shaped bivalves that draw in water through one valve, trapping suspended minute food on a mucus-covered pharyngeal basket, and then exhale the water through the second siphon. *Halocynthia papillosa*, about 100mm (4in) tall, is red-orange in colour with many bristles around the siphons. It is common in the Mediterranean.

Sea urchins
Like their tropical relatives, sea urchins from temperate waters can also make interesting aquarium species. The Black Urchin, *Arbacia lixula*, from the Mediterranean is a purple-black in colour and looks like a short-spined version of the tropical *Diadema antillarum*.

Shellfish
When you are collecting from rockpools, do not forget that there are some surprisingly active shellfish that will add extra interest to the aquarium. Species of limpet (*Patella*) and winkle (*Littorina*) are quite suitable. Do not ignore empty shells; a collection of shells of various sizes make ideal homes for a growing hermit crab.

Above: **Crossaster papposus**
The Sun Star has more than twice as many 'arms' as other starfishes.

Sponges
Sponges are usually difficult to keep in the aquarium as they are very sensitive to adverse water conditions. They must have well-oxygenated, crystal-clear water and are not at all compatible with sea anemones. They attach themselves to shells, even those that contain hermit crabs. If this happens, they will devour the shell and in turn become the home of the crab. *Suberites domuncula* is a common Mediterranean and Atlantic species.

Starfishes
The following species are among the wide range of starfishes found in temperate waters.

Asterias rubens is commonly found in the northeastern Atlantic, where it feeds on mussels and scallops, prising them apart with its feet and introducing its stomach into the shell. The skin is covered with many tubercles.

Astropecten aranciacus, the Red Comb Star from the Mediterranean and northeastern Atlantic, is a large predatory starfish (up to 500mm/20in) with comblike teeth along the edges of its arms.

Echinaster sepositus, a Mediterranean species, grows to 300mm(12in). Fertilized eggs develop directly into small starfishes.

Ophidiaster ophidianus, another red starfish from the Mediterranean, grows to 200mm (8in). The long arms issuing from an almost non-existent central 'body' of this starfish are cylindrical in section rather than flat, with sharply tapering ends.

Above:
Cerianthus membranaceus
Elegant, but delicate in the tank.

Above: *A whelk shell hosts anemones and a hermit crab.*

FURTHER READING

General

Bianchini, F. et al. *Aquaria*, K & R Books, 1977

Dal Vasco et al. *Life in the Aquarium*, Octopus, 1975

Federation of British Aquatic Societies, *Scientific Names and Their Meanings*, 1980

Frank, Dr S. *The Illustrated Encyclopedia of Aquarium Fish*, Octopus, 1980

Hunnam, Milne, and Stebbing, *The Living Aquarium*, Ward Lock, 1981

Madsen, J.M. *Aquarium Fishes in Colour*, Blandford Press, 1975

Midgalski, E.C. and Fichter, G.S. *The Fresh and Saltwater Fishes of the World*, Octopus, 1977

Mills, D. *Illustrated Guide to Aquarium Fishes*, Kingfisher Books/Ward Lock, 1977

Mills, D. *You & Your Aquarium*, Dorling Kindersley, 1986

Palmer, J.D. *Biological Clocks in Marine Organisms*, Wiley-Interscience, 1974

Sterba, G. *The Aquarists Encyclopedia*, Blandford Press, 1983

Vevers, G. *Pocket Guide to Aquarium Fishes*, Mitchell Beazley, 1982

Wheeler, A. *Fishes of the World*, Ferndale Editions, London, 1979

Whitehead, P. *How Fishes Live*, Elsevier-Phaidon, 1975

Wilkie, D. *Aquarium Fish*, Pelham Books, 1986

Marine Aquariums, Fishes and Invertebrates

Baensch H.A. *Marine Aquarists Manual*, Tetra, 1983

Carcasson, R.H. *Coral Reef Fishes of the Indian & West Pacific Oceans*, Collins, 1977

Cox, G.F. *Tropical Marine Aquaria*, Hamlyn, 1971

de Graaf, F. *Marine Aquarium Guide*, Pet Library, 1973

Denham, K. *Marine Tropical Fish*, Bartholomew, 1977

Federation of British Aquatic Societies. *Dictionary of Common/Scientific Names of Marine Fishes*, 1984

George D and J. *Marine Life*, Harrap, 1979

Hargreaves, V.C. *The Tropical Marine Aquarium*, David & Charles, 1978

Kingsford, E. *Treatment of Exotic Marine Fish Diseases*, Kingsford, 1975

Lundegaard, G. *Keeping Marine Fish*, Blandford Press, 1985

Lythgoe, J and G. *Fishes of the Sea*, Blandford Press, 1971

Melzak, M. *The Marine Aquarium Manual*, Batsford, 1984

Mills, D. *Fishkeepers Guide to Marine Fishes*, Salamander, 1985

Petron, C., Lozet, J-B. *The Guinness Guide to Underwater Life*, Guinness Superlatives Ltd., 1977

Ravensdale, T. *Coral Fishes*, John Gifford, 1967

Spotte, S. *Marine Aquarium Keeping*, Wiley Interscience, 1973. *Saltwater Aquariums*, Wiley Interscience, 1979

Steene, R.C. *Butterflies and Angelfishes of the World*, Vols 1 & 2, Mergus, 1977

Straughan, R.P.L. *The Saltwater Aquarium in the Home*, Thomas Yoseloff, 1969

Thomson, D.A., Findley, L.T., Kerstitch, A.N. *Reef Fishes of the Sea of Cortez*, Wiley-Interscience, 1979

Thresher, R.F. *Reef Fish*, John Bartholomew, 1980

Walker, B. *Marine Tropical Fish*, Blandford Press 1975

GLOSSARY

Activated carbon Material used in mechanical/chemical filtration systems (external 'power filter' canister types) to remove, by adsorption, dissolved matter.

Aeration Act of introducing compressed air to the aquarium; to ventilate the water to facilitate the intake of oxygen and to expel carbon dioxide.

Airstone Small block of porous wood (better than ceramic types) through which air is passed to produce air bubbles in the water for aeration purposes, or to draw water through filters or protein skimmers.

Airline (Tubing) Neoprene tubing to convey compressed air from air pump to aquarium equipment such as airstones, filters, ozonizers, and protein skimmers.

Algae Primitive unicellular plants; marine plants such as *Caulerpa* are strictly algae rather than proper plants. Bright lighting is needed for algae growth. Much appreciated by herbivorous fishes.

All-glass tanks Aquariums made by bonding five otherwise unsupported panels of glass directly together with aquarium silicone sealant to form an aquarium. Their virtue is that they are ideal for marine use having no metal or putty to contaminate, or be corroded by, the salt water.

Ammonia (NH$_3$) First byproduct of decaying organic material; also excreted by the fishes' gills. Toxic to fishes and invertebrates.

Anal fin Single fin mounted vertically below the fish.

Artemia salina Scientific name of brineshrimp.

Barbel Whisker-like growth around the mouth or head; used for detecting food by taste.

Benedenia Trematode parasite similar to *Dactylogyrus* gill fluke.

Biological filtration Means of water filtration using bacteria, *Nitrosomonas* and *Nitrobacter*, to reduce otherwise toxic ammonium-based compounds to safer substances such as nitrates.

Bivalve A mollusc or shell-dwelling animal with two respiratory valves.

Brackish water Water containing approximately 10% sea water; found in estuaries where fresh water rivers enter the sea.

Brineshrimp Saltwater crustacean, *Artemia salina*, whose dry-stored eggs can be hatched to provide live food for fish or invertebrates. There are two main sources: San Francisco Bay and Great Salt Lakes, Utah. The newly hatched San Francisco Bay shrimp is smaller, and more suitable for very young fishes or invertebrate feeding.

Buffering action Ability of a liquid to maintain its pH value, i.e. to resist pH changes. Calcareous substrates may assist in this respect.

Cable tidy Commercial 'junction box' for neat and safe connection of electrical supply circuits.

Calcareous Formed of, or containing, calcium carbonate, a substance which may help to maintain a high pH of the aquarium water.

Carnivore Will eat meat foods.

Caudal fin Single fin mounted vertically at the rear of the fish, the tail.

Caudal peduncle Part of fish's body joining the caudal fin to the main body.

Cirri Crestlike growths found above the eyes in some species, such as *Blennius*.

Coelenterates Family to which corals, jellyfish and sea anemones belong.

Combined unit A heater and thermostat in one unit.

Commensalism Living practical partnership, where one party derives more benefit than the other.

Compost Alternative term for aquarium base covering, or substrate.

Copper Metal used in copper sulphate form as the basis for many marine aquarium remedies. Poisonous to fishes in excess, and even more so, at much lower levels, to invertebrates.

Coral (hard) Natural growths of polyps whose external calacareous skeleton form the decorative material for the aquarium.

Coral (soft) Live, more flowerlike, corals with retractable tentacles, kept for their colours, fantastic shapes and decorative beauty.

Coral sand Sand for the marine aquarium made from crushed coral.

Counter-current More efficient design of protein skimmer where the water flows against the main current of air, giving a longer exposure time for sterilization.

Cover glass Panel of glass to form an anti-condensation, anti-evaporation protection placed on top of the aquarium immediately below the hood.

Crustacean Type of aquatic animal with a jointed 'body shell', such as the shrimp.

Cryptocaryon Parasitic infection, often referred to as the marine equivalent of the fresh water white spot disease, *Ichthyophthirius*.

Daphnia Freshwater crustacean, the water flea, used as food in the marine aquarium. Remove dead specimens if uneaten.

Demersal Term usually applied to eggs or to spawning action of fishes. Demersal eggs are heavier than water and are laid in prepared spawning sites on the sea bed. The fertilized eggs are then guarded by one or both adult fishes until hatching occurs.

Diffuser An alternative name for airstones.

Direct-current Design of protein skimmer where the water flows with the main current of ozonized air. May provide too short an exposure time for efficient sterilization.

Dorsal fin Single fin mounted vertically on top of the fish; some species have two dorsal fins, one behind the other. Many marine species have poisonous rays in the dorsal fin, so handle them with care.

Dropsy Disease, where body fluids build up and produce a swollen body.

Enchytraeids Small terrestrial worms (whiteworms, grindalworms, etc.) that can be cultured by the hobbyist for food. Very fatty foods; do not give them in excessive amounts as they can cause internal disorders.

Estuarine Fishes that frequent estuaries, able to tolerate changing salinities.

Euryhaline Ability of some species, such as eels and salmon, to enter both fresh water and salt water.

Filter Device for cleaning the aquarium water. May be biological, chemical or mechanical in form, internally or externally mounted. High rate of water flow recommended for marine aquariums.

Filter feeder Animal (fish or invertebrate) which sifts water for microscopic food, e.g. pipefishes, tubeworms.

Filter medium Materials used in filtration systems to remove suspended or dissolved materials from the water.

Fin rot Bacterial ailment; the tissue between the rays of the fin rots away.

Fins Collapsible, erectile membranes attached to the fish's body: used to produce propulsion or provide manoeuvrability.

Fluorescent Type of lighting; glass tube filled with fluorescing material which produces light under the influence of an electric discharge. Cool-running and recommended for aquarium use; several tubes will be needed if luxuriant algae growth is required.

Foam fractionation Method of separating out proteins from water by foaming action. Also known as protein skimming.

Fry Very young fish.

Fungus Parasitic infection, causing cotton-wool-like growths on the body.

Gallon (Imp) Measure of liquid volume (1 Imperial gallon = 1.2 US gallons = 4.55 litres.)

Gallon (U.S.) Measure of liquid volume (1 US gallon = 0.83 Imp gallons = 3.8 litres.)

Gill flukes Trematode parasites, such as *Dactylogyrus*, that in severe infestation cause rapid breathing and gaping gills.

Gills Membranes through which fish absorb dissolved oxygen from the water during respiration.

Gravel tidy Plastic mesh fitted between layers of gravel to protect biological filtration systems from being exposed (and thus rendered ineffective) by digging fishes.

Grolux Brand name of fluorescent lighting with emphasized red and blue

wavelengths; ideal for encouraging plant growth.

Heater Submersible device for heating the aquarium water; must be controlled by a thermostat.

Herbivore Vegetable or plant eater.

Hood Cover of aquarium containing the light fittings, also known as the reflector.

Hydrometer Device for measuring the specific gravity (S.G.) of the salt water, especially useful when making up synthetic mixes. May be either a free-floating or swing-needle type.

Impeller Electrically driven propeller that produces water flow through filters.

Invertebrate Literally 'animals without backbones', such as sea anemones, corals, shrimps, etc.

Irradiation Method of exposing food to gamma rays to sterilize it.

Lateral line Line of perforated scales along the flanks which lead to a pressure-sensitive nervous system. Enables fish to detect vibrations in surrounding water caused by other fishes, or reflected vibrations of their own movement from obstacles.

Length (standard) Length of fish (SL) measured from snout to end of main body; excludes caudal fin.

Litre Measure of liquid volume (1 litre = 0.22 Imp gallons = 0.26 US gallons).

Lymphocystis Viral ailment that causes cauliflower-like growths on the skin and fins.

Marine Pertaining to the sea.

Mercury vapour Type of high intensity lamp.

Mimicry The close resemblance of one creature to another. Specifically, the resemblance of predatory fishes to 'safe' fishes allowing them to gain unfair advantage over other animals.

Mollusc Group of animals that includes shellfish and nudibranchs.

Mouthbrooder Fishes that incubate fertilized eggs in the mouth until they hatch.

Mysis Commercially available marine shrimp used as live food.

Nauplius Term used generally for the newly hatched form of brineshrimp.

Nitrate (NO_3) Less toxic ammonium compound produced by *Nitrobacter* bacteria from nitrite. Nitrate levels can be kept to a minimum by regular partial water changes; in 'total systems', anaerobic trickle filters convert nitrate back to free nitrogen.

Nitrite (NO_2) Toxic ammonium compound produced by *Nitrosomonas* bacteria from ammonia. Toxic to fishes, and even more so to invertebrates.

Omnivore Eats all foods.

Oodinium Single-celled parasite causing coral fish disease. Highly infectious, but curable with proprietary remedies.

Osmosis Passage of liquid through a semi-permeable membrane to dilute a more concentrated solution. Accounts for water losses through the skin of marine fishes, i.e. to the relatively stronger sea water, which then have to constantly drink to replenish these losses.

Ozone (O_3) Three-atom, unstable form of oxygen used as a disinfectant. Best used in conjunction with a protein skimmer, which prevents direct ozone contact with fishes or invertebrates.

Ozonizer Device that produces ozone by high-voltage electrical discharge. Air from an air pump is passed through the ozonizer on its way to the protein skimmer.

Pectoral fins Paired fins, one on each side of the body immediately behind the gill cover.

Pelagic Strictly meaning 'of the open sea', this term is also applied to eggs and spawning methods. Pelagic eggs are lighter than water and are scattered after an ascending spawning action between a pair of fishes in open water. The fertilized eggs are then carried away by water currents.

Pelvic fins Paired fins on the ventral (lower) surface, usually immediately below the gill covers. Not all marine fishes have pelvic fins; often only a rudimentary stub is present, or perhaps a flap of skin.

pH Measure of water acidity or alkalinity; the scale ranges from 1 (extremely acid) through 7 (neutral) to 14 (extremely alkaline). Sea water is normally around pH 8.3 and aquarium water should be kept in the range of pH 7.9 to 8.3. A falling pH indicates a partial water change is necessary.

Polyps Living filter-feeding animals whose accumulated dead skeletons produce decorative coral.

Power filters External canister-type filtration devices, usually fitted with an electric impeller to drive aquarium water through the enclosed filter media. Often used to prefilter water in 'reverse-flow' biological filtration systems.

Power head Electric impeller system fitted to biological filter return tubes to increase water flow.

Protein skimmer Device which removes protein material from the water by foaming: may be air-operated or electrically powered. Also used in conjunction with ozonized air for further water sterilization purposes.

Quarantine Mandatory period of separation for new fishes, to screen them from any latent diseases. Quarantine tanks must be maintained to the same high standard as the main aquarium to reduce stress when fishes are moved from one to the other. Can double as a treatment tank.

Rays Bony supports in fins.

Reaction tube Part of protein skimmer where foaming occurs. When used with ozonized air, the reaction tube effectively isolates fishes from harmful ozone.

Reef Outcrop of coral growths in the sea, often large enough to protect the shore from wave action. May form lagoons, atolls or larger offshore formations, e.g. Australia's Great Barrier Reef.

Reflector Alternative name for aquarium hood.

Reverse-flow Alternative design of biological filtration system in which water flows up through the base covering instead of the more usual downward direction. Best powered by external power filters.

Salinity Measure of saltiness of the water. Quoted in terms of gm/litre. Natural sea water has a salinity of about 33.7 gm/litre.

Salt Sodium chloride, but more usually the salt mix to make synthetic sea water.

Salt mix Materials to make synthetic sea water. Commercially available in standard packs to make up specific quantities of water. Always follow manufacturer's instructions carefully, and use non metallic containers for mixing and storing.

Scales Bony overlapping plates covering the fish's skin, providing physical protection and streamlining.

Shimmying Condition of shivering; usually the result of a chill.

Shoal Group of fishes of the same species. Fishes in nature shoal for mutual protection and this gregarious behaviour should be encouraged in the aquarium, but obviously only with fishes that tolerate the company of their own kind.

Silicone sealant Adhesive used to bond glass or stop leaks. Use it to create rocks and coral formations, caves, etc. Use in well-ventilated conditions, it gives off heavy vapour smelling of vinegar. Allow at least 24 hours for it to cure. Be sure to use proper aquarium sealant, not the type sold for domestic use.

Siphon A length of tube with which to remove water from the aquarium; may also refer to inhalant organ of molluscs

Spawning Act of reproduction involving the fertilization of the eggs. Many marine species have been observed spawning in captivity, but very few young fishes have been raised. Best chances so far are with Clownfishes and Neon Gobies.

Specific gravity Ratio of density of measured liquid to that of pure water. Natural sea water has an S.G. of around 1.025, but marine aquarium fishes are normally kept in slightly lower density water (1.020-1.023) to avoid osmotic stress.

Starter Circuit necessary to initialize ('start') the discharge in fluorescent lighting.

Substrate Alternative term for aquarium base covering.

Swimbladder Hydrostatic organ enabling fish to maintain chosen depth and position in water.

Symbiosis Relationship between two parties, each deriving mutual benefit; i.e. Cleanerfish and their 'customers' or, less strictly, Clownfishes and sea anemones.

Tail Caudal fin

Temperate Non-tropical areas; in this encyclopedia, the term 'coldwater marines' refers to fishes and inverts from these cooler locations.

Territory Area chosen by a fish as its own.

Thermometer Device for measuring temperature. Floating, stick on or electronic versions available. External liquid crystal types are inexpensive and reasonably accurate, but may be affected by ambient temperatures or even direct sunlight.

Thermostat Device for controlling the supply of electricity to a heater. Usually mounted with heater in combined unit, but separate micro-chip external versions are available.

Total system Term given to aquariums with built-in sophisticated filtration and other management systems providing full water treatment.

Trickle filter Slow filter, often involving inert granules, sand or algal system. Anaerobic types convert nitrates back to free nitrogen.

Tropical Warm water areas, applied to fishes and invertebrates from such locations.

Tubifex Freshwater aquatic worm used as food. Often suspected of carrying disease. Clean well and store under running water before use.

Tungsten Incandescent filament wire type of lighting. Not recommended for aquarium use: inefficient, 'unbalanced' spectral output and produces too much heat.

Ultraviolet (UV) Type of light used as disinfectant, produced by a special tube usually enclosed in a surrounding water jacket through which aquarium water is passed. DO NOT LOOK AT AN OPERATING UV LAMP WITHOUT PROTECTIVE GOGGLES.

Undergravel filter Alternative name for biological filter fitted beneath the substrate in an aquarium.

Ventral Undersurface of a fish. May be especially flattened in bottom-dwelling species.

Ventral fins Alternative name for pelvic fins.

Water change Regular replacement of a proportion (usually 20-25%) of aquarium water with new synthetic sea water. Helps to maintain low nitrate levels, correct pH levels and replaces trace elements. Aerate any stored synthetic sea water before use.

Water flea Common name for *Daphnia*, a freshwater crustacean sometimes used as a live food.

Water turnover Water flow rate through a filter. For marine aquariums a high turnover is recommended.

Wattage Unit of electrical consumption used to classify power of aquarium heater or brightness of lamps.

GENERAL INDEX

INDEX TO SPECIES

Above: The feathery tentacles of the fanworm *Sabella* sp.

Both indexes prepared by Stuart Craik.

PICTURE CREDITS

Artists

Copyright of the artwork illustrations on the pages following the artist's name is the property of Salamander Books Ltd.

Paul B. Davies: 21, 22, 29(T), 34(B), 36, 38, 41, 51, 53

Stephen Gardner: 13, 16-7(B), 19, 29(B), 30, 34(T), 37, 49, 50, 56

Hans Wiborg-Jenssen: 14, 15, 17, 20, 26, 27, 31, 43

Stonecastle Graphics: 57 and the line artwork illustrations on pages 64-185

Photographs

The publishers wish to thank the following photographers and agencies who have supplied photographs for this book. The photographs have been credited by page number and position on the page: (B)Bottom, (T)Top, (C)Centre, (BL)Bottom left etc.

David Allison: Contents page, 33(B), 44(T), 63(T), 72(B), 73, 77, 78, 80(B), 99(T), 103, 110(B), 118(B), 123(B), 127(B), 129(T), 130, 134, 138(B), 147, 165, 170, 191(BR)

Peter Biller: 26, 35(TC), 74, 84, 98, 116(T), 118(T), 131(T), 141(BR), 146(T), 154(B), 164(B), 167(T), 168, 178(B), 189(TR), 190(BR), 191(BL), 192(C)

Heather Angel/Biofotos: Title page, Contents page (Ian Took), 10(B), 20(T), 32(T), 60-1(Ian Took), 104(T), 106(B), 111(T), 115(T, K.Sagar), 133(T), 142, 143, 151(T), 167(B, Ian Took), 180(T), 194-5, 195, 196, 199(TL,BL,TC,BR)

Dieter Brockmann: 150, 173(B), 193(CR)

Eric Crichton © Salamander Books: 8-9, 17(T), 30, 32(BL,BR), 33(TL,TR,CL,CR), 36, 38, 39, 40, 41(T), 42, 49(T)

Bruce Coleman: 67(T, Jane Burton), 71(TR, Alan Power), 108(B, H. Rivarola), 114(Jane Burton), 137(B, Alain Compost), 145(T, Bill Wood), 149(T, H. Rivarola)

Max Gibbs: 12(B), 44(B), 76(T), 88(B), 91, 104(B), 117(B), 122, 137(T), 140-1(BL), 153, 158, 159(T), 160, 161, 163(T), 164(T), 176(B), 179(B), 180(B), 183(B)

Joachim Grosskopf: Half-title, 48, 55(TL), 83(TL), 92, 95(T), 97(B), 99(B), 101(T), 105(B), 107(B), 117(T), 120, 121(T), 123(T), 127(T), 154-5(TL), 171, 187(T), 189(CL,BR), 190(TL,BL)

Andy Horton: 11(B), 43

Jan-Eric Larsson: 12(C), 20(B), 35(TR), 62-3, 68(B), 70(B), 72(T), 80(T), 96, 100(B), 106(T), 119, 121(C), 128(B), 156-7(T), 177(TR), 183(T), 184, 185

Dick Mills: 45, 47(T), 93(B), 100(T), 108(T), 126, 133(B), 138(T), 151(B)

Arend van den Nieuwenhuizen: 64, 65, 66, 67(B), 69, 71(TL,B), 75, 79(B), 81, 82, 83(TR), 85, 86(B), 87, 88-9(T), 93(T), 95(B), 97(T), 101(BL), 102, 107(T), 109, 112, 113(T), 115(B), 116(B), 124, 125, 129(B), 131(B), 132(B), 139, 140(T), 144, 145(B), 149(B), 152, 155(B), 157(B), 159(B), 162, 172, 174, 175, 177(B), 181, 182(T), 189(CR,BL), 191(C), 193(T)

Mike Sandford: 11(T), 121(B), 132(T), 148, 156(B), 163(B), 166, 173(T), 179(T), 182(B), 190(TR,C), 198(T,C)

David Sands: 47(TC,BC), 56, 58, 70(T), 128(T), 135

Gunther Spies: 12(T), 55(TR), 89(B), 16

Stonecastle Graphics © Salamander Books: 16, 17(B), 22-3, 24, 25(T), 31, 32(C), 41(B), 42, 49(B), 51, 52

William A. Tomey: Endpapers, Copyright page, 10(T), 13(T), 14, 18, 25(B), 28, 35(TL,C,BL,BR), 37, 47(B), 54, 68(T), 79(T), 86(T), 90, 94, 110(T), 111(B), 113(B), 136, 155(T), 186-7, 188, 189(TL), 191(T), 192(TL,TR,B), 193(CL,BL,BR), 197, 198(BL,BR), 199(TR), 207

F L Trutnau: 76(B), 101(BR), 176(T)

Uwe Werner: 146(B), 177(TL), 178(T)

Acknowledgements

The publishers wish to thank the following individuals and organizations for their help in the preparation of this book:

Algarde; John Allan Aquariums Ltd.; Ron Allum, Hounslow and District Aquarists Society; Aquarium Systems Inc.; Jim Chambers; Graham Cox, Waterlife Research Industries Ltd., Terry Evans and Derek Whiting, Wet Pets; Andy Horton; Interpet Ltd.; Dave Keeley, Underworld Products; Max Gibbs, The Goldfish Bowl; Hockney Engineers Ltd.; Lahaina Tropical Aquariums; Minireef Aquarium Systems; Chris Rawlings, Aquamagic Ltd./Tunze; Erwin Sander; Seabray Aquariums; Technical Aquatic Products; Tetra UK; UNO Aquatic Products; Vera Rogers (Editorial).